# Winter Gardens

*Other Publications:*

# Winter Gardens

by
OLIVER E. ALLEN
and
the Editors of TIME-LIFE BOOKS

TIME-LIFE BOOKS, ALEXANDRIA, VIRGINIA

**THE TIME-LIFE ENCYCLOPEDIA OF GARDENING**

EDITORIAL STAFF FOR WINTER GARDENS
EDITOR: Robert M. Jones
*Assistant Editors:* Sarah Bennett Brash, Betsy Frankel
*Text Editor:* Bonnie Bohling Kreitler
*Picture Editor:* Jane Jordan
*Designer:* Edward Frank
*Assistant Designer:* Edwina C. Smith
*Staff-Writer:* Reiko Uyeshima
*Researchers:* Diane Bohrer, Margaret White Dawson,
Sheila M. Green, Marilyn Murphy,
Betty Hughes Weatherley

EDITORIAL PRODUCTION
*Production Editor:* Douglas B. Graham
*Operations Manager:* Gennaro C. Esposito,
Gordon E. Buck (assistant)
*Assistant Production Editor:* Feliciano Madrid
*Quality Control:* Robert L. Young (director), James J. Cox
(assistant), Michael G. Wight (associate)
*Art Coordinator:* Anne B. Landry
*Copy Staff:* Susan B. Galloway (chief),
Elise Ritter Gibson, Ricki Tarlow, Celia Beattie
*Picture Department:* Barbara S. Simon

CORRESPONDENTS: Elisabeth Kraemer (Bonn); Margot
Hapgood, Dorothy Bacon, Lesley Coleman (London); Susan
Jonas, Lucy T. Voulgaris (New York); Maria Vincenza
Aloisi, Josephine du Brusle (Paris); Ann Natanson (Rome).
Valuable assistance was also provided by: Loral Dean
(Atlanta); Rosemary Caldwell (Buffalo); Diane Asselin (Los
Angeles); Carolyn T. Chubet, Miriam Hsia (New York);
Mimi Murphy (Rome); Carol Barnard (Seattle). The editors
are indebted to Patricia Bangs, Margaret M. Carter, Susan
Perry Dawson, Maggie Oster, Suzanne Seizas and Michael
McTwigan, writers, for their help with this book.

THE AUTHOR: Oliver E. Allen is a former staff member of *Life* and of Time-Life
Books, where he served as editor of the *Life* World Library and the TIME-LIFE
Library of America. He also wrote *Decorating with Plants, Wildflower Gardening,
Pruning and Grafting* and *Shade Gardens* for The Encyclopedia of Gardening.

CONSULTANTS: The late James Underwood Crockett, author of 13 of the volumes
in the Encyclopedia, co-author of two additional volumes and consultant on other
books in the series, was a lover of the earth and its good things. He graduated
from the Stockbridge School of Agriculture at the University of Massachusetts and
worked all his life in horticulture. A perennial contributor to gardening magazines,
he also wrote a monthly bulletin, "Flowery Talks," distributed through retail
florists. His television program, *Crockett's Victory Garden,* shown all over the
United States, won countless converts to his approach to growing things. Robert L.
Baker is an Associate Professor of Horticulture at the University of Maryland,
College Park. Miklos Faust is Chief of the Fruit Laboratory at the U.S. Department of Agriculture, Agricultural Research Center, Beltsville, Md. Robert G.
Haehle is an urban agriculture agent with the Maryland Cooperative Extension
Service. Conrad B. Link is Professor of Horticulture at the University of Mary-
land, College Park. William Louis Stern is Chairman of the Department of Botany
at the University of Florida, Gainesville. Carl A. Totemeier Jr. is Director of Old
Westbury Gardens, New York.

THE COVER: A frozen man-made pool meanders through the gently landscaped
garden of a home near Orting, Washington. Photographed just after a sleet storm,
the garden's every detail stands out in sharp relief, etched by ice crystals and
sugarings of snow. The tree in the foreground is a Japanese maple surrounded by
wintergreen ground cover. Clumps of bear grass and sword fern dot the middle
distance, and in the background a native vine maple stands on a slope planted
with heath, juniper and a snow-covered triangle of creeping thyme.

Library of Congress Cataloguing in Publication Data
Allen, Oliver E.
  Winter gardens.
  (The Time-Life encyclopedia of gardening)
  Bibliography: p.
  Includes index.
  1. Winter gardening.  I. Time-Life Books.  II. Title.
SB439.5.A39    635.9'53    79-18814
ISBN 0-8094-3210-2
ISBN 0-8094-3209-9 lib. bdg.

For information about any Time-Life book, please write: Reader Information,
Time-Life Books, 541 North Fairbanks Court, Chicago, Illinois 60611.

CONTENTS

# Pleasures and perils of the fourth season

Many gardeners, even experienced ones, think of winter as a down time for their gardens. The flowers are gone, the leaves have fallen, evergreens huddle against the cold. Nothing is happening. In fact, quite the opposite is true. While blizzards rage and freezing winds lash the landscape, many other things are going on. Below the ground, in the roots and soil, the garden is stirring with activity. Early bulbs are swelling and putting out their first shoots, preparing to burst into the open air. Perennial plants, aided by the cold, are undergoing vital chemical changes that will equip them for a new cycle of growth. Seeds are similarly reacting to the cold and getting ready to sprout. Nutrients from fallen leaves and dead stems are working their way down into the soil with the water of melting snow and winter rain, enriching the underground environment.

Aboveground, winter is a time of special beauty. Berries sparkle on some shrubs, while the leaves of others take on the appearance of burnished bronze. The leafless branches of trees etch filigree patterns against the leaden sky or cast hard-edged shadows across freshly fallen snow in the slanting rays of a late afternoon sun. Their bark, hidden in summer by leaves, comes into its own in winter: silvery gray, white, green; deeply fissured, sleek as a seal or curiously pocked by a peeling surface.

Color is everywhere, and not always subdued. The winter stems of some young dogwood shrubs are bright red, others are yellow, purple or green. The wheat gold of dried grasses stands out in brilliant contrast against a backdrop of dark evergreens. As an unexpected bonus, there is even the surprising yellow of ribbon-like witch-hazel flowers, which bloom in midwinter, or the delicate lavenders and blues of tiny species crocuses crowding up through the January snow. "Lots of people don't believe me," one winter gardener reports, "but I have plants blooming outdoors every month of the year." He lives in the cold Northeast.

*In the forecourt of a Baltimore home, winter emphasizes the graceful form of a yellowwood tree and the interplay of textures and greens in clipped mugo pine, creeping juniper and dwarf Norway spruce.*

Whether brightened by flowers or colored with a more subdued palette of greens, grays and browns, the sights of a garden in winter are so rewarding that one couple in a New York suburb set aside a corner of their garden simply for winter viewing. It is framed by the window of an upstairs sitting room where they often talk and read, and its scale is small. At its back is a clifflike ledge into which they have tucked a few winter-hardy rock-garden plants, evergreen candytuft and thyme. At the base of the ledge they have constructed a small pool and surrounded it with creeping lily-turf, a grasslike plant that stays green all winter. Christmas ferns, a few Johnny-jump-ups and some winter aconites complete the garden's horticultural elements, but there are still other visual attractions.

**A JANUARY WATERFALL**

There is in this garden a small stone sculpture that collects a picturesque mantle of snow, and a redwood garden chair — a reassuring sight in the dead of winter and an inviting one on a sunny day during a January thaw. Feeding the pool is a waterfall that can be turned on at any time during the winter, its water warmed by a heating cable wrapped around a pipe where it passes through the garage. The trickling water adds movement and sound to the garden, and also attracts birds. At night the garden can be gently floodlit, but this is a feature its owners seldom use. "There is a family of raccoons living up on the ledge," one explained. "At night they like to come down to the pool to drink — quite a sight when the moon is out and there is snow on the ground."

Creating a garden to be enjoyed in winter, as this couple has learned, means coming to terms with nature. Where winters are mild this accommodation is relatively easy. Southern gardeners sometimes contend with sudden changes in the weather at least as treacherous as those of the North, but their lawns remain green and so do many of their plants. Leaves linger longer on shrubs and trees and something is always in bloom — indeed, there are some plants that bloom at no other season *(pages 58-69)*. In the North, however,

*Nature's winter palette can be as handsome as the brighter colors of summer, as in the warm tobacco brown of the leaves of a European beech hedge in Buffalo, New York. The leaves will remain until new growth in spring forces them off.*

gardeners must provide landscape interest with far fewer plants and rely far more on the garden's "bare bones" — its basic plantings, such as hedges and tall trees, and constructed elements such as walls and paths — to satisfy the eye.

A winter garden in the North is seen largely as a composition of rectangles and circles, horizontals and verticals. There are the stark outlines of plant beds, the sinuous curves of terraces and hedges, the bold uprights of fences, trees and walls. For its decorative effects it may draw upon the fleeting patterns of melting snow on an undulating lawn or the long shadows cast by the slanting winter sun. A well-conceived plan allows enjoyment of the garden from a cozy vantage point in the house but also lures the viewer out for a wintry stroll. The 19th Century English poet John Clare evoked the quiet pleasures of a snowy garden,

> . . . where gravel pathways creep between
> Arches of evergreen that scarce let through
> A single feather of the driving storm;
> And in the bitterest day that ever blew
> The walk will find some places still and warm
> Where dead leaves rustle sweet and give alarm
> To little birds that flirt and start away.

A leisurely walk also brings into view subtler, finer details — the angular twigs of the winged euonymus or the swelling catkins of the pussy willow — that elude the arm-chair gardener.

The plants themselves, with their varied colors and textures, give life and harmony to the geometrics of the basic design. Evergreens are appreciated for the differences in their colors — green, purple, silvery gray — or for the way their branches catch and hold the snow. The bare silhouettes of deciduous trees are admired for their distinctive characteristics, whether staunchly upright, gracefully pendulous or strangely contorted. And when frost strikes, beauty

*With a rhododendron next to the door, this home has no need of a thermometer: the plant's leaves curl up when the temperature dips below freezing. Swelling buds of two other plants, a red-twigged dogwood and a pussy willow, will signal winter's end.*

is to be found in what is left behind — in the reddish-bronze foliage of the drooping leucothoë, the angular lantern-like seed pods of the golden rain tree, the cinnamon-brown patches exposed by the peeling bark of the paperbark maple. A broad expanse of shiny-leaved bearberry dusted with snow is a study in bronze, green and white.

WEATHERING THE COLD

But this winter beauty is accompanied by responsibilities. For a garden to get through the cold months in good health, an extra measure of care must be taken to give the plants a fighting chance against the elements. In the North, plants need to be protected from the dangers of sudden thaws, winterkill and sunscald; in the South they need protection from sudden frosts. Indeed, a sudden winter chill can be more devastating to gardens in South Carolina and California than to those in Minnesota and Maine. In the North, cold is relatively uniform; in the South it fluctuates so much that plants have a hard time adjusting to it. Gardeners in western Georgia still remember the winter of 1950-1951, when the hardest freeze in 52 years sent the temperature plummeting 72 degrees in one 24-hour period. "There we were, enjoying 68° weather one day," recalls one Georgian, "and by the following morning the thermometer had gone all the way down to four below zero." The sudden cold snap blew in on harsh north winds, and many broad-leaved evergreens — mainstays of Southern gardens — were so badly injured that they lost all of their leaves. Some plants recovered, but many others did not survive the glacial temperatures.

All these winter-related concerns — as well as the measures for dealing with them — touch upon the question of hardiness, the ability of a plant to survive the lowest temperatures that occur in the

(continued on page 15)

# Winter's heaths and heathers

*The bonny heather that covers the moors of England and Scotland has long charmed American tourists. Now these hardy evergreens are gaining popularity in this country. They grow best in light, acid soil, and because they need a lot of moisture, they do well in areas that are snow-covered all winter but not bitterly cold.*

*In these climates, similar to those just south of the Great Lakes, their wide range of foliage colors makes heathers ideal for winter gardens. Some keep the same color all year, but in late October the green foliage of others turns purple, and their gold becomes deep orange, red or rust. These hues stand out in spectacular contrast against the snow.*

*If you prefer flowers in your winter garden, try heaths. These low-growing evergreens are so closely related to heathers that many gardeners call them by that name (page 80). But heaths include many winter-blooming varieties, like those shown opposite. Hardy heaths bear white, lavender, pink and purple blooms throughout winter and early spring.*

*Pink clusters of King George heath and the pale flowers of Springwood White heath perk up a snowy landscape.*

# Bright hues for gray days

Heathers and heaths (or *Calluna* and *Erica,* to give their generic names) are strikingly effective when interspersed in mass plantings of irregular shapes, so that their different foliage, flowers and heights create billowing mounds of varied colors and ragged outlines. The plants will do best in partial shade, sheltered from icy winds.

They should be deeply planted in the early spring, in moist but not wet soil, and watered several times weekly until their roots have taken firm hold. Early in spring, all winter-damaged wood should be trimmed away. Heathers and heaths lend themselves well to casual gardens that have winding paths along which winter wanderers can stroll to enjoy these bright shrubs on a leaden gray day.

*Clusters of bell-shaped blooms spring from the foliage of Erica tetralix, a heath so hardy that it grows in Iceland.*

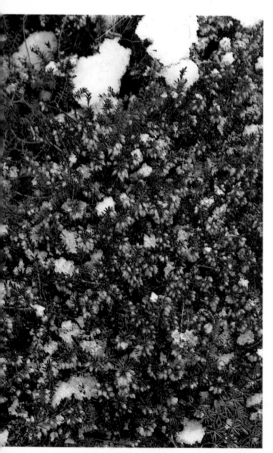

*The cheerful flowers of King George heath bloom from December to April.*

*Unlike heathers that change color, Calluna vulgaris alba remains bright green throughout the winter.*

*In a late-arriving winter, the normally dark foliage of Bronze Beauty heather retains its green coloration.*

*Feathery sprays of red foliage rise from a bed of Blaze Away heather to form a pattern in the snow.*

*Double flowers of a soft rose color cover H. E. Beale, a heather that grows up to 18 inches high.*

13

region where it grows. What makes a plant hardy? How does it adjust to cold? What actually happens when it is hit by frost? And how do plants "know" when it is safe to emerge from dormancy?

For most hardy plants, the ability to survive cold is closely linked to dormancy, a condition roughly comparable to human sleep. During dormancy plants are alive; indeed, they are somewhat active. Evergreens, for example, continue to transpire moisture through their leaves or needles. A dormant plant's metabolic processes continue but at a very slow rate. A dormant plant is also far less responsive to the external stimuli that promote new growth. What blocks this response continues to baffle scientists, but they do know that this period of reduced activity occurs in all plants; even those in the tropics have a period of dormancy during the dry season. Wherever it occurs, dormancy enables plants to survive a prolonged period of stress.

Dormancy lasts in plants for varying lengths of time and begins at varying seasons of the year. Spring-flowering bulbs, for example, start to become dormant when the foliage dies back in midsummer and do not emerge from their period of rest until midwinter, when the chilling of the soil coupled with the increasing amount of sunlight stimulates them to resume their annual cycle of growth. But however long it lasts, dormancy always occurs in several stages, the first few of which are more or less invisible.

**THE SPAN OF DORMANCY**

To prepare for their rest period, plants enter a period of intense activity. First they manufacture and store extra proteins, sugars and fats in their cells to tide them over the lean months and give them the energy they need to burst forth in the spring. Then if they are to bloom early the following year, they will set flower buds so they will be ready to move quickly as soon as their dormant period is over. Leaf buds too are formed, many of which contain in miniature all the preformed leaves and stems for the next year's growth. Only after these preliminaries do they begin to show signs of slowing down: stems stop growing, and deciduous plants shed their leaves. As winter sets in, some perennial plants vanish from sight, leaving only the crown to indicate their continued presence in the garden.

Underlying these various physical maneuvers is a series of chemical changes in the plant. Some of these changes are central to hardiness and help to explain why certain plants can survive subfreezing temperatures while others, the tender plants, cannot. Like much else in nature this ability, or lack of it, is a product of evolution. Scientists think that the ancestors of all of today's plants originated when the earth's climate was warm and humid and temperatures varied little in the course of a year. In the eons that

**WINTRY ADAPTATIONS**

*In exuberant full bloom, Vivellii and Springwood White heaths cover the terraced slope of a Seattle home. The bare trees above are Italian plums.*

# Turning plants off and on

Evolution has programed cold-climate plants to survive winter by going into a period of dormancy. Tissues gradually harden as days grow short and temperatures decline in autumn. Chemical activity continues within the plant at a slow pace until the growth-inhibiting hormones of fall and winter give way to the growth-promoting hormones of spring. This prevents the catastrophe of a seed or bud sprouting too early, only to greet a killing frost. Evolution has also ordained that the winter-to-spring chemical changeover be completed only after a specific period of chilling. Without enough hours of the right degree of cold, a plant cannot fully break its dormancy.

## DRESSED FOR THE COLD

*As winter approaches, plants protect embryonic tissues with tight coverings over compact shapes: buds with scales (near right), bulbs with tunics (center right) or seeds with coats (far right). These coverings contain hormones that inhibit germination of embryonic parts until the danger of freezing has passed. They also maintain a precise water balance that reduces susceptibility to frost and keeps the plant from drying out.*

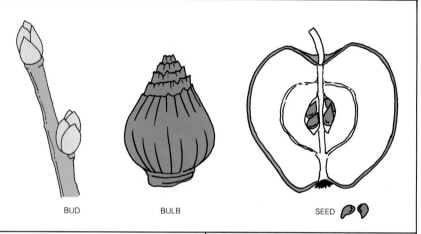

BUD · BULB · SEED

## A CHILLING REVIVAL

*The chemical changes that enable plants to break dormancy occur at temperatures ranging from 32° to 49° (near right); each plant needs a measurable period of chilling in this critical range to produce full growth in spring (far right). The hours of chilling needed depends on the climate of the plant's native region. Insufficiently chilled plants produce weak growth, bloom sporadically, and die after a few seasons.*

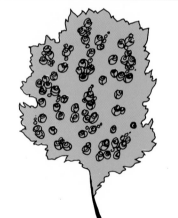

## NIPPED IN THE BUD

*When temperatures suddenly drop before a plant is fully dormant, the heart of a bud (near right), the cambium tissue or even the pith of a branch (far right) dies and turns brown. These tissues will not produce new growth in spring. Plants need a gradual drop in temperatures in order to harden properly, a process involving reduction of water content and storage of enough nutrients to carry them through dormancy.*

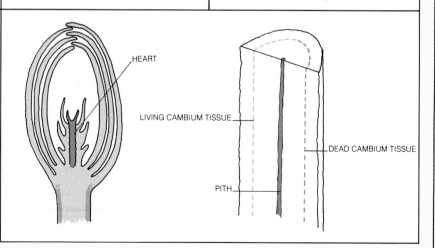

HEART

LIVING CAMBIUM TISSUE

DEAD CAMBIUM TISSUE

PITH

followed, the climate cooled, and plants that could adapt to cyclical changes in temperature were the ones that persisted and reproduced. Some plants, the annuals, survived the winter in the form of seeds, which the parent plants produced and distributed in a single season before they died. Others persisted in the form of bulbs into which were packed in embryonic form all the flowers, stems, leaves and other plant parts. Still others kept their woody structure intact but went through a hardening process that protected them from being injured by cold.

Not all plants of a particular kind are equally hardy everywhere. To be more precise, they are hardy in their natural environment. If this happens to be in an area where winters are extremely cold, they may also be hardy in areas less cold. But there is a risk in trying to grow many northern plants too far south. A crab apple tree in Florida, for instance, will fail to flower and fruit because it actually requires a certain period of cold weather to enable its normal growth cycle to continue. It may live for a few years, but will eventually succumb to the balmy climate *(page 18)*. And a plant grown in an area where winter temperature readings go below those to which it is accustomed will also have difficulty surviving. Some tropical plants, for example, cannot tolerate temperatures in what is called the chilling range, between 32° and 49°. In the subtropics, roughly equivalent to Zones 9 and 10 on the hardiness map *(page 148)*, plants suffer if temperatures fall below 20°. On the other hand, there are plants such as species of primrose, lupine and cinquefoil that live in the frigid cold of Antarctica and survive temperatures as low as -30°, bursting into bloom in the relative 34° warmth of the brief Antarctic summer.

Certain favorable conditions — a moist, well-drained soil, for instance, and shelter from the wind — will occasionally combine to let a plant grow in temperatures that drop below its usual hardiness limit. Gardens frequently contain a plant or two like this, being pushed to the limit of its endurance. It may live through several winters, albeit with protection, but then succumb during an especially severe one. The term half-hardy is sometimes used to describe such plants, but strictly speaking it is erroneous — a plant is either hardy in a particular climate zone or it is not. (If a plant is not hardy, the correct term for it is tender.)

The terms semideciduous or semievergreen are often used to describe plants that normally lose their leaves, but will hold them if grown in climates warmer than those to which they are accustomed. An evergreen plant such as abelia, hardy to Zone 6, may lose its leaves in winter at the northern limit of its hardiness and may even

**VARIATIONS IN HARDINESS**

**BRANCHES BARED BY COLD**

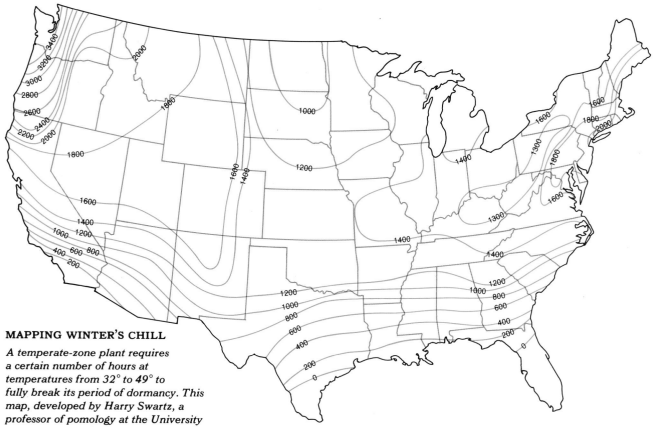

**MAPPING WINTER'S CHILL**

*A temperate-zone plant requires a certain number of hours at temperatures from 32° to 49° to fully break its period of dormancy. This map, developed by Harry Swartz, a professor of pomology at the University of Maryland, charts the average hours of effective winter chilling in various parts of the United States. A plant grown too far south of its native area will grow poorly or die because it does not get sufficient chilling; a plant grown too far north of its range will suffer winter injury.*

be killed to the ground, then send up new stems the following season.

The critical temperature in determining hardiness is slightly below the freezing point of water. Water is the main component of most plant cells, which also contain chemicals that act rather like antifreeze, lowering the freezing point a bit. Most gardeners are aware of the swift damage a sudden frost can bring: overnight, plants go limp and may even turn brown or black. It was once thought the plants were being killed by ice forming in their cells and expanding, rupturing the cell walls. But botanists now think that the damage is actually caused by dehydration. Ice forms between the cells, rather than inside them, and the water inside the cells passes through the cell walls and into the spaces between cells. Thus plants are injured or killed not simply by cold but by a lack of water caused by cold.

Plants that are hardy routinely resist this water loss — and sometimes supposedly tender plants do too, surviving temperatures that dip as low as 20°. What saves them in many cases is the larder of proteins, sugars and fats that the plant stores for winter in its cells. These chemicals make the cell sap more concentrated than it is in other seasons of the year, and water is less likely to be drawn out of the cells. In addition, tender plants sometimes survive freezing temperatures if the weather has been dry. Annuals, for example, often live through the dry cold nights of Indian summer, even though temperatures drop to freezing.

DWINDLING DAYLIGHT

A plant's ability to endure cold also varies with its condition at the time cold strikes. Indeed, if you subjected a supposedly hardy plant to freezing temperatures in midsummer, it would not be hardy at all but would die. Plants become hardy only when they have had a chance to acclimate themselves gradually to cold, a process that takes a long time. For most woody plants the prime trigger that sets the hardening process in motion is not the falling temperature, as most people suppose, but the shortening of days and lengthening of nights. Even if an autumn is unusually warm, these plants will prepare themselves for winter. This is clearly a better arrangement for plants, since the seasonal change in the length of days is constant, year in and year out, while temperatures are not. If plants took their hardening cues from the warm days of Indian summer they would be in deep trouble. On the other hand, the number of hours of daylight on September 1 in Des Moines, Iowa, is exactly the same every year. On September 2 that daylight will always diminish by exactly the same amount, and by, say, October 18, the day's length will be identical to that of every other October 18.

The light-activated changes in a plant's growth process affect many functions besides hardening. So hardening can scarcely be separated from the processes that cause plants to set leaf and flower buds for the next year and to ripen seeds. In the particular changes that affect hardiness, the plant shifts from the production of flowers and vegetative growth to the development of protective mechanisms. This is why fertilizing and pruning in the late summer are ill-advised — both encourage plants to keep on producing vulnerable new growth that will not have sufficient time to harden before the arrival of winter.

A PROCESS COMPLETED

In the final stages of the hardening process, leaves of deciduous woody plants turn color and then drop; the plant is dormant and its hardening is complete. The danger now is not from winter cold but from thaws. As the days lengthen after the winter solstice and the plant begins the long process of preparing for spring, it will be most vulnerable during periods of midwinter warmth. Alternate freezing and thawing cause the soil to heave, thus breaking or exposing the roots, which are more sensitive to cold than the parts aboveground. For plants, as well as for virtually all other forms of life on earth, the daily weather report is of profound interest — and sometimes a matter of life and death.

JANVIER

# Getting the garden ready for a rest 2

Just as the normal human reaction to cold is to bundle up, many gardeners assume that plants need to be kept warm in winter. Almost the exact opposite is true. To survive the icy blasts of a Northern winter, plants must be allowed to become accustomed gradually to cooling weather and then, when winter arrives, must be *kept* cold. The danger to guard against is sudden warmth — a midwinter mild spell, an early February thaw. Mulches, contrary to general belief, do not protect plants so much from the cold as from the damaging effects of rapidly thawing and freezing soil; this causes frost heaving, which breaks plant roots and exposes them to the frigid air. Similarly, the villain in winterkill and sunscald, two related phenomena, is not cold but the heat of the winter sun.

Winterkill, to which broad-leaved evergreens such as azaleas and rhododendrons are especially susceptible, occurs when the sun's heat, coupled with wind, removes moisture from leaves faster than the shallow, frozen, almost dormant roots can replace it. Unfortunately, the condition is often invisible until spring, when the leaves turn brown. Sunscald occurs when an unexpectedly hot sun thaws the living cambium tissues just under the thin bark of young trees as well as under that of certain older trees such as beeches, sycamores and fruit trees. Sunscald is a special danger for trees that developed in shade and were then transplanted into direct sunlight. The tissues are simply burned, much as a fair-skinned person gets sunburned when abruptly exposed to too much sun.

Plants that are particularly vulnerable to winterkill or sunscald should be planted where they have natural protection from the sun — against a north wall, for example, or on the shady side of a tall hedge. You can also protect them with a special wrapping tape, available at garden centers, or burlap *(pages 24-25)* or, in the case of evergreens, by spraying with antitranspirant compounds, as described on pages 23-24. But the best protection against winter

*Bundled up against the January cold, an intrepid gardener cultivates soil around a holly in this 1896 print from La Belle Jardinière, a French calendar depicting the activities of a gardening year.*

damage is choosing plants that are hardy in your area, planting them in a spot compatible with their needs, and then following a program of plant care that goes on all year long.

It is a truism of gardening, but one that cannot be ignored, that a healthy plant is more likely to get through a tough winter than an unhealthy one. Healthy plants store food more abundantly and harden themselves against winter damage more effectively. Their root systems are also more resilient to the stresses of cold. So prepare your plants for winter by watering them whenever they need it in summer, by giving them adequate fertilizer, and by treating insect and disease problems as soon as you notice them. It is also vital, and never more so than in winter, for plants to have good drainage. A plant in waterlogged soil may limp through summer, but it will not survive long after the first frost because the soil heaves when it freezes, breaking the plant's roots. If you suspect that an area of your garden is poorly drained, till the soil to a depth of at least a foot and mix in builder's sand or perlite plus compost or leaf mold.

**FALL FERTILIZING**
As summer wanes, plants need to slow their growth. New tissue is sensitive and fresh green shoots hit by frost will be killed. Plants in general should not be fertilized after midsummer, although in late fall after a hard frost you can ring them with a sprinkling of nitrogen-rich fertilizer such as one labeled 10-6-4. Better yet, top-dress them lightly with an organic substance such as leaf mold, compost or dried manure. The plant's still-active roots will be fortified for winter by this extra-late feeding. Scratch the material into the ground at the outer edge of the root area, underneath the ends of the branches where the feeder roots are located.

Do not prune in early fall except to remove dead or diseased branches, because this too stimulates tender new growth. After a hard frost it is safe to prune, and actually preferable for plants such as maples, beeches and yellowwood that bleed if pruned in spring. Water sparingly in early fall, but once growth has stopped, keep track of the frequency of rainfall. In many areas, late fall is a dry period, and plants should not enter the cold season lacking sufficient water, even if you must provide it.

**BEDDING DOWN PERENNIALS**
Although many gardeners cut perennials down to ground level in the fall to neaten a flower border, this practice is not always horticulturally necessary. In fact, the appearance of some dried stalks can be quite decorative *(pages 40-41)* and some even have seeds that will attract birds. These stalks and stems also serve to hold a mulch in place. On the other hand, many spent stalks are unattractive, like those of day lilies, or are refuges for insects, like the hollow stems of dahlias. These should be removed and discarded. So should

any diseased or mildewed stems, so that the plant can start the following year uncontaminated.

Fall is also the best time for lifting and dividing summer-blooming perennials, such as phlox and Shasta daisies, that have become overcrowded. Be sure to set the newly divided plants so their crowns, at the top of the root structure, are level with the soil surface. Firm the soil around the plants, mulch them and soak them every few days if there is no rain.

As autumn leaves begin to fall, give some thought to making compost or leaf mold. Both are priceless as mulches or for soil conditioning. To make leaf mold, you can simply dump the leaves into a bin 3 or 4 feet across, made of wire fencing or chicken wire. The leaves will compact in time but you can hasten the process by pressing them down as you dump them and by wetting them with a hose if the surface of the pile begins to dry. In a year or so, nature will have done its work and you will have a dark brown, nutritious, soil-lightening material for your garden. For the compost pile, construct an enclosure at least 2 feet high of wire fencing, wood or concrete blocks. Into it can go not only leaves but dead stalks and other garden refuse. Vegetable garbage from the kitchen, including eggshells, is acceptable as is virtually any biodegradable material.

Perfectionists say the compost will break down and be ready to use more quickly if it is assembled in layers, alternating a layer of leaves, for instance, with one of kitchen and garden refuse, followed by a thin layer of soil. But since you are unlikely to acquire these substances in such rigid order, you may safely ignore that dictum. You can speed up the pile's development, however, by turning it over from time to time with a spading fork, by making the top dish-shaped so rain water will collect there, and by adding commercially available chemicals that are specially formulated to speed the decay process. You can also hasten the process by shredding leaves before you add them. Leaf-shredding machines are expensive, but they can be rented. If you adopt all of these speed-up techniques, you may have usable compost in three or four months; if you let nature take its course, your compost will be ready in a year or two.

At some point in fall before the ground freezes, apply an anti-transpirant to your choicest or most vulnerable evergreens, both needled and broad-leaved. Although some gardeners think that these sprays are not worth the trouble and are not very protective — they often wash off in rain or snow — they do slow down the transpiration that causes the loss of moisture and thus go a long way toward preventing winterkill.

Marketed under various trade names, these antitranspirants

come ready-mixed in pressurized spray cans or in concentrated forms to be mixed with water and applied with your own sprayer. They must be applied on a windless day when the temperature is above 40° so the solution will dry properly. Although some manufacturers claim that their brands will last all winter, most antitranspirants eventually wear off and should be reapplied on a mild day in midwinter. Christmas trees or other holiday greens treated with an antitranspirant will hold their needles longer.

Sometimes winter protection needs to be even more substantial. Though burlap-wrapped plants are unsightly, in exposed areas the coat is almost imperative — near the sea, for example, where plants are exposed to the salt spray of winds and winter storms. You

### PROTECTING EVERGREENS

1. *To remove light, newly fallen snow from a needled evergreen without damaging its branches, brush gently upward with the flat side of a broom. If the tree or shrub is heavily laden, use the broom handle to poke through the branches and comb off the snow.*

2. *To protect a broad-leaved evergreen shrub planted in an exposed location, construct a two-sided windbreak of stakes and burlap. Drive three 1-by-1 stakes into the ground, forming a V shape that points into the wind. Wrap a sheet of burlap around the stakes and staple as shown (inset).*

3. *Evergreen shrubs planted beneath the eaves of a house may need to be shielded from ice and snow that slides off the roof. Cover them with A-frame shields made of snow fencing, boards or sheets of plywood. Hinge the A-frame panels at the top for easy storage.*

4. *To keep branches of a tall, upright arborvitae or yew from breaking under heavy snow, drive a 1-by-1 stake slightly taller than the plant into the ground beside it. Beginning at the bottom, loosely wind garden twine around both shrub and stake so snow will not force branches downward.*

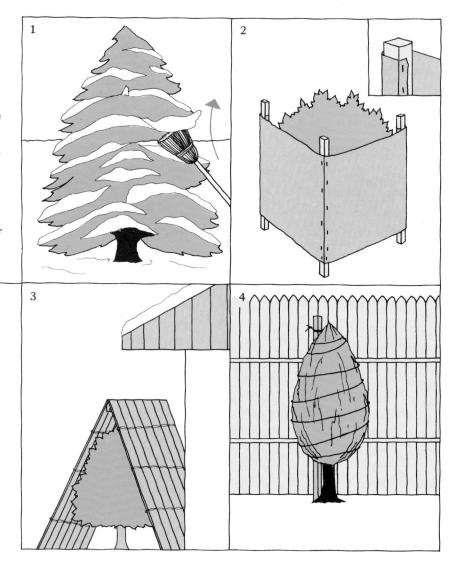

can stretch the burlap around stakes driven into the ground beside the plant, or wrap it around the plant and secure it with staples or with nails used as pins. Do this neatly and the results will not be offensive; otherwise, your shrubs may take on the appearance of a scruffy collection of Snow White's dwarfs.

Hedges and shrubs along paths and roads may also need extra winter protection from salt, pedestrians and cars. Salt, used to keep sidewalks or streets free of ice, is one of the worst winter enemies of plants — a tree can be fatally injured in a single season if salt is applied frequently nearby. To provide traction on icy walks, use sand, cat litter or gritty urea fertilizer, which benefits plants as it washes into the soil. To prevent stems from being broken, tie them together in a clump or shield them with a snow fence. Tender shrubs like roses have the best chance of surviving deep cold and winter winds if they are both tied and burlaped. Very young or recently transplanted trees should have their trunks wrapped with burlap or a wrapping tape to protect them against sunscald. For good measure, they should also be staked for a year or two after planting so they will not be blown over. To do this, use heavy wire leading down to stakes in three or four directions around the tree, and be sure to protect the branches and trunk by enclosing the wire in a piece of old garden hose where it loops around the tree.

Wherever there is the probability of large amounts of snow sliding off the roof, it pays to protect foundation plantings with wooden frames that can be set over the plants in winter, and removed in spring. Such frames need not be unsightly. One of the simplest models looks like an A-frame house; it is made of two panels hinged at the top and thus folds flat for summer storage (left).

One final chore before freezing weather arrives concerns concrete garden pools. A straight-sided pool may be cracked by ice and should either be drained or equipped with a small electric pool heater to keep part of the surface free of ice. You may also have to drain recirculating fountains and waterfalls if you cannot keep the water moving in freezing weather. Never solve this problem with antifreeze if there is any likelihood that animals will drink the water. (Freezing water usually does not damage a pool with sloping sides, since the ice moves upward rather than exerting its pressure against the sides of the pool.)

With the arrival of temperatures below 32°, it is time to think about winter mulches. One of the best is, of course, snow. A winter-long snow cover acts like an insulating blanket, preventing wide temperature fluctuations in the soil beneath. This explains why plants in the coldest parts of Minnesota, where snow remains on the

**ALTERNATIVES TO SALT**

**AN INSULATING BLANKET**

ground all winter, have a better chance of coming through unscathed than do plants in New England, where the snow cover, because of frequent sudden thaws, is apt to be intermittent. Soil under snow may freeze only 1 inch deep, while adjacent exposed soil freezes a foot down. Furthermore, in areas where air temperatures fluctuate as much as 30 degrees during cold snaps, a snow cover keeps the temperature of the soil constant.

**LIGHT THROUGH THE SNOW**

It is not dark beneath this blanket of snow. Though its consistency is constantly changing, growing denser as it settles, snow is almost always able to transmit a surprising amount of light and air to the plants beneath. A layer of dry, fluffy snow may contain as much as 97 per cent air, old granular snow as much as 50 per cent. The light that penetrates a layer of snow enables the plants to carry on the vital process of photosynthesis. This explains the ability of winter-blooming bulbs such as aconites and snowdrops to thrust their shoots through the snow. In fact, melting snow may even act like a fertilizer, carrying valuable nutrients such as nitrates into the soil.

In cold areas where snowfalls are infrequent or irregular, other forms of winter mulch are generally necessary. Bear in mind that these winter mulches, while they may deliver nutrients to the soil as they decompose, are primarily intended to keep the temperature of the soil constant. Consequently, anything that shades the soil from the sun will suffice, from living ground covers to evergreen boughs from a discarded Christmas tree. The mulch must not, however, cut off moisture from the roots of the plant. This excludes the use of certain potential mulches such as peat moss, grass clippings and the leaves of poplar and maple trees, all of which form mats that shed water like shingles on a roof.

**THE ORGANIC MULCHES**

Wood chips, compost and pine needles are all suitable organic winter mulches but should generally be applied no more than 2 inches thick. If the wood chips are fresh from a tree trimmer's chipping machine, they may, as they decompose, remove nitrogen-fixing bacteria from the soil; you may have to add supplemental nitrogen fertilizer. The leaves of oak, birch, hickory, beech and linden trees also make good winter mulches. Unlike the leaves of maple and poplar, they curl as they dry and therefore do not mat when it rains. Salt hay, the marsh grass found near the ocean, is an excellent mulch if available, but ordinary hay usually contains too many weed seeds. Other locally available mulch materials that work well include cocoa-bean hulls, peanut shells, buckwheat hulls and pine or fir bark. Salt hay and leaf mulches do tend to blow around in windy areas and it may be necessary to anchor them with fallen branches or evergreen boughs.

The need for mulches varies with the plant. Native wildflowers and shrubs need scarcely any mulch at all if they are already supplied, as they should be, with a forest-floor environment that is in itself a natural mulch. Other plants such as shallow-rooted camellias, azaleas and rhododendrons need more than the normal amount; this mulch should remain in place year round. But other plants that keep their leaves all winter, such as primroses, hellebores, foxgloves and sweet William, should be mulched lightly so their leaves are not covered. In fact, mulch should never cover the foliage of any plant, but should be tucked beneath the leaves. Keep mulch about an inch away from the main stems to prevent rot.

Roses are in a class by themselves. In addition to having their canes tied together in a bundle to prevent breakage, they need to be mulched to a point 8 to 10 inches up the canes north of Zone 7. This protects the delicate bud graft just above the soil level, where the plant was originally propagated. Some rose growers simply pile soil around the canes to this depth, but soil can wash away. It is safer to construct a foot-high collar of wire mesh, tar paper or plastic around the plant, and to fill the intervening space with leaves, leaf mold or compost. You can also use a splint basket for this purpose, with its

**PROTECTION FOR ROSES**

**A MULCH FOR ALL SEASONS**

Cultivating the soil around azaleas and rhododendrons may damage their shallow roots, so it is best to keep the soil loose and open with a mulch that is permanent, instead of one that goes on in the winter and comes off in the spring. To confine this year-round covering, mound soil around the plant's drip line to a depth of 2 or 3 inches, forming a water-retaining saucer. Fill this saucer with wood chips, oak leaves, pine needles or other light organic material. Keep the mulch watered well to prevent the roots, which may grow into it, from drying out.

bottom cut out. Or you can buy, at many Northern garden-supply stores, a ready-made, tepee-shaped cover made of foam plastic.

In very cold or windy areas, climbing tea roses need even more elaborate treatment to protect their long canes. Untie the canes from their support and bend them over so that they nearly touch the ground, anchoring them with stakes and soft twine. Then cover the entire plant with soil or a mulch of evergreen boughs, salt hay or similar light material. Alternatively, you can dig a trench next to the shrub and tilt the whole plant into the trench for the winter, covering it with light, loose soil.

DISCOURAGING RODENTS

Roses and other woody plants, as well as some fruit trees, are subjected in winter to a special danger associated with mulches. Mice and rabbits like to make their winter homes in mulch and feed on the tender bark of plants. By winter's end the animals may have girdled the stem or trunk, cutting off a plant's food supply and killing it. If you hold off applying mulch until the ground has frozen, you can usually avoid this problem, for the mice and rabbits will have taken up winter quarters elsewhere. Nevertheless, for safety's sake, you may want to discourage such marauders by installing an 8-inch-high collar of screening around the stems or trunks of favorite plants.

One place you are less likely to need a winter mulch is in the

SHIELDING AGAINST THE SUN AND WIND

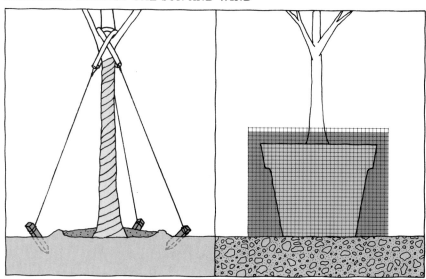

To brace a young tree against wind, sink three equally spaced stakes in the ground and run a guy wire from each stake to a low branch. Thread the wire through rubber hose to protect the bark. Wind tree wrap around the trunk to prevent sunscald.

To winter a hardy deciduous tree growing in a pot outdoors, place around it a ring of hardware cloth 6 inches larger in diameter than the pot and wide enough to extend several inches above its rim. Fill the ring with damp peat moss or shredded bark.

vegetable garden, though mulching will prevent rich soil from eroding if the garden is on a slope. Perennial vegetables, such as rhubarb and asparagus, are generally sturdy enough to require little in the way of winter protection beyond a light covering of salt hay or leaves. Before you mulch a food plant, sprinkle compost and perhaps a spoonful of superphosphate around it. This will improve the quality of the crop the following year. Some gardeners turn over the soil of the entire vegetable garden in fall, incorporating the spent plants into the soil to enrich it and getting a head start on spring planting. If you follow this practice, make sure the plants are free of pests and disease.

Although mulching is the standard method of preparing most plants for winter, container plants may require other safeguards. Mulching just the surface of the soil is of little use, since the roots would still be vulnerable to alternate freezing and thawing temperatures through the sides. A mulch that surrounds the container can insulate the roots of a hardy plant (left). Another effective protection for a hardy container plant is to lift it from its pot and sink it in garden soil over the winter. If it is impractical to remove the plant from its pot, it may be possible to sink it into the soil, pot and all, depending upon the composition of the container. Clay and terra-cotta pots are impractical, because the freezing soil will crack them. Plastic and metal containers are less likely to crack but they provide little protection against temperature changes. Fiberglass is better in this respect, but the best material is undoubtedly wood. Not only does it protect plants well, but it is also flexible enough to absorb the stresses of alternately freezing and thawing soil. Styrofoam panels, which can be cut to fit inside the container, keep the soil at a more even temperature.

Of course this protection will vary with the dimensions of the container you use. In general, the larger the container is, the less danger the plant will suffer winter damage. Experienced terrace gardeners agree that any container that is left outdoors all winter should be at least 14 inches deep, and preferably 18 inches. Furthermore, the thicker its walls, the better: a container made of 2-inch lumber will see your plants through the winter more securely than 1-inch lumber. Be careful to provide good drainage at the base, since soggy soil freezes more quickly than open, porous soil.

If you are gardening on a city terrace, you will also want to make sure that your container-grown plants are protected from winds that funnel between tall buildings. Antitranspirant sprays are useful. You might even want to consider wrapping both plants and containers in burlap. Finally, be prepared on windy terraces to water

PLANTS IN CONTAINERS

ON WINDY TERRACES

*Cold air naturally drains downhill and will harm tender shrubs or perennials if it is trapped by a wall or dense hedge or by the close proximity of other plants. To avoid damaging plants of doubtful hardiness, do not place them near a barrier at the bottom of a slope, and always leave enough space between the plantings at the bottom of a hill to permit cold air to drain through.*

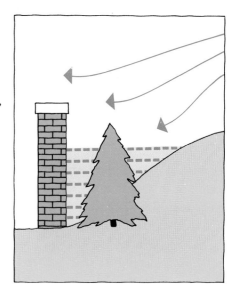

evergreens even during winter, if neither rain nor snow is copious enough to keep the soil moist.

In the warmer winter gardens of Zones 8-10, where persistent cold is not a problem, mulching will help keep the weeds down and the soil moist, but is of limited usefulness as protection against weather. In these zones, severe sudden frosts, driven by brisk north winds, sometimes strike. Protective mulches do little to allay such conditions. If mulches are applied, they should be loose, light and removable. More practical is some sort of covering that can be placed around the entire plant for a brief period, perhaps just overnight. Some gardeners use burlap, others old bed sheets or light plastic. Whatever the material you use, it should cover the plant but should not touch the leaves. To manage this, support the covering with stakes or some kind of temporary frame. You can heat the enclosure with a single light bulb if the cold snap is expected to be particularly severe. And remember always to remove the covering promptly when the danger is past.

**FENDING OFF FROST**

When plants are too large for such protective measures, a constant play of water from a hose or sprinkler may keep frost from forming on the leaves or stems. This should only be done when the temperature is above 32° and rising. If you spray when the temperature is falling, you run the risk of adding a layer of ice to the stems, breaking them and injuring the plant. By the same token, an ice-clad plant exposed to the sudden warmth of the morning sun may thaw so rapidly that its flower buds are ruined; winter- or spring-flowering shrubs that are vulnerable to this damage, such as daphnes, rhododendrons, camellias and azaleas, should be planted where they will be shaded in the morning and will thaw gradually. Similarly, all plants benefit from being planted where there is good air circulation — frost collects first in hollows.

As winter runs its course, gardening chores are largely confined to snow removal. Soft accumulations on hedges and broad-leaved evergreens should be gently brushed off as soon as possible *(page 24)*. If the snowfall is heavy, it may break stems or branches. Even a light snowfall can cause extensive damage if it turns to ice — and when ice forms on branches, there is not much to do except hope that it melts in time. Do not attempt to remove the ice, since shaking icy branches does more harm than good. Snow tossed onto shrubbery from passing snowplows should also be removed as soon as possible, since it often contains harmful salt. Be on guard against snow that plummets from your roof onto foundation plantings, perhaps protecting them with the same wooden A-frame structures that are recommended for use in areas of heavy snow.

For you and for plants, lengthening days and rising temperatures of late winter signal the approach of spring. Buds begin to swell, stems elongate and the first spring flowers appear. This is the time when you may want to apply a dormant oil spray onto some of your plants, especially woody plants vulnerable to scale attacks later in the year. But withhold this spray until the temperature reaches 40 to 45°. Late winter is also the time to consider removing winter mulches from perennials and spring-flowering bulbs. The question of when — and whether — to do this is a tricky one to answer. Late winter weather can be quixotic, and tender plants need protection until the last frost, especially if young growth has started. On the other hand, leaving the mulch on too long can slow young growth and make it too tender.

To be on the safe side, it is best to remove a winter mulch from your plants in two stages. When all but the tag end of winter seems to be past — just as new growth first appears — you can remove about half the thickness of the mulch. After three or four days, remove the remainder of the mulch. If possible, do this on a cloudy day so that the newly exposed areas are not exposed too abruptly to the sun. This gradual removal allows your plants to become accustomed to the chilly air without being damaged.

Many plants, of course, do not need a special mulch for the winter. Instead, the same mulch of compost, wood chips or leaf mold is left in place winter and summer, and is simply replenished when it becomes thin. With shallow-rooted plants that have sent rootlets up into the mulch, disturbing the mulch at any season of the year will do more harm than good.

**FROM WINTER TO SPRING**

**REPLENISHING MULCH**

# The tranquil beauty of dormant nature

"Gardener, if you listen, listen well: plant for your winter pleasure, when the months dishearten," wrote the English gardener and essayist Vita Sackville-West. But such planting requires careful thought and much imagination. The winter garden, bereft of flowers, relies more on shape and texture than on color. It draws upon nature's bare essentials, and on the arrangement of these essentials. A silver-barked birch tree is played against a backdrop of evergreens; a tall, narrow juniper is set amid a circle of smaller rounded ones. When color does surface, it is subdued, often a mere pinprick in the prevailing palette of grays, greens and browns.

Evergreens form the backbone of a winter landscape, and are arranged to highlight their contrasting shapes and sizes, from the ground-hugging Wilton carpet juniper to the tall, shaggy Hinoki false cypress. Their leaves, whether needled or broad, come in a variety of shades of green and often reach beyond to gold, red, copper or silver gray. Some, like variegated Japanese aucuba, have beautiful two-toned leaves. Still others, like wintergreen and English holly, display bright, decorative berries.

The herbaceous perennials can also play a role in a winter landscape. With the advent of frost, ornamental grasses turn warm shades of tan and the dense flower heads of many sedums darken to rich hues of brown and red. Coneflowers retain their chocolate-brown centers while the crisp green leaves of sweet woodruff soften to gold. Left untouched, these plants rise from the snow-crusted ground like natural dried arrangements.

On a larger scale, so do the bare branches of deciduous trees and shrubs. After their leaves have fallen, they reveal the beauty of their forms — round, conical, columnar, weeping or spreading — and many have added beauty when colorful bark is exposed. The paperbark cherry tree's trunk is a shiny, almost metallic-looking red; the stems of the Siberian dogwood fan out in sprays of scarlet. Lacy twigs and decorative bark, set against a contrasting wall or a dark background of evergreens, create a study in stark contrasts.

*Japanese holly, sarcococca and a Japanese andromeda (left to right) combine to sculpt a wintry entrance wall with a bas-relief of evergreen. A second holly is espaliered above.*

# The ever-useful evergreens

Plants whose leaves stay green year round come into their own in winter when their color dominates the landscape. Among them are the two large classes of evergreens: those with needle-like foliage, such as pines and junipers, and the broad-leaved plants, such as rhododendron and holly. Both groups contribute interest to a winter garden either as accents or as backdrops for deciduous plants.

But the green that graces a winter garden can come from sources other than trees and shrubs. Ivy can cloak a fence or a wall, a host of low-growing ground covers can carpet the frozen soil, and the winter-hardy leaves of succulents like the yuccas opposite can punctuate a frigid landscape with shapes that are dainty or bold.

*The silver-tipped leaves of a blue carpet juniper and the reddish-brown rosettes of a common houseleek sparkle under a shaft of winter sunlight. The plants are set among rocks whose surfaces hold and radiate heat.*

*The sword-shaped leaves of yucca, weighted down with snow, cascade over a winter garden like frozen fountains. Their gray-green color sets off the golden clumps of calamagrostis grass in the background.*

A decades-old boxwood hedge, sculptured by nature into strong undulating shapes, wraps a winter garden in privacy and shelters

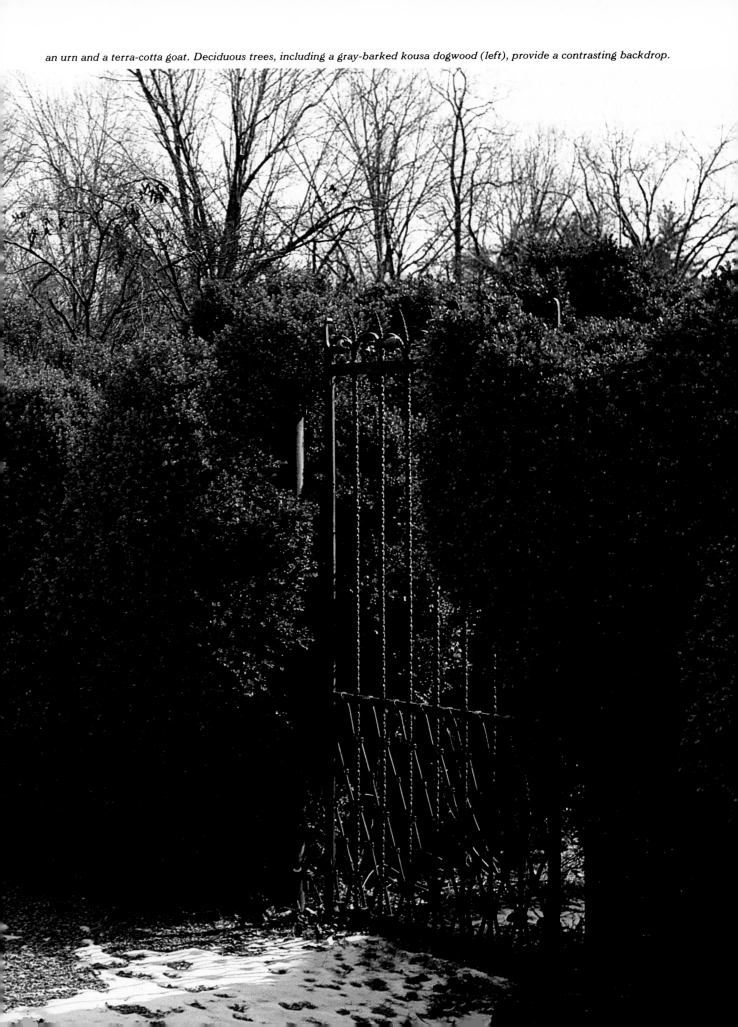

an urn and a terra-cotta goat. Deciduous trees, including a gray-barked kousa dogwood (left), provide a contrasting backdrop.

A circle of evergreen lily-turf and the upright branches of a Japanese yew (left) echo the architectural lines of a formal garden.

Topiary evergreens, including a Chinese-juniper bird in a ring of lavender cotton, demarcate pathways of this formal garden.

# Plants that tan in winter

In winter, many herbaceous perennials turn warm shades of tan and brown; if left uncut, they decorate the winter scene with natural dried bouquets. The ornamental grasses are among the most useful of these plants, especially tall grasses with plumed feathery seed pods. The wheat-colored stems are notably handsome against evergreens.

To provide accent, the grasses are often used with succulents such as stonecrop, whose dense flower heads darken in winter to the russet brown of well-polished leather. Like the grasses, they are easy to grow, resisting pests, drought and diseases.

*Tall, luminous clumps of golden reed grass, combined with the brown flower heads of showy stonecrop and the silky white seed pods of giant silver grass (background), rise from an island in the middle of a circular driveway. The plants are cut back to the ground in early spring, just before the new growth begins.*

41

# Focusing on form

Deciduous trees and shrubs, stripped of their leaves in winter, reveal the beauty of their bare bones. Shapes, outlines, bark textures and colors hidden or overlooked in summer suddenly come into sharp focus: the fantastically twisted branches of a curly hazelnut shrub, the silver tracery of beech-tree branches, the deeply ridged bark of an Amur cork tree. Complementing them in a snowy landscape are deciduous vines, whose intertwined stems enhance garden structures in winter as much as in summer.

*A century-old European beech tree spreads its fanlike form against a blue winter sky. Its smooth, silver-gray bark is clearly visible only in winter; during the rest of the year it is hidden under a thick veil of leaves.*

*A wisteria vine, its trunk twisted with age, crowns a gazebo like a giant bird's nest. Supporting it are the posts of old gas lamps set in concrete. In late fall and early winter, stems that no longer flower are pruned away.*

*The slender gray trunks of a stand of quaking aspens, mottled with green moss, are as beautiful in winter as in summer. These*

native trees of the Pacific Northwest are valued for their resiliency in strong winter winds as well as for their decorative bark.

# Ornaments for a wintry landscape 3

In contrast to summer gardens, a winter garden is mostly savored from indoors, looking out. "Let's face it," says one realistic gardener, "how many of us will tramp across the yard through a foot of snow to inspect our Christmas roses?" So in designing your winter garden, begin from the vantage point of a room with a view.

Where, in the winter, do you sit most often and look out? The answer may surprise you. Quite often it is not in the living room, which may face the street rather than the garden. For one family it is an upstairs sitting room. For another it may be the kitchen, the family room or a bedroom.

In fact, you may discover that you spend more time at a window in winter than you thought you did. True, the days are shorter and darkness comes early, but the view in winter is often clearer than in summer. The leaves are off the trees, the light is frequently brighter, and you may even see the horizon. "There's all that sky," says one gardener, "plus the neighborhood vistas that open up. And the bird-watching is particularly good — in summer we lose sight of most of their comings and goings."

Your winter garden, then, will be part of this scene. But how you choose to introduce and develop it depends on several variables. You could, for example, create a design for a winter garden that extends throughout your property, or you might decide to confine the garden to a separate area that is visible from a single window. If your land is flat, you might extend the winter garden to your property line. If, on the other hand, the ground slopes away, you might prefer to end your garden a few feet beyond the window.

However you resolve such questions of design, your winter garden should blend harmoniously into the landscape throughout the year, but at the same time should emphasize plants that are particularly beautiful in the winter. There are an astonishing number of choices. Among them are trees and shrubs with unusual shapes or

*Refreshed by a granular crusting of late-winter snow, the perky berries and bronze-stained leaves of a patch of wintergreen ground cover enliven a garden in the Pacific Northwest with eye-catching color.*

with foliage that turns surprising colors. Other qualities that contribute to what is sometimes called "winter interest" are colorful stems, buds or trunks, bark that peels or flakes attractively, handsome berries or decorative seed pods.

By the same token the winter garden should exclude from view those plants that are far from their best at this season. Forsythia, for example, is a glorious sight in spring but rather nondescript in winter. Some gardeners give rhododendrons poor marks in winter because their leaves roll up like cigars when temperatures drop below freezing. For one gardener, however, the rhododendron's leaves are an indispensable feature of his winter landscape. "All I have to do is look out the window at my rhododendrons to see what the temperature is," he says.

**SILHOUETTES AND SHADOWS**

Bear in mind, too, that the winter garden presents a different set of visual relationships. In place of the dominant greens of summer, there are now light browns and grays; against these softer hues, bits of color stand out that in summer would be lost. Variations in the texture and color of evergreen foliage are more noticeable. Because the angle of the sun is low, silhouettes and shadows take on strange shapes; shining through foliage or bare branches, the slanting rays of the sun create interesting patterns on the ground or on snow. In fact, snow itself provides a succession of different effects as it progresses from soft powder to a more solid blanket and finally through a gamut of melting stages.

But while subtle colors and textures can be endlessly intriguing, the winter garden's primary visual impact comes from the forms of its plants, chief among them solid masses of tall needled evergreens. These plants are an example of what landscape architects call "bare bones"—elements such as walkways, fences, tall trees or hedges that define the garden's structure. If the basic plan of your garden is agreeable, plants appear at their best. This is true throughout the year, of course, but it is particularly true in the winter. As one designer put it, "You can get away with an awkward garden in the summer, when there are flowers that distract the eye, but not in winter when the camouflage is gone."

**ARRANGING THE BARE BONES**

The best-designed gardens are generally based on very practical considerations. First, make a sketch of the area to be developed for your year-round garden, outlining planting areas, walkways, terraces and fence lines as they seem most pleasing to you. Make sure that the planting areas are large enough to accommodate a number of plants and that you have allowed enough room for the movement of people. Sometimes a minor alteration in the shape or placement of a terrace or walk will greatly enhance a garden's usefulness or balance. Then take a closer look at your plan with winter in mind. One thing you will want to consider is how much sunlight the various parts of your garden receive at different times of the day. Winter-flowering plants such as the Christmas rose require shade in the morning so that their flower buds will thaw gradually after the night's freeze; broad-leaved evergreens will benefit from the partial shade cast by a bare deciduous tree, since direct sunshine may cause winterkill.

Fences, walls and hedges are also important considerations because they shield the garden from wintry winds. But they perform this function in different ways. When wind hits the solid barrier of a panel fence or wall, it is momentarily deflected upward but soon continues with unabated force on the other side. Only the narrow area immediately against the barrier's leeward side is protected. But when wind hits a hedge, its force is broken into swirls and eddies and does not rebuild for some distance. A hedge therefore protects a much wider garden area on its lee side.

The type of hedge you choose depends partly on esthetics: it should suit the garden's scale. But if privacy is a consideration, or if you are screening out an unappealing view, an evergreen hedge is an obvious choice. In winter, a deciduous hedge loses much of its effectiveness. Furthermore, a needled evergreen will generally screen more effectively than a broad-leaved evergreen because its foliage is denser. But a row of needled evergreens along the south side of your garden will cut off much of the winter sunlight.

Give special attention to the contours of the ground. Variations in ground level can be appealing in winter snow. The patterns made by melting or windblown snow on a rolling lawn can be quite beautiful, and some homeowners deliberately grade their lawns to accentuate this effect. Snow sometimes creates odd shapes atop walls and fences. With this in mind, you might want to finish the top of a fence with narrow horizontal strips, to catch snow in ribbons that look like decorative icing on a cake.

A number of other elements in the bare bones of a garden's composition deserve special consideration. Trellises should be intrinsically good-looking; in winter, with no greenery to hide them, their design is revealed. Statuary makes the transition into the winter scene easily — provided it is weatherproof. Rocks can be strong focal points in a winter garden. If nature has not supplied them and you are adding some, be sure to set them solidly into the ground with the grain of all the stones running in the same direction.

Finally, the sight of chairs and tables in a winter garden can, rather surprisingly, be very appealing. The most practical furniture

**SHIELDS AGAINST THE WIND**

**MAKING THE MOST OF SNOW**

for this purpose is rustproof wrought iron or plastic-coated metal because these materials dry quickly and are easy to maintain. But rot-resistant wood, although slow to dry after a snowfall, tends to appear warmer and more inviting and blends naturally into the colors of the winter landscape.

A MIXTURE OF PLANTS

With the garden's bare bones determined, you can turn to refining your selection of plant materials. An important question to be resolved is the mix of evergreen and deciduous plants. Some gardeners believe that the more evergreens they have, the better. Evergreens, it is true, are the mainstays of the winter garden, flourishing when everything else around them appears to be dead. But their solid mass can be monotonous and can make the garden seem dark — the very opposite of the effect you want on a gray day in winter. Mixing evergreens with deciduous plants lets in light and air and may introduce such provocative extras as colorful stems, attractive bark or interestingly formed branches. Some of the best winter effects are achieved by placing lacy deciduous shrubs against a banked group of evergreens or, reversing the order, by placing evergreen shrubs where they will be seen against the delicate tracery of deciduous tree branches.

Fully as important as the mix of plants is plant hardiness.

**SHAPING UP SHAGGY CONIFERS**

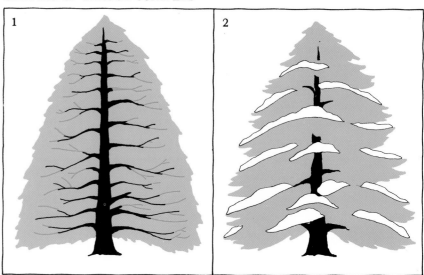

Conifers such as spruce, fir and pine may conceal an attractive framework beneath shaggy foliage. To expose a shapely trunk-and-branch pattern, thin out branches (blue) in late spring or early summer, cutting them back to the trunk with lopping shears.

Careful pruning improves the appearance of these evergreens, especially in winter when they are set off by a light frosting of snow. Pruning also lets more sunlight and air reach the tree's center, producing healthier foliage near the trunk.

Although you may want to include a plant or two that is marginally hardy in your area, it is best to compose the basic framework of your garden with plants that are absolutely reliable. Otherwise, if you have a severe winter the entire garden may be wiped out. The hardiness range of many plants to consider for winter interest is given in the encyclopedia entries in Chapter 5. Even if a plant is cleared for the zone you live in, it is advisable to check with a knowledgeable local nurseryman or an extension agent before buying; your particular neighborhood may be exceptional.

In considering hardiness, you will want to decide early how you feel about wrapping plants with burlap during severe winters. Landscape designers usually are against it. "I don't believe in putting my plants in shrouds," says one. "A plant has to make it on its own and it is odd, to say the least, to hide the green that makes it evergreen." To which one winter gardener on the New England coast replies with some asperity, "That's all very well, but if we had not wrapped our evergreens during one recent winter, we would have lost them all." In the end, to wrap or not to wrap is something you must decide for yourself, based on conditions in your own garden.

**EVERGREENS UNDER WRAPS**

In choosing trees for a winter garden, the possibilities are many. Some can be singled out for grace and elegance of form. There are, for example, the dogwoods and Japanese maples, both notable at other times of year for their foliage, flowers or berries; both have, in addition, a handsome framework of branches that makes them outstanding in winter gardens. The beeches are also splendid in winter, having a special grandeur, but they grow very large. More manageable is the European hornbeam, which has a distinctive oval shape.

There are a number of needled evergreens that also have shapes of distinction. You might want to consider, for example, some of the cedars or firs, which are best suited to large gardens since they may become extremely tall. In the eastern United States, the broad pyramidal shape of the white pine makes it a good choice, while Western gardeners might select the picturesque, spreading bristle-cone pine for their winter settings. For gardens near the sea, the angular asymmetrical Japanese black pine resists damage from both high winds and salt spray.

**FORMS OF DISTINCTION**

For even more distinctive shapes, there are weeping and pendulous trees. The weeping hemlock, some of the cherries and the Red Jade crab apple are good examples; the bright red fruit of the latter may also last into the winter. The white trunk of the European birch, obscured by its drooping branches in summer, is visible in winter. A classic, of course, is the golden weeping willow, whose young branches are yellow. But the weeping willow sheds twigs, creating a maintenance problem, and its invasive roots sometimes clog drainage pipes. Its cousin, the corkscrew willow, looks like a conventional tree in summer when clothed in leaves, but in winter reveals twisted, contorted branches whose shapes must be seen to be believed. Some of the false cypresses also assume unexpected shapes, and the pencil-shaped variety of Virginia cedar called Skyrocket has a uniquely narrow form.

**BARK THAT GETS ATTENTION**

A number of trees are distinguished by bark that peels, or exfoliates, providing interesting textures and mottled colorings. One of the finest of these is the paperbark maple, whose red-brown bark peels off in thin sheets. Another is the Korean stewartia, an exceptional tree in any season of the year. In summer it bears white flowers, in autumn bright orange-red foliage, and all through the year its dark brown outer bark flakes off to reveal light-brown or green bark underneath. Also a splendid sight throughout the year is the peeling bark of the white or paper birch — which should, incidentally, be allowed to peel naturally. Pulling off the bark of any exfoliating tree is likely to injure the plant.

The shagbark hickory certainly belongs in the category of trees with decorative bark and so does the lacebark pine, whose bark peels to reveal gray, cream and white underlayers. The shredding brown bark of the Russian olive is pleasing and calls attention to the angular trunk of the tree. In warmer climates, the peeling light-brown bark of the crape myrtle accentuates the sculptural quality of the tree's clustered trunks. "Tree barks," observes one landscape designer, "are endlessly fascinating. Someday I'd like to design an entire garden around them."

**STALWART MINIATURES**

Among smaller plants the choice for winter beauty is equally wide. In a class apart are the dwarf and slow-growing varieties of needled evergreens — hemlocks, spruces, pines, Japanese cedars, yews and junipers. The foliage of these miniature trees and shrubs often changes color in winter, and may vary from blue-green to gold to bronze-purple. Also useful for dressing up the winter garden are broad-leaved evergreens and deciduous shrubs with unusual shapes, berries, foliage or stem colors. Foremost on anyone's list of shrubs for the winter garden are the broad-leaved evergreens that keep their looks in bitter cold. Among the most handsome and dependable of these are the mountain laurel and the two andromedas, mountain and Japanese. All three have deep green leaves, in both winter and summer. The beloved boxwood is, of course, vulnerable to damage from heavy snow and ice, which may snap its brittle stems. But its look-alike, Japanese holly, is more resistant to snow injury and may be clipped into any shape you wish. When the leatherleaf viburnum is protected from cold drying winds it will keep its handsome, crinkly leaves all year round.

The contorted branches of some deciduous trees have their counterparts among the deciduous shrubs. One of the strangest is the Harry Lauder's Walking Stick, whose gnarled, twisting stems rival the shape of the trademark cane of the famous Scottish entertainer. Another is the vine maple, a shrubby tree whose long, limber branches trail across the ground or can be trained like a vine to grow against a wall. The twigs and branches of the winged euonymus, with their odd, corklike ridges, make this plant arresting even after its brilliant red autumn leaves have fallen.

Fully as useful to the garden are the shrubs with winter color in their leaves and stems. The foliage of drooping leucothoë turns a reddish bronze when the temperature drops, as does that of Oregon holly grape, the P.J.M. rhododendron and several other broad-leaved evergreens. Warminster broom provides the unexpected sight of bright green winter twigs in a sunny spot, and on a cold, crisp winter day, the pale green fluttering leaves of evergreen bamboo make lacy patterns against the snow.

**BRONZES IN THE SNOW**

Probably the most flamboyant winter color is that provided by the stems of the Tatarian dogwood, which may be crimson, purple or coral red, depending on the variety. For the strongest color, however, this shrub must be grown in full sun and heavily pruned in the spring after it has flowered, since only new stems are brightly colored. This is also true of several other plants, notably kerria, whose new growth is a glossy green in winter.

One colorful winter-garden plant that looks tropical but in fact is dependably hardy as far north as Zone 7 is the Japanese aucuba, which may have solid green or green-and-gold leaves, depending on the variety. If you plant both male and female aucubas, you will get a winter bonus of large red berries — a dividend also offered by a number of other shrubs. Chief among them, of course, are the hollies. Except for the few self-fertile species and hybrids such as Chinese holly, these need male and female plants in order to produce berries, at least one male to 10 females — but the expense of acquiring a berryless male plant is well worth it. The shiny leaves and berries of the holly turn the winter garden into a scene straight out of a Christmas card.

Usually the berries of the holly are shades of red and orange, but several varieties have yellow berries, and one, the inkberry, has glossy black fruit. Also, though most hollies are evergreen, there are two deciduous species that bear abundant fruit. One is the possum

**A SPECTRUM OF BERRIES**

haw, a Southern shrub with large orange-red berries; the other is the winterberry or black alder, whose stems are lined with coral-red berries, which birds relish.

Other plants besides hollies produce fruit, of course, and many of them last into winter. Pyracantha's orange or red berries cling to its branches through much of the winter, and so do those of cotoneaster and barberry. The scarlet hips of two hardy shrub roses, multiflora and memorial, are also long-lasting. A number of other shrubs put out berries of various colors: sea buckthorn bears bright yellow-orange berries that last through the winter; snowberry has white or pink-and-white berries, depending on the variety.

Perhaps the most dazzling berry display is put on by skimmia, a low-growing, well-proportioned shrub that is hardy in Zone 7. In a shady, protected spot, planted by twos, male and female together, skimmia will hold its holly-like berries all winter long, since one of its advantages (or disadvantages, depending on your priorities) is that its fruit is ignored by the birds.

**CARPETS FOR COLOR** For textural variety beneath trees and shrubs you will want a ground cover or two. In a winter garden the choice includes a number of favorites from other seasons of the year. The spring-blooming epimedium, though it eventually loses its leaves, puts on an impressive autumn foliage display that extends well into the cold months. Wintergreen's bronze-tinged foliage also performs well in winter, as do the purple-red leaves of the wintercreeper. Among evergreen ground covers, it is important to identify those that provide a pleasing winter carpet without stifling any of the winter-blooming bulbs. Myrtle, for example, is sufficiently airy for a bulb bed, but English ivy and pachysandra permit virtually no sunlight to warm the ground beneath them.

Especially useful as evergreen ground covers along the edges of walks or to establish isolated spots of green are sarcococca, paxistima and evergreen candytuft; all three are shrublike rather than creeping. Several low-growing ornamental grasses also make excellent winter ground covers. One of the best is blue fescue, a true grass that forms small clumps and keeps its silvery-blue color all winter. Mondo grass and lily-turf, though not strictly grasses, have long, slender grasslike leaves that stay green year round.

**THE SURPRISING FERNS** Finally, there are evergreen ferns, often overlooked as winter ground covers, though in fact some are hardy as far north as Zone 3. Probably the most familiar is the aptly named Christmas fern, but others that should be considered are the soft shield fern, ebony spleenwort, common polypody and the cliff brake fern. Ferns need some shade, even in winter, and in a winter garden should be closely massed, since they tend to become prostrate in cold weather.

To supplement these plant materials in your winter garden consider three other decorative elements: mulches, birds and lighting. Mulches add textural interest where there are no plants, as well as covering areas that would otherwise be muddy in winter. Decorative mulches come in many forms, the choice depending on your taste and on availability. Some mulches are so uniform in color and size — buckwheat hulls, for example, or fir and pine bark — that they can be monotonous over large areas. Pine needles are attractive, if you can get them, but they can be a fire hazard in summer. Wood chips, often available from tree maintenance crews, tend to bleach to a silvery-gray color as winter progresses. Pebbles and stones create fascinating effects and, though expensive, need replenishing less often than organic mulches.

Birds can be mesmerizing — they provide life, color and movement in the otherwise subdued winter landscape. Attracting birds to your winter garden means providing food for them and giving them protection from the elements, from predators such as cats and from competitors such as squirrels. Birds value security, and any feeder should be placed not far from trees or shrubs that offer them refuge. As for protecting the feeder from cats and squirrels, numerous

**REFUGE FOR THE BIRDS**

**A MARRIAGE OF CONVENIENCE**

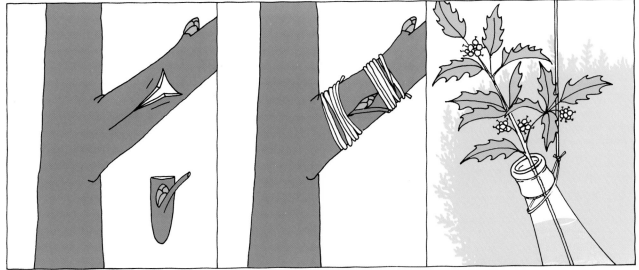

To produce berries on a female holly without planting a male holly, graft male buds onto a female's branches. Cut a 1½-inch-long T in the female's bark. Slice an inch-long wedge with a leaf bud from a young male; pinch off the leaf but not its stem.

Pry up bark at the sides of the T-shaped cut and push the male bud down into it, using the leaf stem as a handle. Bind the graft with cotton string. As the holly matures, prune the faster-growing male branches in order to keep them within bounds.

Another way to obtain holly berries without planting berryless males is to cut several flowering branches from a male plant. Place them in a water-filled container hanging among the branches of a female holly. The pollinating bees will do the rest.

55

# Inviting birds to your garden

Birds will brighten a winter garden with their color, movement and sound if you keep them supplied with food and water. It is better not to start feeding them, however, unless you intend to continue all winter, because birds soon learn to depend on your generosity and will perish if it is withheld. The devices shown below will keep birds coming to your garden even if you go away for a few days. A seed hopper (1) provides food for several days, whenever birds need it. Even early birds have trouble catching worms when the ground is frozen, but you can feed insect eaters suet, a high-protein insect substitute, on logs (2) suspended from tree branches. Birds need unfrozen water (3) to drink, clean their plumage and stimulate oil glands in the feathers that insulate them from cold. A metal baffle (4) mounted beneath a feeder will keep cats and squirrels at bay.

## THE LURE: FOOD AND WATER

1. *Attract birds with seeds that pour automatically onto a platform from openings near the bottom of a hinge-topped box. The hopper is a piece of curved sheet metal fastened to the back wall of the box. Drill ¼-inch holes through the platform so rain will drip through, and attach the feeder to the window ledge for easy refilling.*

2. *Present suet on a log in which wedges are cut with a hatchet or a saw. To hold suet in place, stretch wire or weatherproof twine across it, wrapping the wire or twine around nails placed at opposite sides of the wedge.*

3. *Winterize a birdbath placed near the shelter of a tree by equipping it with an aquarium-type immersion heater weighted down with stones that also serve as perches. Birds, unlike human beings, do not suffer from exposure to frigid air when damp.*

4. *To encourage timid birds, put food in full view on a platform with a roof that you can add to keep the seeds dry after the birds feel safe. Attach the roof by slipping bolts through the holes in the feeder edges and roof supports. A sheet-metal collar makes the feeder cat- and squirrel-proof.*

devices have been designed to thwart these creatures. They are usually available at garden-supply centers and they work with varying degrees of success.

In choosing a feeder, consider the kinds of birds you wish to attract. Some are seedeaters — and some seedeaters prefer to pick up seeds from the ground rather than from a feeder. Others are insect eaters that prefer suet to seed in winter; you can set suet out for them in a wire-mesh feeder. Most birds welcome the wild-bird seed mixture that you can buy in supermarkets, but for smaller birds like the tufted titmouse and the chickadee you might rig up a separate small tube of sunflower seeds, so they can eat without being pushed aside by blue jays or starlings.

Planting certain trees and shrubs will also draw birds to your garden. The winter fruits of dogwood, hawthorn, holly, pyracantha and bayberry are particular favorites; indeed, dogwood berries are popular with more than 75 different kinds of birds. The colder the winter, the more the birds will dip into this food supply.

But even as you watch your holly berries disappear, remember that birds cannot survive on berries alone. Once you start feeding them seeds, keep feeding them until spring arrives. Birds also continue to need water. If you have a birdbath, keep it filled; otherwise, set out a pan of water. In freezing weather, some wildlife enthusiasts set out warm water every morning for birds to use. Others install immersion water heaters in their birdbaths.

Night lighting can similarly run from the makeshift to the elaborate, but it is best and safest to use low-voltage weatherproof wiring and fixtures. They can be purchased at most hardware stores. Before installing these fixtures permanently, you should try various combinations and angles of light, keeping in mind that a winter garden should be lit somewhat differently from a summer one. A winter garden is viewed primarily from indoors, whereas a summer garden is lit for outdoor sitting and strolling. Usually a small adjustment will suit the lighting needs of both seasons.

Where you place the lights varies with each garden. Sometimes a tree looks better illuminated from above, sometimes from below. Some shrubs may be effectively lit from the front, others silhouetted from behind. Often sculpture is enhanced by side lighting, bringing out its modeling. The intensity of the light also makes a difference — you may discover that a 15-watt bulb with its soft light does more for your garden than a brighter one. One thing, however, is essential: do not install an outdoor light so that it shines in your neighbor's eyes. The winter scene you create to view from your windows should be delightful from his windows, too.

**A NATURAL FOOD STORE**

**LIGHTING THE NIGHT SCENE**

# Brilliant color under balmy skies

Gardeners in areas where winters are mild may have to contend with occasional frost, but with luck they are never without flowers. Many of these flowers bloom on evergreens, often the stalwarts in Southern gardens just as they are in the North. Indeed, they may be identical with evergreens that flower later in Northern gardens. If you go to Savannah in February, for example, you will be greeted by azaleas in full bloom. In the antebellum gardens of Charleston, South Carolina, the rhododendrons will be out.

Azaleas and rhododendrons by no means exhaust the possibilities. A glorious array of other broad-leaved evergreen plants bursts into bloom in winter in the gentle climates of Zones 8-10. A few are trees, several are vines, a great number are shrubs. Winter is the flowering time of the sweet-smelling Carolina jessamine and of the frothy pink-and-white strawberry tree. In Southern California a succession of acacias flower through the winter, and all through the Old South the beautiful camellia unfolds its breathtaking blooms in a multiplicity of colors and shades. Sweet osmanthus, which Deep South gardeners call tea olive, has small flowers but such a delicious fragrance that it is a favorite winter-bloomer.

Like most evergreens, these Southern plants often need special growing conditions. Many need the filtered sunlight found beneath the branches of tall trees or the shade of a protective wall. Year-round moisture may also be a requisite. Their foliage, vulnerable to cold, drying winds, fares better where it is humid year round, and many need mulches to keep shallow roots moist. As a group they are tender plants, but some are more so than others. The large, lush flowers of the Chinese hibiscus, for example, are safe only where temperatures remain above 50°. On the other hand, a number of Southern evergreens actually need a period with some chilling to produce the best blooms. To Northern gardeners, accustomed to equating swelling buds with the zephyrs of spring, it may be a surprise that the delicate camellia is forced into flower when brushed by the brisker air of a Southern winter.

*Rhododendron cilpinense, a hybrid that is hardy to Zone 8, brightens an entranceway in Seattle with winter blooms. The flowers open pale pink, then gradually fade to white.*

## Trees ablaze with color

Among the most spectacular Southern evergreens that flower in winter are the small trees. Although some are technically shrubs with multibranching trunks, they reach heights of 30 feet, spread even wider, and possess an ornamental value so great they are commonly used as centerpiece plants. The acacia, for example, is prized for feathery gray-green foliage as well as flowers, the evergreen pear for thick, shiny, leathery leaves, the aptly named strawberry tree for bright red strawberry-like fruit.

*An Acacia baileyana, laden with fragrant yellow flowers, decorates a winter garden in the mild climate of Zone 9 in Southern California.*

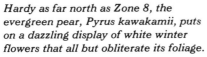

Hardy as far north as Zone 8, the evergreen pear, Pyrus kawakamii, puts on a dazzling display of white winter flowers that all but obliterate its foliage.

Last year's fruit and this year's winter flowers hang on the branches of the strawberry tree, Arbutus unedo, which is hardy as far north as Zone 8.

# Wallflowers to catch your eye

Winter-flowering evergreens that cling to walls, cover trellises and spill from wrought-iron balconies are so common in Southern gardens that they are virtually a trademark. Some are vines, like the scarlet-flowered bougainvillea of Zones 9 and 10, and the equally tender and luxuriant flame vine, whose orange blossoms often crown terra-cotta roofs. Others, like the calliandra and Carolina jessamine shown here, are shrubs with such long, trailing branches that they lend themselves well to being espaliered.

Carolina jessamine, trained to grow
on a garden wall, perfumes the winter
air with yellow flowers. A Southern
favorite, it is grown in Zones 8-10.

Years of careful pruning translated
this red-flowered calliandra into a wall-
wide evergreen cloak. Frequently
called the powder-puff shrub,
calliandra is hardy in Zones 9 and 10.

# The versatile Southern belles

The winter-flowering shrubs of Southern gardens are versatile as well as decorative, serving either as focal points or as formal or informal hedges and privacy screens. Their foliage can be delicate or sturdy, their ultimate shape compact or sprawling, their blossoms demure or vibrant. Some are adaptable, like Indian hawthorn, which survives despite poor soil and ocean spray. Others are demanding, none more so than winter daphne, which repays intensive care with a pervasive fragrance that makes all the work worthwhile.

*Indian hawthorn, clipped into a formal hedge, lines a broad, outdoor stairway. These popular evergreens bloom all winter long south of Zone 8.*

*A variegated winter daphne, hardy to Zone 8, brightens a terrace garden; the dainty pink flowers fill the late-winter air with roselike perfume.*

*Bright red funnel-shaped flowers and glossy foliage decorate a neatly pruned Cape honeysuckle all winter in Zones 9 and 10.*

*Clusters of tiny winter flowers rest like snow on the branches of laurestinus, a care-free viburnum that grows in Zones 8-10.*

A Camellia japonica shares a shaded patio garden in Charleston, South Carolina, with a Nandina domestica whose berries echo

the scarlet blossoms of the camellia. Japonica is probably the most popular of all the winter-flowering evergreens in Zones 8-10.

# In pursuit of year-round bloom 4

A gardener who lives in northern Maine has winter aconites in bloom in early February. Another gardener in upstate New York enjoys violas and winter-flowering heaths straight through the cold months. A Long Island gardener reports having a crocus in bloom the day before Christmas; an Indiana gardener cuts forsythia that will bloom indoors weeks ahead of schedule. Admittedly winter flowers are no match for the spectacular displays of summer, but that never seems to matter. "There's as much joy in finding a single flower in February," says one veteran, "as a whole border in June."

Getting plants to flower in winter is a tantalizing game, especially for gardeners living in the broad central belt of the United States represented by Zones 5-7 *(map, page 148)*. What will come up? And if it comes up, will it flower? There is always an element of adventure. South of this belt, in Zones 8-10, there are plenty of opportunities for winter flowers. North of Zone 5, there is often little chance of seeing flowers until spring.

Nevertheless, even the cooler parts of the United States and southern Canada have a number of plants that will flower in winter. Some do so naturally. Others normally flower in late autumn or early spring but have been induced to extend or advance that period of bloom. Zealous winter gardeners narrow the gap in their gardening calendars to a few weeks around the turn of the year. With luck and weather permitting, they sometimes bridge the gap completely by creating conditions that mimic Indian summer or early spring.

The key to successful mimicking is warmth. To flower ahead of or beyond their normal schedule, plants need to be shielded from the harshest rigors of winter. Some gardeners use the shelter of a pit greenhouse *(page 72)*. But if you have a garden of average size, you should have little trouble providing propitious conditions in the open air. First, look at your garden and identify places that are warmer than others, where the snow melts soonest and there is ample winter

*A spray of winter-flowering witch hazel, brought inside to be forced into early bloom, reflects the shape of a witch-hazel bush in the snow-filled garden. On the bush, buds are just beginning to show color.*

# A solar-heated underground greenhouse

A pit greenhouse is basically a hole in the ground roofed with glass and warmed by the sun. Insulated by the surrounding soil, it needs little or no artificial heat to keep temperatures above freezing. There the winter gardener can raise vegetables, start seedlings or store tender perennials.

Choose a sunny, well-drained site; the greenhouse can be either freestanding or adjoin a house wall. Excavate to a depth of 5 feet and line the walls with concrete blocks. Extend one end of the pit to allow for a door and stairway. Put down a 1-foot layer of stones graded from large to small and cover with 6 inches of tamped-down soil. Plastic drain tiles outside the base of the walls improve drainage.

Roof the south side of the pit with greenhouse glass or plastic panels and the other sides with fiberglass insulation between boarding. A window opposite the door and a vent in the north roof keep the pit from becoming too warm. Provide electricity for a small fan, a light and a heater. On cold nights and gray days a layer of straw covered by a tarpaulin insulates the glass roof.

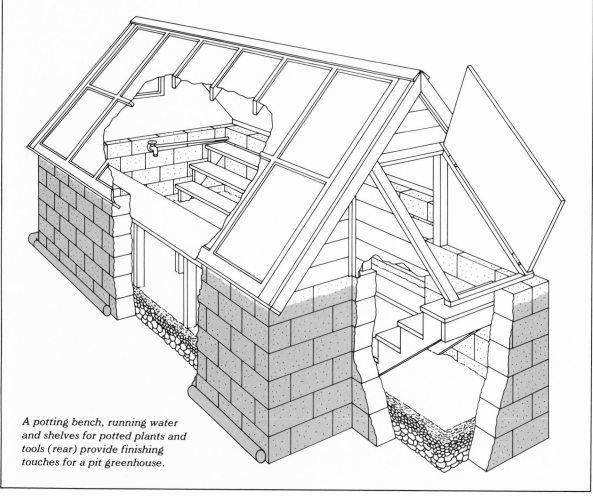

*A potting bench, running water and shelves for potted plants and tools (rear) provide finishing touches for a pit greenhouse.*

sunlight. If there are rocks or a south-facing masonry wall to absorb the sun's heat and radiate it through the day and into the evening, so much the better. A furnace or fireplace chimney will radiate some heat through the bricks, and a ground-level window may leak enough warm air to affect plants growing immediately outside.

Second, be sure this area is protected from cold prevailing winds by a house wall, a solid fence or a dense evergreen hedge. Third, shun low areas that trap down-flowing cold air and are subject to early-fall or late-spring frosts *(page 30)*. Fourth, take advantage of structures that will trap or convey heat. Finally, improve the soil by digging in a mixture of compost, peat moss and sand; loose, well-drained soil will not freeze as hard as damp clay soil.

*(page 30)*

These ideal conditions are often found in a rock garden, particularly one that faces south and has a light, well-drained soil. In addition to offering the warmth of the rocks, a rock garden is a logical setting for many of the small plants that flower in winter, especially bulbs native to mountainous areas. For many gardeners the hardy bulbs are the first choice for winter bloom. A dozen or so can be tucked into a space no larger than a man's handkerchief and, blooming in succession, provide color almost all winter.

After roses, chrysanthemums and the other floral vestiges of summer have faded, two kinds of bulbs — crocuses and colchicums — bring color to the garden from fall until the end of the year. Until a week or so before Christmas the late-flowering fall crocus, *Crocus laevigatus fontenayi,* produces flowers that are buff-colored on the outside and lilac inside. It is quickly followed by the bright orange *Crocus vitellinus* and *Crocus imperati,* with purple stripes on its white or lilac petals. Colchicums look like large crocuses, and one species, *Colchicum speciosum,* is almost a foot tall and resembles a tulip, though the plants are not related. Colchicums are available in shades of mauve, lavender or white, and have one curious feature. Their foliage, nonexistent when the bulbs are in bloom, suddenly appears in spring and grows about a foot tall, dying back in midsummer. You will want to plant colchicums where their broad, rather coarse foliage will be disguised by other plants.

These bulbs may not be available at garden centers, but can usually be bought by mail from firms that specialize in bulbs. They should be ordered in late summer and planted when they arrive, so roots will have time to develop before the ground freezes. Plant each at a depth equal to three times its maximum diameter.

The earliest spring crocuses appear while snow is still on the ground. If the snow is only a few inches deep and the bulbs get enough sunlight, they may even win the flowering sweepstakes and

**CAPITALIZING ON WARMTH**

**THE SPECIALTY BULBS**

appear in early January, before their close rivals, the snowdrops and winter aconites. Note, however, that these are not the familiar Dutch hybrid crocuses but species crocuses, and they are marvelously varied. One of the earliest to bloom is *Crocus sieberi,* a handsome lilac-to-purple flower from the mountains of Crete and Greece.

Another species crocus is *C. chrysanthus;* varieties range from cream color and orange-yellow to various shades of light blue. Or you may want to try *C. susianus,* the cloth-of-gold crocus, with stripes of brown on a golden-yellow background.

**DEFYING WINTER SNOWS**

Species crocuses should be planted in late summer or early fall so the bulbs will have a chance to go through a warm period to develop their roots, followed by a cold period to start top growth. If this cold period is delayed by a late winter, flowering will also be late. The bulbs should be allowed to bake in summer through a period of dry heat; they should never become waterlogged. Properly cared for, they are marvelously sturdy. They will sprout through snow and flower above it, and if buried by fresh snow, they will bloom anew when they have full access to sun. In fact, they are so dependent on light that they will not open on a cloudy day.

Shortly after the crocuses, and sometimes simultaneously with them, the snowdrops and winter aconites make their appearance. True to their name, the snowdrops are undeterred by snow, and will last for several weeks. If temperatures drop below freezing they may become limp, but they will resume their jaunty demeanor as soon as the weather improves. Most gardeners are familiar with the diminutive variety, *Galanthus nivalis,* but may be unaware of the larger *Galanthus elwesii,* with stalks 10 inches tall and white flowers an inch or more wide marked with emerald green on the inside.

Unlike crocuses, snowdrops need some shade for strongest growth. So too do winter aconites, whose bright yellow flowers look like overgrown buttercups — a plant to which they are related. Winter aconites differ from crocuses and snowdrops in being unusually dependent on moisture. If their bulblike corms seem dried out when you get them, soak them overnight before planting them in soil that remains moderately moist all year.

**THE STURDY CYCLAMEN**

By February, assuming the weather has moderated a bit, these pioneering stalwarts are likely to be joined by a number of other early-flowering bulbs. One of the loveliest is the Coum cyclamen, a small relative of the florist's cyclamen. In fall it produces attractive kidney-shaped foliage, and then in late winter it bears a clump of small, elegant white, pink or red flowers. The Coum cyclamen needs excellent drainage and, in cold areas, a protective mulch.

Several dwarf irises that grow from bulbs can also be expected at this point. Most notable are *Iris reticulata,* with deep violet flowers, and *Iris danfordiae,* with bright yellow flowers. The flower stalks of these plants are only 6 inches high, but their leaves may be a foot or more long and have sharp tips for pushing through frozen ground or snow. The irises may develop a fungus disease in summer unless they are kept bone dry. They can usually be protected by surrounding them with sand, but you may dig them up in spring after their foliage has yellowed and store them indoors until fall.

Another group of early-blooming bulbs that needs to be protected from excessive moisture belongs to the narcissus clan. The earliest is the tiny *Narcissus asturiensis,* just 2½ inches high, which looks like a conventional daffodil seen through the wrong end of a telescope. Its bulbs are often hard to find. Slightly larger is the hoop-petticoat daffodil, with funnel-shaped flowers. Although most varieties of this species do not bloom in Northern gardens until March, two varieties, *foliosus* and *romieuxii,* may flower during a February thaw — but they will disappear for the year if the temperature drops again. A third daffodil that may flower at this time is February Gold, which grows to a more standard size.

As the winter-flowering bulbs come and go, you may wish for the constancy of longer-lasting color. The wish can be fulfilled in part by a handful of perennials and two somewhat bizarre annual

**FINDING GOLD IN FEBRUARY**

**PRUNING SHRUBS FOR INDOOR BLOOM**

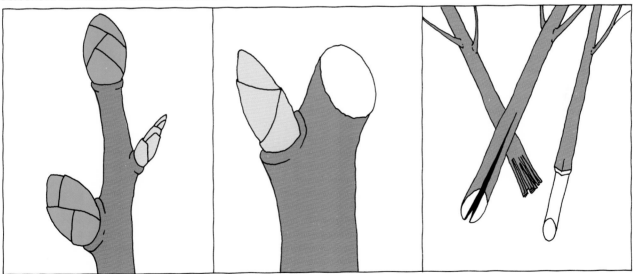

*To obtain bountiful winter flowers indoors, cut branches from early-blooming shrubs that bear numerous large, rounded flower buds (dark green). The smaller, pointed buds (light green) will produce leaves.*

*Cut the branches just above a leaf bud at a 45° angle in the same direction that the bud is pointing, using sharp pruning shears. This angled cut is not as likely to damage the leaf bud as a cut made straight across the branch.*

*To help cut branches absorb more water, slit the ends of slender stems to a depth of 3 to 4 inches. For thicker stems, crush cut ends with a hammer, or shave outer bark to expose the water-absorbing layer just beneath.*

vegetables, ornamental kale and ornamental cabbage. These look-alike plants, which resemble nothing else in the flower garden, have tight heads of leaves, opening from the centers, which may be off-white or deeply tinged with pink, rose, red or purple at the centers, shading to emerald around the edges. When started from seeds in midsummer, they put on a startling display that may last into January. The color of individual plants cannot be predicted, however, so it is best to keep seedlings in pots until they begin to show color. Then place them in the garden to suit your color scheme.

**THE RELIABLE HELLEBORES**

Of the several perennials that flower in winter, the most valuable for winter gardeners of the North are probably the hellebores. These plants from the Alps can be grown as far north as Zone 4 and as far south as Zone 9. The most striking is the Christmas rose, which is not really a rose but like all hellebores is a member of the buttercup family. Its blooms are dazzling white, 2 to 3 inches across, with yellow stamens. As they age, the petals turn pink or green.

With luck and moderate weather, the Christmas rose may indeed bloom at Christmas, but an appearance in late January or February is more likely. "No one ever told my Christmas rose that we celebrate the event in December," one gardener said. A few weeks later the flowers of three other hellebores appear. The cream-colored Lenten rose almost always blooms by March; there are also hybrids with green, brown or purple flowers. The green flowers of setterwort and Corsican hellebores bloom in time for St. Patrick's Day. All hellebores have lustrous, evergreen foliage.

Hellebores can be difficult to start, but once established, they are extremely hardy. They are best begun from clumps bought from

*(continued on page 80)*

# Harbingers of winter's end

*A number of early-blooming bulbs are so hardy that they flower even before the soil has fully thawed, opening their bright petals against patches of glistening snow. If they are planted in sun-catching, south-facing sites, snowdrops and winter aconites, the earliest of the bulbs, may bloom in January in the North — sometimes as early as New Year's Day. Typically, species crocuses appear in February, followed by squills, chionodoxas and a handful of the hardier daffodils. Most of these bulbs can survive a late storm quite handily, emerging from under a layer of newly fallen snow. They have a still better chance if they are planted in the quick-draining soil of a rock garden or on a slope.*

*To ensure that they get enough light to promote early flowering, early-blooming bulbs should not be planted under evergreens or against a north wall. Dense ground covers such as ivy may also shade them from sufficient light. It is safer to plant them among the more open-growing periwinkle, or alongside low-growing wildflowers.*

*Early-blooming crocuses like these, emerging in late winter, are most striking when planted in drifts of 25 or more.*

# Flowers that flout the cold

The round cups of winter aconites pop out of the ground by mid-March in bitter-cold climates.

Looking like purple-dyed daisies, Greek anemones unfold their petals under the first rays of the March sun.

The glory-of-the-snow resembles Siberian squill (opposite), except that its petals face up to the sky.

In its early stages, this white squill's flowers are a soft, silvery blue color that pales as the foliage ages.

The sharp leaves of snowdrops can push up through ice and frozen soil, before the bell-like flowers open.

Harput irises, the gold spots on their petals flashing in the sun, typically rise out of the gray slush of March.

Star-shaped Siberian squills, which bloom in March, are notably prolific, spreading with each passing year.

With broader petals than its violet counterpart above, the yellow Danford iris may bloom in late February.

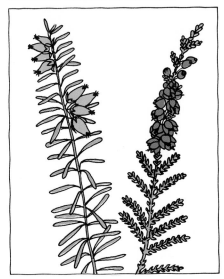

*From a distance, heaths and heathers look very much alike and in fact the two plants are related. But a close look will reveal differences. Heath (left) is the common name for the genus Erica, which is noted for its needle-like foliage and urn-shaped flowers. Heather (right), or Calluna, has scalelike leaves and bell-shaped flowers that divide at the rim into four parts. Most heaths bloom in winter and spring, while heather blooms in late summer and early fall.*

**COLORFUL RELATIVES**

a reputable nursery. Shade is essential, especially in midsummer, and they need a rich neutral-to-alkaline soil deep enough to accommodate a long taproot. Because of the root, hellebores do not usually survive transplanting. The plants may take several years to reach flowering size, but the wait is worth it. A mature hellebore not only puts on a good midwinter show but provides cut flowers for bouquets that last up to 12 days.

Another plant that will bloom in the coldest months of the year is the Johnny-jump-up, a relative of violets and pansies. Few things are more astonishing than the sight of its dainty blue, yellow or white flowers nestled against the ground when the weather is at its worst.

By late winter the Johnny-jump-ups and hellebores compete with several other perennials. One of the most rewarding is the Amur adonis, with fernlike foliage and cup-shaped yellow or apricot blossoms up to 3 inches wide, that may remain fresh for two months. Others are two pulmonarias, cowslip lungwort and Bethlehem sage, which grow a foot or more and have blue or reddish-violet funnel-shaped flowers. Completing the list is a Himalayan import, *Primula denticulata,* the earliest of the primroses. Himalayan primrose has dainty ½-inch flowers that are violet, purple or white.

Just as the cool, misty slopes of the Alps and Himalayas are the source of many of the winter-flowering bulbs and perennials, so the cool, misty moors of Scotland are the source of another group of favorites: the winter-blooming evergreen heaths. One of the prettiest of these low-growing shrubs, *Erica carnea,* produces tiny white, red, pink or purple flowers right into spring. It comes in many varieties, perhaps the sturdiest being King George. Writer-photographer Mildred Graff tells of going out to take a picture of King George's rosy flowers in 15° weather in a gale-force wind. In the time it took to brush snow off the plants, her fingers stiffened and the camera shutter refused to work properly. Her picture was useless — but the King George stayed sprightly and unperturbed.

The heaths are closely related to the heathers, but the two plants are quite different in appearance and behavior. Heaths have needle-like leaves and bloom in winter and early spring; heathers have scalelike leaves and flower in summer — although the winter foliage of some varieties is so spectacular that it too is an important source of winter color. When hit by frost, a hillside of heather becomes a kaleidoscope of reds, yellows, purples, bronzes, oranges, browns, pinks and olive green. Indeed, a gardener must exercise restraint to avoid gaudiness. Furthermore, as you walk around a clump of heather it changes hue, for its colors characteristically develop most vividly on the side facing the sun. Heather seen as

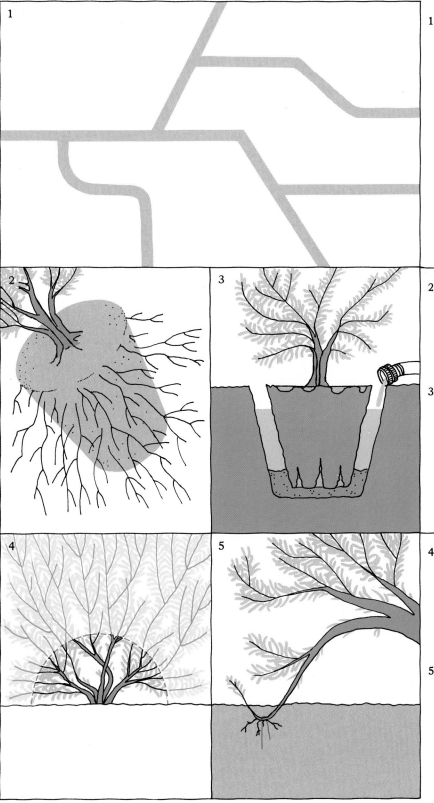

## DESIGNING DRIFTS OF COLOR

1. *Beds of heath and heather look most natural when planted in irregular drifts across a sunny slope protected from winter winds. First sketch the drifts on paper, allowing enough room in each drift for at least three plants. Then transfer the plan to the garden, outlining each area with sand or clothesline. Although no two adjacent drifts should contain the same plant variety, the whole bed will look more unified if no more than a total of five different color varieties is used. Heaths and heathers grow best in a sandy soil enriched with peat moss or other organic material.*

2. *If plants come from the nursery in plastic containers, remove the containers and gently loosen the fine, fibrous roots with your fingers. Roots will then penetrate the new soil more easily, becoming quickly established.*

3. *If plants are in peat pots, crush the pot bottom to hasten root penetration, and set the pot directly in the prepared hole. Water well and fill the hole with equal parts of soil, peat moss and sand. Break off the pot rim if it extends above the soil; otherwise it will act like a wick, drawing off water. Plants will die if the roots dry out.*

4. *To keep heaths and heathers bushy and to stimulate blossoming, shear back dead growth to healthy green wood, removing one half to two thirds of the plants' height. Shear spring heath right after flowering, other species in spring just before new growth begins.*

5. *Propagate new heath and heather plants by bending a low branch of an established plant to the ground and burying it so the branch tip extends upward. Hold the buried branch in place with a bent wire until roots develop, then snip the new plant from the parent and transplant to the desired location.*

orange from one point may be green when viewed from another side.

Heaths and heathers like sandy, acid soil and the cool, moist conditions of their natural environment. They are hard to grow in dry parts of the United States and in the warm, humid Southeast, where they live for only four or five years. They also need sunlight but at the same time protection from winter sun and wind, a condition that can usually be met with an eastern exposure and by interspersing them with other shrubs. A heavy mulch is often necessary to keep the roots from drying out. Otherwise, they are relatively trouble-free, needing only annual pruning — in late winter or very early spring for heathers and just after flowering for winter-blooming heaths — to keep the plants from looking scraggly.

**BEWITCHING BLOSSOMS**

A number of other shrubs, both small and large, also contribute bloom to the winter garden. Chief among them are the witch hazels, a group of large gray-barked deciduous shrubs the size of small trees. Witch hazels grow from Zone 8 north, and open their yellow or red-to-yellow blossoms at various times all through winter, depending on the species. The earliest to flower is the Virginia witch hazel; its small yellow flowers appear as the leaves drop in fall, and remain on the tree into December. During a mild spell in January, you may see the yellow-to-red flowers of the vernal witch hazel, which unrolls long ribbon-like petals in good weather and rolls them up again when temperatures drop; it will continue to do so, with increasing frequency, until early spring. While the vernal witch hazel is still performing, it will be joined by the Chinese and Japanese witch hazels. The Japanese is the hardier of the two, but the Chinese has the more spectacular blooms; its branches are thick with red or golden-yellow ribbon-like flowers that are fragrant and last for weeks.

Yellow flowers abound on winter-blooming shrubs. Winter jasmine, a trailing deciduous shrub, exhibits small tubular yellow blossoms from midwinter to early spring. Not sturdy enough to stand alone, it looks best trained on a trellis or cascading over a wall. The Cornelian cherry, a shrubby relative of the flowering dogwood, also has a profusion of yellow flowers in late winter. Wintersweet and winter honeysuckle, neither a particularly elegant shrub, make up for their lack of shape with extremely fragrant flowers that bloom in mild spells from December to March. And the yellow-flowered evergreen shrub, leatherleaf mahonia, blooms as early as February.

**FROM YELLOW TO WHITE**

Color other than yellow can be obtained from the silver-pink catkins of the pussy willow, which may emerge in February on the native American shrub, and later but more luxuriantly on the French pussy willow. The evergreen shrub *Sarcococca hookerana* bears white blossoms in February — even earlier in the South.

Southern gardeners, in fact, have a cornucopia of winter bloom not available to gardeners in the North. The familiar springtime bloom of azaleas in Northern gardens emerges in Zone 9 in the South and along the West Coast in the middle of winter. Two hybrid evergreen groups in particular, the Kurume and Indica azaleas, will bloom from late December through early spring. And few Southern gardeners can resist the opportunity to have magnolias in bloom a month after Christmas. Although the evergreen magnolias bloom in late spring and summer, the smaller deciduous star magnolia puts on a display of fragrant, snowy-white flowers in February in Zone 8 and as early as January in Florida and other parts of Zone 9.

But for winter bloom in Southern gardens probably no plant can surpass the camellia, the finest of all winter-flowering shrubs. Originally brought from China to Europe, the camellia prospered in areas where summers were warm and winters were cool enough to give them some chilling. Well before the Civil War more than 100 varieties of camellia were being cultivated in the gardens of Charleston, South Carolina, and today they are widely grown in many parts of Zones 8 and 9, and even (though rather unpredictably) in Zone 7.

The best-known camellia is probably the *Camellia japonica*, often called simply japonica. Its large white, pink or red blossoms begin to appear in December or January and put on a show at least

**THE FINEST OF ALL**

**CARING FOR CAMELLIAS**

To ensure that a camellia, which has shallow roots, is not smothered under too much soil, set the plant in a prepared hole so the root crown is 1 inch above ground level. The plant will settle, but not enough to harm it.

During their first winter, protect the newly planted camellias from strong winter wind and sun by erecting a shelter of 1-by-2s covered with bamboo or burlap. The shelter should especially block the morning sun.

To stimulate extra-large camellia flowers, remove the leaf bud closest to the flower bud you wish to enlarge, leaving the leaf calyx in place. Put a drop of gibberellic acid solution, a growth hormone, in the leaf calyx.

## Selections for a mild climate

For the gardeners who live in southern Florida and Texas, and along the coast of Southern California, winters are so mild that it is possible to have annuals and perennials that bloom in December and January. The annuals selected for this purpose are called winter-hardy, meaning they are likely to survive occasional short bouts of cold. A list of favorite annuals and perennials is at the right, along with the best time for planting.

**AEONIUM ARBOREUM ATROPURPUREUM** (*black tree aeonium*) *Set out plants in early spring or early fall.*

**ANTIRRHINUM MAJUS** (*snapdragon*) *Set out seedlings in early fall.*

**BELLIS PERENNIS** (*English daisy*) *Sow seeds in late summer or early fall.*

**CALENDULA OFFICINALIS** (*calendula, pot marigold*) *Sow seeds in late summer or early fall.*

**DIMORPHOTHECA HYBRIDS** (*Cape marigold, star-of-the-veldt*) *Sow seeds in late summer or early fall.*

**IBERIS UMBELLATA** (*globe candytuft, annual candytuft*) *Sow seeds in fall.*

**KALANCHOE LACINIATA** (*kalanchoe*) *Sow seeds in spring.*

**LAMPRANTHUS SPECIES** (*ice plant*) *Set out plants in early spring or early fall.*

**LATHYRUS ODORATUS** (*sweet pea*) *Sow seeds in late summer or early fall.*

**LOBULARIA MARITIMA** (*sweet alyssum*) *Sow seeds in fall.*

**MATHIOLA INCANA ANNUA** (*common stock*) *Sow seeds in early fall.*

**NEMESIA STRUMOSA** (*nemesia*) *Sow seeds in fall.*

**PAPAVER NUDICAULE** (*Iceland poppy*) *Sow seeds in late summer or early fall.*

**PRIMULA POLYANTHA** (*polyanthus primrose*) *Set out plants in early fall.*

**SCHIZANTHUS WISETONENSIS** (*butterfly flower, poor man's orchid*) *Sow seeds in fall.*

**SENECIO CINERARIA** (*cineraria*) *Set out plants in spring or fall.*

**SEDUM SPECIES** (*sedum*) *Set out plants in early spring or early fall.*

**VIOLA TRICOLOR HORTENSIS** (*pansy*) *Set out plants or sow seeds in late summer.*

*A midwinter border that includes annual calendulas blooms in a California garden against cypresses and a bare elm.*

until the middle of March. Second in popularity is the *Camellia sasanqua,* which has smaller though more abundant flowers and blooms in late fall and early winter. The sasanqua camellias do equally well in sunlight or shade — unlike the shade-loving japonicas. A third species, *Camellia reticulata,* with large flowers but fewer leaves than the other two, has become a favorite of California gardeners. It blooms in late winter or early spring in Zones 8 and 9.

For winter gardens in the South and on the West Coast there are also flowers of another plant category: hardy annuals. These plants bloom in summer in Northern gardens, but can withstand the frosts that sometimes descend even on the subtropical gardens of Zones 9 and 10. Among them are such favorites as calendulas, Cape marigolds, sweet alyssums, sweet peas, stocks, hollyhocks and petunias. Seeds planted in fall will flower by December or January.

ANNUALS FOR THE HOLIDAYS

To match this performance, a Northern gardener would have to resort to a bit of subterfuge. He could, for example, move his winter gardening activities into the relative warmth of a pit greenhouse, a kind of cross between a greenhouse and cold frame. In this underground haven heated by the sun, he could extend the blooming season of such autumn plants as chrysanthemums or fall-blooming irises and crocuses, to provide midwinter bouquets. Or he could advance the season of certain spring-blooming trees and shrubs by cutting branches still in tight bud and forcing them into early bloom indoors. Forsythia is commonly forced into bloom in this way. Other likely candidates are flowering dogwood, flowering quince, azalea and spirea, and such flowering fruit trees as apple and pear.

The technique of forcing plants into bloom in advance of their season is simple. The cut branch is split, peeled or crushed to improve its water intake *(page 75),* then wrapped in newspaper and placed in a vase of tepid water in the coolest room in the house for several days, until the buds begin to open slightly. At that point remove the newspaper and move the vase to a brightly lit place, though not in direct sunlight, which would dry out the buds. The flowers last longer if the air is cool and moist.

Successful forcing is a matter of timing. How soon you can move cut branches indoors is largely up to nature, and depends on the plant's cycle of growth as well as the vagaries of the weather. Achieving winter flowers indoors can be a matter of chance. One Northern gardener watched in dismay as a child broke a branch from a spring-flowering azalea in mid-February. On an impulse, he carried the branch indoors and put it in water. Ten days later he was handsomely rewarded when the azalea burst into a blaze of pink flowers, two months ahead of its normal schedule.

A MATTER OF TIMING

# An encyclopedia of plants for winter gardens 5

Winter offers a time to enjoy subtle features of a garden that are overshadowed in other seasons. No longer burdened by pressing maintenance chores, the gardener has the leisure to appreciate the varied textures of bark and dried grasses, the sculptural silhouettes of deciduous trees, and the many shades of evergreen foliage.

Since winter is a time of dormancy for plants in most climate zones, outdoor gardening is not so much done in winter as it is done for winter. To help in choosing plants that will be attractive through the cold months, the encyclopedia on the following pages describes 94 kinds of plants with desirable winter traits. Some are at their best in early winter when berries punctuate their branches with color. Others offer distinctive shapes or furled flower buds for winter-long interest. There are also bulbs and shrubs that respond quickly to a few extra hours of warmth after the sun has passed its December solstice and burst into bloom in mid- or late winter. The encyclopedia describes growing conditions for each plant, as well as its principal features during other seasons. There are also suggestions on where to place a plant for maximum visual impact.

You may notice that some familiar species are not listed among other members of a particular genus. The plants recommended here have been specially chosen for their winter attractiveness and inbred tolerance to colder weather, qualities that their near relatives may not possess. Each encyclopedia entry is keyed to the climate zone map on page 148, which shows the depth of winter cold each plant can survive. The maps on page 149 broadly define the span of winter in a given region, indicating the dates when the first and last frosts can be expected.

Planning a garden for winter is a relatively new landscaping idea, and a few of the species described may require a search among specialized nurseries. But each one will reward you for the effort by extending your gardening pleasure into a fourth season.

*The subtleties and surprises that await a winter gardener are evident in this sampler of plants, which includes the purple Bar Harbor juniper (center) and the golden flowers of winter aconite (bottom center).*

**WHITE FIR**
*Abies concolor*

**PAPERBARK MAPLE**
*Acer griseum*

# A

## ABIES

*A. concolor* (white fir, Colorado fir, concolor fir); *A. veitchii* (Veitch fir)

Dense, conical trees with flat, aromatic needles that may be either blue-gray or dark green, firs are striking specimen trees and can also be used as screens or background plantings. The closely spaced branches spread out in stiff and formal horizontal layers. Upright cones ripen on the topmost branches in the fall and disintegrate by midwinter. The dark gray bark of young trees is smooth and thin, but it becomes deeply fissured as the trees get older and lose their lower branches. Both firs are hardy in Zones 3-6, although the Veitch fir withstands extreme cold and late-spring frosts better than the white fir.

The colorful white fir has 2-inch-long needles that are blue or gray-green. There are varieties with yellow, silvery white, or blue-white foliage. The 3- or 5-inch cones are green tinged with purple or yellow; young twigs are yellow-green. Although it grows 100 to 120 feet in the wild, the white fir usually gets no taller than 60 feet when it is in a garden.

The Veitch fir is a compact tree that reaches 25 to 50 feet in height. Only ½ to 1 inch long, the dark green needles are banded with silver underneath. In winter, the buds at the tip of each branch are purple; the 2- to 2½-inch cones are blue to purple.

HOW TO GROW. Firs grow best in full sun in moist but well-drained soil with a pH of 5.0 to 6.0. Plant trees in spring or fall and maintain a 3- to 4-inch mulch of shredded bark, oak leaves or pine needles to keep the soil cool and moist. Feed each spring with cottonseed meal or 5-10-5 garden fertilizer. Because of their naturally symmetrical outlines, firs need very little pruning except to remove competing leaders from young trees in early spring. If lower branches are removed, new ones will not develop. Propagate from seeds.

## ARBORVITAE, AMERICAN See *Thuja*

## ACER

*A. davidii* (David maple); *A. griseum* (paperbark maple); *A. palmatum* 'Dissectum' (threadleaf Japanese maple); *A. palmatum* 'Sangokaku' (coral-bark Japanese maple); *A. pensylvanicum* (striped maple, moosewood); *A. rufinerve*

Unusual bark colors and textures coupled with distinctive silhouettes make the maple species listed above especially ornamental in winter. In addition, they all have brilliant fall leaf colors. The group includes maples suited to climates ranging from Zones 3-10.

The David maple is a snakebark maple, so called because its smooth gray-to-green bark is striped with white cracks. Best grown in Zone 6, this tree becomes 30 feet tall with branches that spread as much as 30 feet. The leaves are red when they emerge in spring, turn dark green as they grow to a length of 8 inches, then blaze yellow and purple in fall.

The paperbark maple has distinctive, colorful, shaggy bark in winter as thin shavings of light reddish-brown outer bark curl back to expose new orange-brown bark beneath. In Zones 6-9, this maple slowly develops a rounded silhouette; it seldom grows taller than 25 feet. The fan-shaped summer leaves are deeply cut into 3-inch leaflets that are green above and silvery below; they turn brilliant red in fall.

The Japanese maples have short, often multiple trunks and graceful branches that form lacy, broad winter silhouettes. The two Japanese maples listed here grow slowly to 15 feet in Zones 5-10. The threadleaf Japanese maple has deeply cut, fernlike leaves composed of many tooth-edged leaflets; some varieties have leaves that are red, yellow or tricolored throughout the growing season. Coral-bark Japanese maple is notable for its young shoots of brilliant coral red in winter.

A snakebark maple native to the Eastern United States, the striped maple grows from 15 to 35 feet tall in Zones 3-8. Its 7-inch, three-lobed leaves turn clear yellow in fall. Like the David maple, *A. rufinerve* is a snakebark maple suited only for Zone 6; it grows 30 to 40 feet tall with green leaves that turn reddish in autumn.

HOW TO GROW. Plant maples in any moist, well-drained garden soil where they will receive full sun or partial shade; full sun heightens autumn leaf color and bark color. Shelter the smaller species from wind. Plant nursery saplings in the spring; select grafted varieties of the Japanese maple to ensure desired characteristics. You can prune maples to ensure that small species have multiple trunks, to remove branches from the lowest third of a trunk to display ornamental bark, or to thin older branches from species with colorful young growth. But always prune in late summer or early fall; maples bleed profusely if pruned in spring.

ACONITE, WINTER See *Eranthis*
AMERICAN ARBORVITAE See *Thuja*
AMERICAN BEECH See *Fagus*
AMERICAN CRANBERRY BUSH See *Viburnum*
AMERICAN FILBERT See *Corylus*
AMERICAN HAZEL See *Corylus*
AMERICAN HORNBEAM See *Carpinus*
AMERICAN PLANE TREE See *Platanus*
AMUR CORK TREE See *Phellodendron*

## ANEMONE

*A. blanda* (Greek anemone, Grecian windflower)

Greek anemones provide as much as a full month of color at winter's end, filling in just after the first round of the earliest bulbs. Hardy in Zones 6-9, Greek anemones grow from twiggy tubers into 6- to 8-inch mounds of fernlike leaves topped by 2-inch flowers resembling white, pink, blue or purple daisies. The flowers open in sunlight and close at night or in cloudy weather. The foliage dies down soon after flowering ends. Among the varieties are White Splendour, pure white with yellow centers; Atrocaerulea, clear blue; Ingramii, deep purple; Radar, pink; and Blue Pearl, violet. Greek anemones make an attractive display in perennial borders or among ground covers. The blossoms are longlasting as cut flowers, but the short stems should be cut cleanly with a sharp knife to avoid damaging the tubers.

HOW TO GROW. A deep mulch of salt hay or wood chips in winter will allow Greek anemones to grow north of their usual range, but winter protection is usually unnecessary. Plant the tubers in well-drained, neutral to slightly acid soil enriched with dried manure or compost. Greek anemones grow in full sun or partial shade; shield plants from the sun in the South. Water well during the growing period and add a mulch of leaf mold after the foliage dies to nourish the tubers. Plant Greek anemones in fall, soaking the tubers in water for one or two days, then setting them 4 to 6 inches apart and 2 inches deep. Propagate in late summer by dividing tubers, or grow from seed to bloom in about 18 months.

ANDROMEDA, MOUNTAIN See *Pieris*

## ARCTOSTAPHYLOS

*A. stanfordiana* (Stanford manzanita); *A. uva-ursi* (bearberry, kinnikinick)

*For climate zones and frost dates, see maps, pages 148-149.*

THREADLEAF JAPANESE MAPLE
*Acer palmatum* 'Dissectum'

GREEK ANEMONE
*Anemone blanda* 'Radar'

**BEARBERRY**
*Arctostaphylos uva-ursi*

**RED CHOKEBERRY**
*Aronia arbutifolia*

Winter gardeners cultivate Stanford manzanita and bearberry for the year-round color of their evergreen foliage and the seasonal accents provided by their berries and bark. A shrub that reaches about 6 feet in height and has a similar spread, Stanford manzanita is hardy in Zones 7 and 8 on the West Coast. In winter, its smooth brown bark takes on a distinctive red hue that contrasts attractively with the glossy, bright green 1½-inch oval leaves. Stanford manzanita bears clusters of pink flowers each spring that ripen into ½-inch red-to-brown berries in autumn.

Growing from coast to coast in Zones 2-7, bearberry is a trailing ground cover that becomes 6 to 12 inches tall. Its shiny green leaves turn an attractive bronze in winter if the plant is grown in full sun. The ½-inch scarlet berries, which ripen in fall, cling to the branches well into winter. By rooting at each branch joint, bearberry spreads about 1½ feet a year to form mats up to 15 feet in diameter. In spring, clusters of small pink flowers dangle from its branches.

Both Stanford manzanita and bearberry tolerate coastal winters. Stanford manzanita requires some protection from wind, but bearberry often grows in rocky, exposed seashore areas or on sand dunes where little else survives.

HOW TO GROW. Stanford manzanita grows best in full sun in a well-drained soil. Bearberry grows best in sandy, acid soils with a pH of 4.5 to 5.5. Both plants produce the most berries when grown in full sun, but bearberry will also do well in partial shade. Stanford manzanita loses its naturally rounded form and becomes leggy if planted in shade. Because of their extensive root systems, neither shrub is easily transplanted. Set container-grown nursery plants out in early spring or late fall. Bearberry plants should be spaced about 2 feet apart. Prune the creeping stems of bearberry to confine the shrub to its allotted space.

## ARONIA

*A. arbutifolia* (red chokeberry); *A. melanocarpa* (black chokeberry); *A. prunifolia* (purple chokeberry)

The chokeberries, deciduous shrubs with red, black or purple fruits, hold their decorative berries through much of the winter, thanks to the bitter flavor that makes them unpalatable to birds. The red chokeberry has masses of shiny, bright red ¼-inch berries that appear in fall as the dull green oval leaves turn a brilliant red. The leaves remain on the branches well into fall. Clusters of ½-inch white flowers bloom in late spring. Red chokeberries, which grow 6 to 10 feet tall, are handsome when grown as hedges or planted at the edge of a woodland garden. Like the red chokeberry, the black chokeberry and the purple chokeberry grow from Zones 4-9, but their shining fruits do not persist past fall except in Zones 7-9. Both of these species have red leaves in fall. The black chokeberry grows only 1½ to 3 feet tall; the dense, upright growth of the 10- to 12-foot purple chokeberry makes it a good screening plant.

HOW TO GROW. Chokeberries grow in any good, well-drained garden soil and the red chokeberry will tolerate wet conditions. The shrubs produce the most fruit and the brightest fall leaf color when grown in full sun, although they will grow in partial shade. Mulch the shrubs with 2 inches of wood chips, shredded bark or pine needles to protect the roots from deep frost, and maintain cool and moist soil conditions during the growing season. Pinch new growth in spring to encourage branching; thin out a few of the oldest stems every third or fourth summer to promote good fruiting and flowering. Remove suckers when they appear. Chokeberries can be propagated by rooting cuttings of new growth or by digging and transplanting suckers with their roots.

## ASARUM

*A. europaeum* (European wild ginger); *A. shuttleworthii* (mottled wild ginger)

Wild gingers carpet winter gardens with spicy-smelling mats of heart-shaped evergreen leaves. European wild ginger, hardy in Zones 4-9, grows 5 inches tall and has 2- to 3-inch glossy green leaves. Mottled wild ginger, which grows up to 8 inches in height, has 6-inch-wide leaves marbled or veined with silver. In both species the dull brown or purplish-green flowers appear beneath the leaves, almost at ground level, in late spring and are followed by large, thick seeds. These wild gingers make excellent ground covers and are also favorite rock-garden plants.

HOW TO GROW. Wild gingers grow best in deep to medium shade in moist, humus-rich, slightly acid soil with a pH of 5.5 to 6.5. They are often planted under evergreen trees or shrubs, such as mountain laurel and rhododendrons, that require similar soil conditions and provide the necessary shade. Set the plants out in spring or fall, spacing them 12 inches apart; mulch new plants with oak or beech leaves or hay during their first year. Wild gingers are easily propagated by dividing older plants or by taking cuttings in spring and rooting them in sand for fall planting. These two species also seed themselves freely.

## ASPLENIUM

*A. platyneuron* (ebony spleenwort); *A. trichomanes* (maidenhair spleenwort)

Small and delicate species of ferns, spleenworts are hardy in Zones 3-8. They have two different kinds of fronds. The fertile fronds, which carry reproductive spores on the backs of their leaflets, grow upright and do not last the winter. The ground-hugging rosettes of sterile fronds, on the other hand, are evergreen.

The 8- to 15-inch-long fronds of the ebony spleenwort have polished, purple-to-brown stalks that are lined with narrow, slightly toothed leaflets that each have a distinctive hump on its upper edge near the stalk. The dark green fertile fronds appear first in the spring; rosettes of new, lighter-green sterile fronds appear later.

Growing only 5 to 8 inches long and an inch across, the fronds of the maidenhair spleenwort have round, toothed leaflets. Rosettes of low-growing, sterile fronds emerge first in the spring; the upright, fertile fronds appear later.

Easy to grow, spleenworts are useful in rock gardens and for planting in wall crevices or along stone ledges, especially limestone ledges.

HOW TO GROW. Spleenworts benefit from a light winter mulch of leaves to keep the soil from drying out and to protect their roots. They do best in gravelly or sandy soil that has a pH of 7.0 to 8.0 and is enriched with leaf mold. The soil should be well drained but constantly moist since spleenworts will tolerate only short dry periods. Select a site with partial-to-deep shade. Before planting, prepare the soil by mixing 1 part garden soil, 1 part builder's sand and 2 parts peat moss or leaf mold with 2 tablespoons of ground limestone per cubic foot of soil mixture. Plant in the spring, setting maidenhair spleenworts 6 to 8 inches apart and ebony spleenworts 10 to 12 inches apart. Place the crown — where the roots and leaves meet — 1 inch below the soil surface. Feed the ferns each spring thereafter by working bone meal into the soil around the plants at the rate of 1 ounce per square yard, or use water-soluble fish-emulsion fertilizer at half strength. Prune dead fronds off at any time the plants are actively growing. Propagate by dividing the plants in the spring or fall.

*For climate zones and frost dates, see maps, pages 148-149.*

EUROPEAN WILD GINGER
*Asarum europaeum*

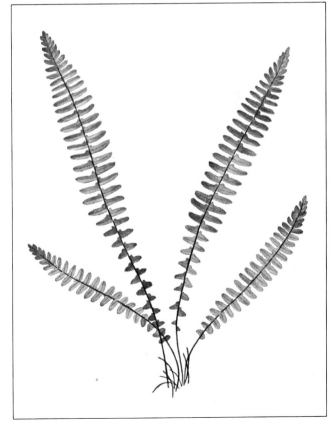

EBONY SPLEENWORT
*Asplenium platyneuron*

JAPANESE AUCUBA
*Aucuba japonica* 'Picturata'

JAPANESE BARBERRY
*Berberis thunbergii*

## AUCUBA
*A. japonica* and varieties (Japanese aucuba)

Colorful the year round, Japanese aucuba is an especially cheerful shrub in winter with its splashy evergreen foliage and, on female plants, large clusters of scarlet berries. The glossy serrated leaves, 4 to 6 inches long, are narrow and willowy or broad and oval depending on the variety, each of which is distinctively spotted, streaked or mottled with yellow or white. The foliage of Variegata, sometimes called the gold-dust tree, is spotted with yellow; that of Crotonifolia is spotted or barred with white; Picturata has leaves with yellow centers and green edges, while the variety Sulfur reverses that color pattern. On female plants, the small purple flowers that bloom in 2- to 5-inch clusters each spring develop into erect, oval red berries that last all winter. In its range from Zone 7 southward, the Japanese aucuba is a tough, durable shrub that grows 10 to 15 feet and about half as wide in only 10 years.

HOW TO GROW. Japanese aucubas grow best in partially shaded areas and do well even in deep shade; full sun will burn the foliage. The shrubs grow in almost any kind of soil but they thrive in those that are moist but well drained; established plants will withstand drought. Plant Japanese aucuba in spring or fall, setting out a ratio of about 1 male plant to every 10 female shrubs to ensure good fruit production. To encourage leafy growth, apply a light top-dressing of a high-nitrogen fertilizer such as cottonseed meal to the soil in early spring. Japanese aucuba seldom needs to be pruned but the shrubs can be shaped with hand clippers in early spring; make cuts just above the buds at the base of leaf joints. Propagate additional plants by rooting cuttings of new growth in moist sand.

## AZALEA See *Rhododendron*

# B
BAMBOO, HEAVENLY See *Nandina*
BARBERRY, JAPANESE See *Berberis*
BARBERRY, WINTERGREEN See *Berberis*
BAY, BULL See *Magnolia*
BAY, SWEET See *Magnolia*
BAYBERRY, See *Myrica*
BAYONET, SPANISH See *Yucca*
BEARBERRY See *Arctostaphylos*
BEECH, AMERICAN See *Fagus*
BEECH, EUROPEAN See *Fagus*

## BERBERIS
*B. julianae* (wintergreen barberry); *B. thunbergii* (Japanese barberry)

Tough, vigorous shrubs, the wintergreen and Japanese barberries have stiffly arching, thorn-covered stems adorned in winter with either glossy leaves or bright berries. The wintergreen barberry forms a dense mound of 7- to 10-foot stems lined with 3-inch, spiny evergreen leaves. Hardy in Zones 6-9, this Chinese native produces masses of small yellow flowers in the early summer, followed by a crop of blue-black berries.

The more upright deciduous Japanese barberry offers a winter display of shining red berries clustered along grooved, 4- to 7-foot stems. Yellow blossoms precede the tiny berries in late spring and the 1½-inch leaves provide a brilliant red display before dropping in autumn. Grown in Zones 4-10, varieties of this species include Atropurpurea, with purple leaves; Atropurpurea Nana, a dwarf 1 to 2 feet tall; Erecta, with a compact, conical form; and Minor, a dwarf only 12 to

18 inches high. All of the barberries make excellent barrier hedges but their use is prohibited in some areas because they serve as alternate hosts for wheat rust.

HOW TO GROW. Barberries are noted for their vigor in poor soils, but wintergreen barberry grows best in a moist but well-drained soil with full sun. Japanese barberry will flourish anywhere under virtually any growing conditions except deep shade. Both benefit from a 2-inch organic mulch such as wood chips, shredded bark or pine needles left in place the year round. Thin a few of the oldest canes every second or third winter. To better display the berries of Japanese barberry, prune the outermost twigs. If barberries become overgrown, they can be cut back to the ground to rejuvenate them. Barberry hedges can be sheared. Plant Japanese barberry and wintergreen barberry in fall or early spring; set 1-foot-tall plants 2 feet apart in a hedge. Propagate from cuttings at any time.

## BERGENIA

*B. cordifolia* (heartleaf bergenia); *B. crassifolia* (leather bergenia, Siberian tea)

The thick, leathery leaves of bergenias remain green during the winter in Zones 7-9. The foliage turns an attractive red-to-bronze in Zones 4-6, although extremely cold temperatures combined with exposure to wind may wilt or sunburn the leaves. Because their rosettes of bold, glossy leaves have a strong visual impact, bergenias are frequently planted along walks as edgings, used as ground covers or mixed with other plants in rock gardens. The leaves are also used in floral arrangements.

The round, 8- to 10-inch-wide leaves of heartleaf bergenia have wavy, serrated edges; the leaves of leather bergenia are similar to those of the heartleaf, but more nearly oval. Both plants spread along thick underground stems, or rhizomes, to form clumps 2 to 3 feet wide. In early spring before the new leaves emerge, 3- to 6-inch clusters of small waxy flowers in shades from pale pink to rose or white, depending on the variety, bloom above the old foliage.

HOW TO GROW. Bergenias thrive in full sun or partial shade but they are largest when grown in the shade; in hot areas, shade is necessary to keep the leaves cool. They do not do well in Florida or along the Gulf Coast. They grow in any soil but do best in moist, well-drained sandy soil enriched with peat moss, leaf mold or other organic matter.

Growth is rapid in moist sites but slow in dry soils. Fertilize bergenias in spring, sprinkling 0-20-20 garden fertilizer or bone meal and wood ashes around the plants and scratching it lightly into the soil. Remove any damaged leaves and faded flowers in spring. Plant bergenias in groups in spring, spacing them 12 to 15 inches apart. After three or four years of flowering, divide overcrowded clumps in the spring or fall. New plants that have been started from seed take two years to reach flowering size.

## BETULA

*B. albo-sinensis* (Chinese paper birch); *B. nigra* (river birch); *B. papyrifera* (canoe birch); *B. pendula* (European white birch); *B. platyphylla; B. populifolia* (gray birch)

Distinctive in the winter garden for their graceful, bold silhouettes and white or red peeling bark, birches often grow in clumps with multiple trunks. While a few species are rugged sturdy trees, most of these rapid-growing trees are short-lived and susceptible to diseases and insect pests, particularly the bronze birch borer and the birch leaf miner. They compensate for these shortcomings, however, by leafing out in spring long before other trees have broken their

**HEARTLEAF BERGENIA**
*Bergenia cordifolia*

**CANOE BIRCH**
*Betula papyrifera*

*For climate zones and frost dates, see maps, pages 148-149.*

winter dormancy, by turning an exquisite golden yellow in fall, and by providing striking winter profiles.

The Chinese paper birch grows to 75 feet with an open, rounded crown. Hardy in Zones 5 and 6, this rare birch is at its ornamental best when planted in a spot where its unique bright orange bark is fully visible in winter.

The river birch is often found in wet lowlands in Zones 4-7. Growing up to 60 feet in height, it has multiple trunks that give it an irregular outline. Young trees have shiny, cinnamon-brown bark that flakes off to reveal pink-to-brown bark underneath. The bark on the lower portion of older trunks becomes red-to-black and has deep fissures.

The familiar canoe birch, with chalky white bark curling back in sheets to expose yellowish-tan patches underneath, is the most widely used birch species for winter settings. Grown in Zones 2-6, a mature canoe birch has either single or multiple trunks and an open, irregular shape spreading to about half of the 60- to 75-foot height of the tree. Its slender trunks and delicate twigs give this birch a lacy winter outline that is enhanced by the small, inch-long seed clusters dangling from its outer twigs.

The European white birch grows up to 60 feet in Zones 2-6. Pyramidal in shape, with either single or multiple trunks, this Eurasian counterpart of the canoe birch has pendulous branches that sometimes sweep the ground. The white bark, distinctive though not as striking as that of the canoe birch, is most ornamental in winter when the leaves that obscure it in summer drop from the pendulous branches. Several well-formed varieties of the European white birch include Fastigiata, with a columnar shape; Tristis, with slender branches and a more rounded form; and Youngii, with an irregular outline and branches that droop more noticeably than those of the other varieties.

*B. platyphylla,* an ornamental birch from Japan with thin, ruffled white bark, grows 60 feet tall in Zones 4-6. This species is noteworthy for its resistance to pests.

A young gray birch might be mistaken for a canoe birch, but when mature, it is a much smaller tree, rarely over 30 feet tall, and lacks the peeling bark of the canoe birch. The common name of this tree alludes to the color of areas where its white bark meets dark triangular patches, which are actually scars left by branches that have fallen off. Its multiple trunks often lean at sharp angles after they have been bent under the weight of winter ice and snow. It is attractive in small winter gardens where trees of limited size are needed.

HOW TO GROW. All birches do best in a moist, but well-drained soil in full sun. The roots of the river birch and the European white birch can stand in water for short periods without harm. Since both the bronze birch borer and the birch leaf miner are difficult to control in their destructive phases, the best cure is prevention. After planting balled-and-burlaped trees in spring, wrap their trunks to prevent borer entry and keep them watered well. Top-dress the soil under the trees annually with compost to provide nutrients necessary to keep the trees healthy, and water during dry spells. If insects attack, clean up leaf debris in fall and prune and burn infested branches. Always prune birches in summer or fall; trees pruned in winter or spring bleed excessively.

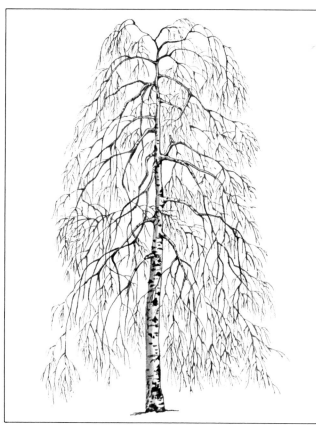

YOUNG'S WEEPING BIRCH
*Betula pendula* 'Youngii'

BIG BLUE LILY-TURF See *Liriope*
BIRCH, CANOE See *Betula*
BIRCH, CHINESE PAPER See *Betula*
BIRCH, EUROPEAN See *Betula*
BIRCH, GRAY See *Betula*
BIRCH, RIVER See *Betula*
BLACK GUM See *Nyssa*

BLACK TUPELO See *Nyssa*
BLUE BEECH See *Carpinus*
BLUE FESCUE See *Festuca*
BOX, COMMON See *Buxus*
BOX, ENGLISH See *Buxus*
BOX, LITTLE LEAF See *Buxus*
BOX, SWEET See *Sarcococca*
BOXWOOD See *Buxus*
BRAMBLE, WHITEWASHED See *Rubus*
BROOM, COMMON See *Cytisus*
BROOM, SCOTCH See *Cytisus*
BROOM, WARMINSTER See *Cytisus*

## BULBOCODIUM
*B. vernum* (spring-meadow saffron)

Despite their name, the 4-inch funnel-shaped flowers of the spring-meadow saffron break through the ground in midwinter in the Southern portion of its wide range. Similar in appearance to crocuses, these early rose-to-violet flowers fade, then are followed by narrow, grassy leaves that reach 5 inches in height. This foliage withers in the early summer. Suitable for rock and woodland gardens from Zone 3 southward, spring-meadow saffron grows from tiny corms that multiply readily.

HOW TO GROW. Spring-meadow saffron grows best in full sun with sandy, well-drained soil. Set the corms out in early autumn, planting them 3 inches deep and 4 inches apart. Allow the foliage to ripen and wither before removing it, in order to replenish the corms for the next season's bloom. Propagate additional plants every three years in midsummer or fall after the foliage dies by removing the tiny new offsets that grow beside older corms; replant the old corms in fresh soil to renew their vigor.

BULL BAY See *Magnolia*
BUTTONBALL See *Platanus*
BUTTONWOOD See *Platanus*

## BUXUS
*B. microphylla* (littleleaf boxwood or box); *B. sempervirens* (common box, English box)

Box forms dense masses of evergreen foliage that can be sheared into elegant, formal shapes or allowed to spread into billowy mounds of small oval or tongue-shaped leaves set in pairs along the twiggy branches. Littleleaf box is a 3- to 4-foot-tall, cold-resistant species hardy in Zones 5-10, but its leaves sometimes turn brown in severe cold weather. A variety that reliably retains its dark green leaf color all winter long is Wintergreen, which grows 2 feet tall and spreads about 4 feet wide. Common box, with its fragrant dark green leaves, grows from Zone 6 southward. It may reach a height of 15 feet or more but can easily be kept smaller with pruning. Cold-resistant varieties include Vardar Valley, a 2-foot shrub that spreads 4 to 5 feet; Northern Find, which forms a 3-foot-tall, rounded mound; and Northland, which grows 4 feet tall and about 5 feet wide.

HOW TO GROW. Box grows in full sun or partial shade in any moist, but well-drained soil. Since box is sensitive to extremes of either heat or cold, choose a site protected from both winter winds and full summer sun. Plant balled-and-burlaped shrubs in spring and mulch them with an inch-thick layer of pine needles or wood chips to keep the roots cool and moist. If the leaves begin to lose their deep green color, spread cottonseed meal or lawn fertilizer under the shrubs in the spring. Prune box in early spring before new growth begins, removing any dead branches and shearing into for-

SPRING-MEADOW SAFFRON
*Bulbocodium vernum*

LITTLELEAF BOXWOOD
*Buxus microphylla*

*For climate zones and frost dates, see maps, pages 148-149.*

**FEATHER REED GRASS**
*Calamagrostis epigeios hortorum*

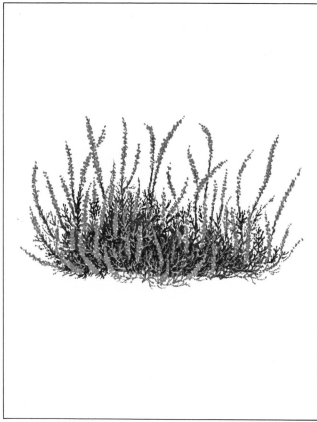

**BLAZE AWAY HEATHER**
*Calluna vulgaris* 'Blaze Away'

mal shapes, if desired. To prevent winter damage in areas with occasional heavy snowfalls, use a broom to sweep snow gently from plants before the weight of it bends or breaks the brittle branches. Do not plant box where it will be hit by snow falling off the roof of a house.

# C

## CALAMAGROSTIS
### *C. epigeios hortorum* (feather reed grass)

Feather reed grass, an ornamental grass that grows from creeping underground stems called rhizomes, forms thick clumps of gracefully arching stems 3 to 4 feet long. Green in summer, feather reed grass turns brown after frost and remains standing through the winter. In summer, the stout flowering stalks that rise about 2 feet above the leaves are so bristly with tufts of flat, rough, ¼-inch spikelets that each of them resembles a hairbrush. These flower stalks also persist through the winter, turning gold in late fall. Feather reed grass is particularly suitable to naturalistic gardens, where evergreen shrubs or trees make an effective backdrop for its brown winter hue and curving lines. It is hardy in Zones 6-9.

HOW TO GROW. Feather reed grass grows best in sandy, dry soils in sunny locations. It will tolerate partial shade and drought and withstands periods of wet weather, provided its soil has excellent drainage and water does not remain standing around its roots. In late winter or early spring, before new growth has begun, cut clumps of feather reed grass to within 2 to 6 inches of the ground. The clumps increase slowly in width and can easily be kept at a constant size by occasionally removing some of the underground stems. No other maintenance is required. Propagate feather reed grass from seed or by division in spring or fall.

## CALLUNA
### *C. vulgaris* and varieties (Scotch heather)

The heathers of the Scottish moors, celebrated in song and legend, grow in twiggy, dense mats of green or golden foliage that, depending on the variety, may turn a bronze or red hue to brighten winter landscapes. In Zones 4-6, which have the cold winters that these plants require, the many varieties of Scotch heather range from 4 to 24 inches high. The branches are covered with tiny scalelike leaves that stay on the plants year round. In summer to early autumn, Scotch heathers bear 1- to 6-inch spikes of tiny, bell-shaped flowers in shades from white-to-red, pink and lavender. When cut and dried, these blossoms last many months in flower arrangements.

Varieties of Scotch heather that are especially appropriate for winter plantings because of their cold-weather foliage colors and flowering habits include Aurea, a dwarf shrub 9 to 12 inches tall with foliage that is russet in winter, gold in summer; Blaze Away, an 18-inch shrub with deep red foliage turning gold in the summer; Bronze Beauty, 18 inches tall with golden-yellow leaves all year that take on a purplish hue near the bottom of the plant; Golden Feather, an 18-inch-tall heather with gold or orange foliage summer and winter on stems that resemble tiny plumes; and H. E. Beale, a 24-inch shrub with green foliage all year and pink flowers that bloom in late fall and last until early winter.

HOW TO GROW. Scotch heathers need a poor, moist but well-drained, acid soil with a pH of 4.5 to 5.5; in humus-rich soils, heathers become leggy and eventually die. Though these plants bloom most profusely when grown in full sun, heathers need protective shade in areas with an inadequate snow cover to screen them from the late winter sun, which burns their foliage and can kill plants. A light winter mulch of pine needles or hay protects the shallow roots from thawing and heaving during the winter. To encourage new growth or to limit the height of the shrubs, shear them with hedge clippers to half their height in early spring; pruning in any other season may severely injure the plants. Set heather out in early spring, spacing the plants a foot apart and watering them frequently until the roots are established. In early spring, apply an acid fertilizer such as those sold for hollies or rhododendrons. New plants are easily started by ground-layering branches of older shrubs or by rooting cuttings taken in late summer in sand and then setting them out the following spring.

## CAMELLIA

*C. japonica* and varieties (common camellia); *C. sasanqua* and varieties (sasanqua camellia)

Gardeners from Zone 7 southward treasure the winter-flowering camellias for both their polished evergreen foliage and their waxy pink, white or red flowers that resemble peonies or roses. Early-blooming varieties of both the common and the sasanqua camellias begin to flower in mid-autumn and later-blooming varieties extend the flowering season through early spring.

The common camellia grows into a shrub or small tree 6 to 10 feet tall in 10 to 15 years. Among its glossy, 2- to 4-inch-long oval leaves, flowers bloom in shades from white through pink-to-red or variegated. They vary in form from a single row of petals around prominent yellow stamens to semi-double or double-petaled flowers that have ruffled centers. Among the varieties recommended for the winter garden are Bernice Boddy with pink flowers, Betty Sheffield Supreme with white-and-pink mottled flowers and Kramer's Supreme with deep red flowers.

The sasanqua camellia, a smaller, more open shrub with narrower leaves, grows 5 to 6 feet tall in 8 to 10 years. Its flowers, ranging from deep pink to white, almost always have a single row of petals. Three varieties for good winter color are rose-pink Cleopatra, ruby-rose Sparkling Burgundy and pure white White Dove, also called Mine-No-Yuki.

HOW TO GROW. Camellias require an acid soil with a pH of 6.0. A sandy soil mixed with peat moss is ideal, as it provides the moist but never soggy conditions these plants need. Camellias must be kept evenly moist since too much or too little water causes their buds to drop. In most locales, camellias do best planted in lightly shaded areas beneath deciduous trees such as oaks; in coastal areas with high humidity, they can be grown in full sun. Plant camellias in early spring in Zone 7; spring or fall planting is appropriate in other zones. Set the shrubs so that the soil line at which they previously grew is an inch above the new soil line; this will avoid suffocation of the shallow roots. A 2- to 4-inch mulch of pine needles or shredded bark will protect roots and provide the evenly moist conditions these plants need. In spring, when new growth begins, fertilize camellias with any commercial fertilizer specially prepared for rhododendrons and camellias. To maintain their shape or remove dead wood, prune camellias just after flowering, before new growth begins. Start new plants from cuttings taken in early summer.

CANADA HEMLOCK See *Tsuga*
CANDYTUFT, EVERGREEN See *Iberis*
CANOE BIRCH See *Betula*
CAROLINA HEMLOCK See *Tsuga*

## CARPINUS

*C. betulus* (European hornbeam); *C. caroliniana* (American hornbeam, blue beech, ironwood)

*For climate zones and frost dates, see maps, pages 148-149.*

GOLDEN FEATHER HEATHER
*Calluna vulgaris* 'Golden Feather'

COMMON CAMELLIA
*Camellia japonica*

97

**AMERICAN HORNBEAM**
*Carpinus caroliniana*

**SHAGBARK HICKORY**
*Carya ovata*

A hornbeam tree's smooth bark fits so tautly over its ridged trunk that the tree appears to be muscular. Pointed, cinnamon-colored buds stand out in contrast to the gray bark, and many fine-textured twigs also add to winter interest. The dense green summer leaves turn yellow or orange in fall, then turn brown and sometimes cling through winter.

In Zones 6-9 the European hornbeam grows slowly to a dense conical or oval form 40 to 60 feet tall and 30 to 40 feet wide; older trees become vase-shaped as their aged boughs droop. The pyramidal European hornbeam, Fastigiata, is a variety that develops a more upright profile 30 feet high and 10 to 12 feet across. The American hornbeam has multiple trunks that branch in zigzag fashion to develop a low, broad shape 20 to 30 feet high and wide. Grown in Zones 3-8, it is occasionally called the blue beech because its bark has a blue cast.

HOW TO GROW. The disease- and pest-resistant hornbeams thrive in deep, moist soil. The European species requires full sun but the American tolerates partial shade. Hornbeams are not easy to transplant and should be moved with a large soil ball. Plant young trees no more than 8 feet tall in their permanent locations in spring. Hornbeams can also be planted 2 to 3 feet apart and sheared into a hedge.

## CARYA

*C. ovata* (shagbark hickory)

Ragged-looking trunks and statuesque oval silhouettes up to 100 feet tall make shagbark hickories notable in a winter landscape. The gray bark curls away from the trunk in long, narrow flakes. The handsome, feathery, deciduous leaves of summer, up to 14 inches long, turn golden yellow in fall when thick green husks surrounding edible nuts ripen and burst. Grown in Zones 5-8, hickories reach their ultimate height slowly; saplings bear fruits four to seven years after planting and take 10 years to grow 15 to 20 feet tall.

HOW TO GROW. The brittle branches of the shagbark hickory split under heavy loads of snow or ice. Cut damaged limbs back to an outward-facing bud in late winter before new growth starts. To develop a strong branch structure in a young tree, select a single main trunk when the tree is 4 to 5 feet tall and remove competing branches. As the leader grows, allow side branches to develop at 18-inch intervals. Grow hickories in full sun in moist but well-drained sites with deep soil. Hickories have long taproots, which makes them difficult to transplant. Start trees from seed or transplant very small seedlings to their permanent locations. To increase the nut crop, plant two or more seedlings in the same area to ensure cross-pollination.

## CEDAR See *Cedrus*
## CEDAR, JAPANESE See *Cryptomeria*

## CEDRUS

*C. atlantica* and varieties (Atlas cedar); *C. deodara* and varieties (deodar cedar); *C. libani* and varieties (cedar of Lebanon)

Handsome evergreen trees at any time of the year, the cedars, with their graceful shapes and stiff green, blue or yellow needles, are particularly decorative in a winter landscape. The three species listed here, along with some of their varieties, are all true cedars, although many other trees with similarly aromatic wood are commonly called cedars. The parent species have conical silhouettes when young and mature into spreading, flat-topped trees after 40 or 50 years; grafted weeping varieties and dwarf varieties increase the choice of cedar silhouettes available to winter gardeners.

The Atlas cedar has a form unusual among conifers. The stiff branches of younger trees ascend from a single trunk rather than growing horizontally or drooping. Fast-growing when young, it reaches 40 to 60 feet in about 40 years and can ultimately grow to 120 feet. The parent species has dark green needles less than an inch long and pale green cones that ripen to light brown; *C. atlantica* Glauca, the blue Atlas cedar, is a variety with powdery blue needles and cones. The weeping Atlas cedar, *C. atlantica* Pendula, is a grafted variety with gracefully pendulous branches that sweep to the ground from an arching main stem; growing to 10 feet tall and spreading three times as wide, it is often grown cascading over rocks, walls or banks. *C. atlantica* Glauca pendula, the blue weeping Atlas cedar, combines the attributes of the two previous varieties. It is usually grafted onto a 6- to 10-foot-tall trunk, or standard, and its branches are trained horizontally before the long new shoots are allowed to trail to the ground. All of these Atlas cedars are hardy in Zones 6-9 and can withstand seashore conditions.

The deodar cedar, the least hardy of these cedars, grows in Zones 7-9. Both its horizontal branches and straight central leader droop gracefully at their tips. Red-brown cones are set among gray-to-blue-green needles. The deodar cedar can grow to 40 feet in as many years and may ultimately reach a height of 150 feet. The golden deodar cedar *C. deodara* Aurea is a slower-growing variety with golden-yellow needles. *C. deodara* Nana, the dwarf deodar cedar, very slowly grows to 15 feet and spreads twice as wide; its young needles are an attractive apple green. The wood of the deodar cedar is burned as incense in India and a few twigs added to a winter fire give the well-loved cedar aroma to a room.

An Asia Minor native that was used to build King Solomon's temple, the cedar of Lebanon has wide-spreading, horizontal branches ascending its straight trunk in open tiers. Slow growing, it takes up to 70 years to attain 40 to 60 feet in height. The bright-to-dark green needles are an inch long and the 3- to 4-inch cones are produced only on very old trees. The dwarf cedar of Lebanon, *C. libani* Nana, is a dense plant with horizontal branches that spread as wide as its 5- to 15-foot height. Its branches are sometimes thinned to reveal the trunk and give the cedar a more open appearance. The cedar of Lebanon grows in Zones 5-9 but at the northern end of its range it benefits from the protection of a site on a warmer, south-facing slope.

HOW TO GROW. Gently knock snow from young cedars to prevent its weight from breaking their branches. Plant the cedars in full sun in almost any moist but well-drained soil. Since cedars do not transplant well, choose permanent sites with ample space for the spread of these trees. Plant container-grown trees in spring or late summer, incorporating leaf mold or peat moss and bone meal into the planting hole. Fertilize each spring thereafter with cottonseed meal or a standard 5-10-5 garden fertilizer. Prune cedars in the early spring if necessary, cutting off branch tips to shape the trees and to thicken their foliage; remove competing leaders from young trees.

## CHAMAECYPARIS

*C. lawsoniana* and varieties (Lawson's false cypress, Port Orford cedar, Oregon cedar); *C. obtusa* and varieties (hinoki false cypress); *C. pisifera* and varieties, also called *Retinspora pisifera* (sawara false cypress)

Thick evergreens offering a diverse assortment of heights, shapes and foliage colors, the false cypresses and their varieties are attractive in any season as screening or background plants and as borders or accents in rock gardens. Their forms

*For climate zones and frost dates, see maps, pages 148-149.*

**BLUE ATLAS CEDAR**
*Cedrus atlantica* 'Glauca'

**DEODAR CEDAR**
*Cedrus deodara*

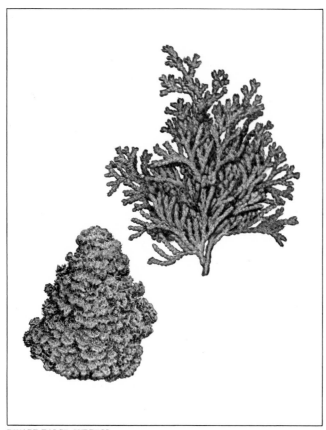

**DWARF FALSE CYPRESS**
*Chamaecyparis obtusa* 'Nana Gracilis'

**THREAD SAWARA FALSE CYPRESS**
*Chamaecyparis pisifera* 'Filifera'

range from squat shrubs and compact pyramids to narrow columns. The tiny overlapping leaves in shades of green, blue-green or golden yellow may be soft and scalelike or sharp and pointed, and are arranged in flattened fans, feathery plumes or whiplike cords.

Capable of reaching a height of 200 feet along the humid coasts of Oregon and California where it is native, the Lawson's false cypress grows to 60 feet or more under cultivation in coastal areas of Zones 5-9 and can grow as much as 2 feet in a single year. A stately, conical tree with branches that may spread horizontally or sometimes ascend slightly, the Lawson's false cypress retains its ground-level branches even in old age. This, plus its long, drooping branchlets, gives it a full silhouette. Older trees have shredding red-brown bark. *C. lawsoniana* Allumii, the scarab false cypress, has stiff, vertical sprays of steel-blue foliage and develops into a compact oval or pyramidal tree that is often used in formal hedges. It reaches 20 feet in 40 years and can be kept smaller by close shearing. The Elwood false cypress, *C. lawsoniana* Elwoodii, is a dwarf variety with blue-gray to blue-green feathery foliage along erect branches; it grows into a compact oval 8 feet tall and 3 feet wide in 10 years.

Native to Japan, the hinoki false cypress grows into a dense, broad pyramid 25 feet tall with a spread about half as wide in Zones 5-9. Its pendulous branches sweep the ground and each drooping branchlet along them is a twisted, curled fan of overlapping, scalelike leaves. These glossy, dark green leaves are marked with white on their undersides and may brown during severe winters. *C. obtusa* Crippsii, the Cripps golden hinoki false cypress, has looser, more open growth and foliage that emerges yellow, then turns green by the end of the season. The slender hinoki false cypress, *C. obtusa* Gracilis, grows into a compact, narrow cone about 6 feet tall with drooping fans of green foliage on slender stems. The dwarf slender hinoki false cypress, *C. obtusa* Nana Gracilis, is sometimes confused with the dwarf hinoki false cypress, *C. obtusa* Nana. They can be distinguished by the sheen of the foliage of young plants; the former plant has shiny young leaves while the latter false cypress has dull ones.

The true dwarf hinoki false cypress with its horizontal sprays of cupped foliage is an excellent rock-garden plant that grows only 10 inches tall and as wide in 10 years; its mature height is 2 feet. The dwarf slender hinoki false cypress has light-colored new growth that contrasts attractively with darker, older foliage. It grows into a conical shape 4 feet tall and 2 to 3 feet wide in 10 years, ultimately reaching 6 feet in height.

In all but the drier areas of Zones 5-7, the sawara false cypress grows into a loose, open conical tree 30 feet tall and spreading about half as wide. Its horizontal branches are lined with plumy fans of dark green, prickly foliage marked with white on its underside. With age, this false cypress loses its lower branches and reveals the shredding, red-brown bark on its trunk. The soft and mosslike foliage of the Boulevard sawara false cypress, *C. pisifera* Boulevard or *C. pisifera* Cyanoviridis, is light-blue to silvery green in summer and gray-blue in winter; it slowly grows to 8 feet in 20 years.

The thread sawara false cypress, *C. pisifera* Filifera, has drooping, cordlike branchlets and forms dense mounds 6 to 8 feet tall after 10 years. The golden thread sawara false cypress, *C. pisifera* Filifera-aurea, is similar but with yellow summer foliage that deepens to gold in the winter. Golden Mop sawara false cypress, *C. pisifera* Golden Mop, is a slower-growing, low form of the golden thread sawara false cypress. *C. pisifera* Squarrosa, the moss sawara false cypress, has a broad, pyramid shape with soft blue or gray-green summer foliage that turns bronze in the winter. With horizontal or somewhat upswept branches, it becomes 20 feet tall in as many years and can be kept smaller by pruning.

HOW TO GROW. False cypresses prefer cool, moist, unpolluted air and protection from both drying winds and strong winter sun. Full sun is tolerated in mild climates, but in areas with hot, dry summers, partial shade is necessary for healthy growth. Foliage color is best in partial shade. Plant false cypresses in the spring or fall in a moist but well-drained, fertile and slightly acid soil; foliage colors may dull in alkaline soils. Space larger false cypresses at least 15 to 20 feet apart in hedges or screens and water newly planted false cypresses at least once a week during their first two summers until their root systems are well established. Maintain a 2-inch layer of organic mulch such as wood chips or shredded bark to keep the soil cool and moist. For fast growth, fertilize in early spring with cottonseed meal or any other fertilizer formulated for acid-loving plants such as hollies or azaleas.

Prune to remove rival leaders in late fall or early winter. If a more open silhouette is desired, remove branches close to the main trunk at any time; false cypresses will not grow new branches to replace lost ones. To keep plants compact and to encourage dense foliage, clip the tips of soft-foliaged varieties with hedge shears in the early spring. Propagate false cypresses from seeds or from cuttings taken in fall or winter.

CHECKERBERRY See *Gaultheria*
CHERRY See *Prunus*

## CHIMONANTHUS

### C. praecox (wintersweet)

Along the bare stems of wintersweet, extraordinarily fragrant pale-yellow flower cups with maroon centers appear in winter from Zone 6 southward. The stemless, 1-inch flowers appear early or late in the season depending on the zone and the severity of the weather. Since the shape of the gray-barked, twiggy bush is not remarkable, wintersweet is frequently trained against a south wall to create a more pleasing silhouette, to provide protection from the wind, and to give it maximum exposure to the sun. Untrained wintersweet grows into bushy mounds 7 to 9 feet high with an equivalent spread. Paired, lustrous leaves 3 to 6 inches long follow the flowers in spring.

HOW TO GROW. Plant wintersweet in any good garden soil where it will receive full afternoon sun. At the northern end of its range, plant it where it is protected from wind and from direct morning sun; the latter can damage flower buds after a frosty night. Mulch the plants with 2 inches of organic material such as wood chips or shredded bark to protect the roots in winter and to keep the soil moist during the growing season. In early spring, after the flowers have faded, prune out a few of the oldest canes and cut back to a few inches the shoots on canes trained against a wall. Propagate wintersweet by soil-layering long shoots in summer; separate the new plants that result from the parent after two years and transplant them to their permanent location in spring.

CHINESE ELM See *Ulmus*
CHINESE HAZEL See *Corylus*
CHINESE PAPER BIRCH See *Betula*

## CHIONODOXA

### C. luciliae; C. sardensis (both called glory-of-the-snow)

Chionodoxa blooms so early in the year that it is not uncommon to see the star-shaped flowers pushing out of the soil along the edges of receding snowbanks. Each of the 3- to

WINTERSWEET
*Chimonanthus praecox*

GLORY-OF-THE-SNOW
*Chionodoxa sardensis*

*For climate zones and frost dates, see maps, pages 148-149.*

YELLOWWOOD
*Cladrastis lutea*

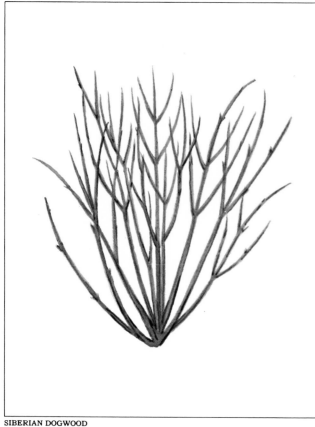

SIBERIAN DOGWOOD
*Cornus alba* 'Sibirica'

6-inch stems bears eight to 10 flowers with lavender-blue petals and white throats that last three weeks in the garden and make excellent cut flowers. There are also varieties with white, lilac, pink or pale purple-blue blossoms. *C. sardensis* bears bright blue ¾-inch flowers. The straplike green leaves of chionodoxas are sometimes edged in bronze. They are hardy from Zone 3 southward, and grow best in the northern parts of their range. The tiny bulbs spread naturally into attractive masses.

HOW TO GROW. Plant chionodoxas in early fall under deciduous trees or along banks where they will receive winter sun. Flowering improves from year to year and beds can be left undisturbed, or some bulbs can be dug every three or four years in fall so the tiny bulblets growing beside older bulbs can be removed and planted.

CHOKEBERRY See *Aronia*
CHRISTMAS FERN See *Polystichum*
CHRISTMAS ROSE See *Helleborus*

CLADRASTIS
*C. lutea* (yellowwood)

When the yellowwood's leaves turn yellow in autumn and drop off, the bare form of the tree, along with its smooth gray-white bark, stands out in the winter garden like an intricate, multibranched candelabrum. Growing up to 50 feet tall and spreading almost as wide in Zones 3-9, the yellowwood has erect boughs that branch into narrow angular forks, and further divide into a fan-shaped pattern of twigs. Flat brown seed pods, 2 to 4 inches long, dangle from the twigs all winter long. The seed pods are profuse every second or third year but they are sporadic in the intervening years, following the tree's fluctuating pattern of summer flowering. The blossoms hang in fragrant white clusters, up to 14 inches long in early summer. Although the large leaves, which are composed of up to 11 leaflets, provide good shade, the root structure of the yellowwood is deep enough to permit other plants to grow beneath it.

HOW TO GROW. Yellowwood grows best in full sun and tolerates poor soil, acid or alkaline, as long as it receives enough moisture to develop its deep root system. Plant saplings in spring. Yellowwoods are vulnerable to wind damage because of their intricate branching, and may need pruning to remove broken branches. Mature trees may also need thinning to lessen their susceptibility. Always prune yellowwoods in summer, since they bleed severely if pruned during any other season.

COLORADO SPRUCE See *Picea*
COMMON BOX See *Buxus*
COMMON BROOM See *Cytisus*
COMMON PERSIMMON See *Diospyros*
COMMON SNOWDROP See *Galanthus*
CORK TREE, AMUR See *Phellodendron*
CORKSCREW HAZEL See *Corylus*

CORNUS
*C. alba* and varieties (Tatarian dogwood); *C. florida* and varieties (flowering dogwood); *C. kousa* (Kousa dogwood, Japanese dogwood); *C. sanguinea* (blood-twig dogwood, pegwood, dogberry); *C. sericea*, also called *C. stolonifera* (red-osier dogwood, American dogwood)

Attractive in any season, dogwood trees are valued in the winter landscape for their lacy silhouettes, red berries and square buds, while the shrub species are noted for brightly colored twigs and fruit. Both trees and shrubs have pointed oval leaves with wavy edges that turn a brilliant red before dropping in autumn. Their showy spring flowers frequently last several weeks.

The shrubby Tatarian dogwood grows into clumps of whip-like bright red stems 7 to 9 feet tall in Zones 2-9. The 2- to 4-inch-long leaves are dark green with pale or white undersides; 2- to 3-inch clusters of tiny white spring flowers are followed in late summer and fall by tiny white or blue-white berries. *C. alba* Siberca, the Siberian dogwood, is an especially vigorous variety with bright coral-red stems. Other recommended varieties of *C. alba* include Westonbirt, with vivid red stems, and Kesselringii, with purple stems.

The flowering dogwood is a 15- to 30-foot tree with either single or multiple trunks and spreading, horizontal branches. As the tree matures, it becomes flat-topped and its gray bark darkens and becomes checkered with deep ridges. When young, the narrow flowering dogwood, *C. florida* Fastigiata, has ascending branches that droop of their own weight after 15 to 20 years and become horizontal. The weeping flowering dogwood, *C. florida* Pendula, has gracefully drooping branches. Appearing in early spring before the leaves come out, the flowering dogwood's 3- to 5-inch-wide white or pink blossoms are composed of a small yellow true flower surrounded by four petal-like leaves called bracts, which each have a characteristic notch. White-flowered varieties include White Cloud, Cherokee Princess, Gigantea and Magnifica.

For pink flowers, Apple Blossom, Spring Song and Cherokee Chief are among the best. The pink varieties are more susceptible to damage from late-spring frosts. Small clusters of shiny red, ¼-inch berries ripen in late summer and fall and cling into winter; square flower buds stand out along the upraised twigs from midwinter on. Hardy in Zones 5-9, flowering dogwoods are useful as accent trees or planted against buildings or tall evergreen backdrops that dramatize their branching patterns.

A small, fine-textured tree, the Kousa dogwood grows 15 to 25 feet tall and as wide. It is hardy in Zones 6-9 but needs protection from winter winds. The ascending branches become horizontal with age and the bark on the trunk and older limbs flakes off in uneven patches to reveal lighter bark underneath. The flowers appear after the foliage is out, about three to four weeks later than that of the flowering dogwood. Clustered along the tops of the branches, the 3- to 4-inch-wide white or pink flowers have four sharply pointed white bracts; the flowers last up to a month. The pink-to-red fruit that ripens in late summer resembles large raspberries, and the narrow oval leaves, up to 4 inches long and an inch wide, turn purple-to-red in the fall. *C. kousa* Chinensis has larger leaves and flowers 5 inches across.

The blood-twig dogwood is a shrub up to 12 feet tall that is hardy in Zones 5-9. Its branches are purple or dark blood-red. The broad leaves are 1½ to 3 inches long and hairy on both sides with the undersides almost woolly. The small green-to-white flowers appear in 2-inch clusters in the early spring and are followed by black or purple berries in the late summer and fall. The variety Viridissima has green stems.

The red-osier dogwood is similar to the Tatarian dogwood except that it spreads by underground stems and thrives in wet areas, making it useful along stream banks or ponds in Zones 2-9. *C. sericea* Flaviramea or golden-twig dogwood, has new stems that are yellow rather than red. *C. sericea* Kelseyi is a dwarf variety with 2-foot red stems. It is sometimes used as a ground cover.

HOW TO GROW. Tree dogwoods grow in partial shade or full sun except in areas with hot summers, where shade is a necessity. Shrub dogwoods also grow in partial shade or full

FLOWERING DOGWOOD
*Cornus florida*

*For climate zones and frost dates, see maps, pages 148-149.*

**HARRY LAUDER'S WALKING STICK**
*Corylus avellana 'Contorta'*

**BEARBERRY COTONEASTER**
*Cotoneaster dammeri*

sun, but their best coloring develops in full sun. Tree dogwoods need a moist, well-drained, acid soil with a pH of 5.5 to 6.5 enriched with peat moss or leaf mold; neither drought nor soggy soil are tolerated. Maintain a 2- to 4-inch layer of organic mulch to conserve moisture and keep their roots cool. To protect the trunks of young dogwood trees from rodents, wrap a 12-inch-wide piece of coarse wire screening around the base of the trunk. Shrub dogwoods grow in almost any soil, and the red-osier dogwood tolerates wet soils. Dogwood trees should be pruned as little as possible because they heal slowly. Prune shrub dogwoods to keep new bright young stems coming each year; thin older stems each year, cutting them back to the ground in early spring. Shrub dogwoods can also be renewed by cutting them to the ground. Plant dogwoods in the spring. Propagate them from seeds.

### CORSICAN HELLEBORE See *Helleborus*

### CORYLUS
*C. americana* (American hazel, American filbert); *C. avellana* 'Contorta' (corkscrew hazel, Harry Lauder's Walking Stick); *C. colurna* (Turkish hazel)

An abundance of male catkins, or flowers, dangling from bare twigs, makes hazel shrubs and trees more decorative in winter than in any other season. In late winter these catkins swell into bright yellow, pollen-laden cylinders 2 to 4 inches long. Inconspicuous female flowers appear simultaneously and ripen later into clusters of hard-shelled, edible nuts.

The American hazel is a rounded shrub that grows 8 to 10 feet tall from Zone 4 southward. In summer it bears oval, toothed leaves 2 to 5 inches long. The corkscrew hazel has a startling winter silhouette: the branches, twigs and even catkins of this 7- to 10-foot shrub twist, curl and spiral into fantastic shapes. From Zone 3 southward this hazel is an outstanding attraction in any winter garden. The pyramidal Turkish hazel tree has a stout trunk covered with corky gray bark; it grows to 70 feet tall from Zone 5 southward.

HOW TO GROW. These hardy hazels will grow in any well-drained soil, acid or alkaline, and the Turkish hazel will even tolerate dry soil. Full sun is best but they will grow in partial shade as well. Mulch the shrubs with 2 inches of organic matter such as wood chips, bark or pine needles to protect their roots in winter and to maintain cool, moist soil during the growing season. Plant shrub hazels in fall or spring. Propagate shrub hazels in fall by transplanting the suckers that appear. Plant Turkish hazel saplings in permanent locations in late fall or spring.

### COTONEASTER
*A. adpressa* (creeping cotoneaster); *C. dammeri* (bearberry cotoneaster); *C. salicifolius* (willowleaf cotoneaster)

Bright orange-red berries pepper the branches of cotoneasters throughout the winter and make an especially lively counterpoint against the glossy green leaves of evergreen species. The berries develop from small white or pinkish flower clusters that bloom in early summer.

Creeping cotoneaster is a deciduous dwarf that grows only 12 to 18 inches high; it will tumble over rocks or down steep banks, slowly spreading into a 6-foot-wide mat. Grown from Zone 4 southward, it has dull green leaves that are flushed with scarlet in fall. Bearberry cotoneaster is a prostrate evergreen shrub with showy fruit; it may spread by rooting at each branch node. *C. salicifolius* is a tall evergreen shrub with arching 16-foot canes. Though grown from Zone 6 southward, it is not reliably evergreen in the northern part of its range. The shrub has 3-inch, willow-like leaves that are glossy green on top and downy white underneath. *C. salicifolius floccosa* is an especially hardy variety with slightly larger berries and ruddy-colored leaves in fall.

HOW TO GROW. Given full sun, cotoneasters will grow in any well-drained soil, whether acid or alkaline. Creeping cotoneaster and *C. salicifolius* tolerate the dry soil, wind and salt air of seacoast gardens. Mulch around the shrubs with 2 inches of organic material such as wood chips or shredded bark to protect the roots in winter and to keep the soil cool and moist during the growing season. Thin out twiggy or crowded plants to improve air circulation, important in forestalling fire blight and spider-mite infestation. Plant cotoneasters in fall or early spring, moving them with soil balls to protect their delicate roots. Cotoneasters have a deep root system that prevents later transplanting.

COTTON, LAVENDER See *Santolina*
CRAB APPLE See *Malus*
CRANBERRY BUSH, AMERICAN See *Viburnum*
CRAPE MYRTLE See *Lagerstroemia*

## CRATAEGUS

*C. crus-galli* (cockspur hawthorn); *C. phaenopyrum* (Washington hawthorn)

Hawthorns enliven a winter garden by bearing clusters of haws — small red, apple-like fruits, which can be cooked into a tangy jelly. The branches themselves provide winter interest because they are covered with a rough, flaky gray bark and studded with formidable 3- to 4-inch bonehard thorns. Hawthorns grow rapidly in Zones 3-8 with saplings reaching 20 feet in 6 to 10 years and trees beginning to flower only two years after planting. The 2- to 3-inch saucer-shaped clusters of small white flowers bloom from late spring to early summer, and the 3- to 4-inch tooth-edged leaves turn red or orange before dropping in fall.

Cockspur hawthorn, which grows 25 feet tall, has zigzag branches that weave flat-topped crowns as much as 20 feet across. Because of its fearsome thorns, dense twiggy growth and receptivity to shearing, it is sometimes planted as a barrier hedge. A thornless variety, *C. crus-galli* Inermis, is also available. The 25-foot-tall Washington hawthorn develops a dense, round head and has an abundant crop of glossy red-orange fruits that usually cling all winter. The variety Fastigiata grows into a more columnar form.

HOW TO GROW. Hawthorns flourish in nearly any type of soil — dry or moist, alkaline or acid — as long as it is deep enough to accommodate their long taproots. They grow best in full sun but tolerate partial shade. Hedges of cockspur hawthorn may be sheared throughout the growing season. Thin the crowns of trees to open them up in early spring. Plant saplings 8 feet tall or less in spring; larger trees are difficult to transplant. Set hedge plants 1 to 2 feet apart.

CREEPING LILY-TURF See *Liriope*

## CROCUS

*C. ancyrensis* (Golden Bunch crocus); *C. chrysanthus* hybrids; *C. imperati* (early crocus); *C. laevigatus; C. sieberi* (Sieber crocus); *C. versicolor* (spring-flowering crocus) (all called crocus)

Blooming earlier than the more familiar Dutch crocuses, the species crocuses that are listed here appear in the winter and open at the first break in the cold weather from Zone 7 northward. The delicately colored, goblet-shaped flowers often have contrasting interiors. The 8- to 10-inch grasslike foliage usually emerges and matures after the flowers bloom.

*For climate zones and frost dates, see maps, pages 148-149.*

WASHINGTON HAWTHORN
*Crataegus phaenopyrum* 'Fastigiata'

GOLDEN BUNCH CROCUS
*Crocus ancyrensis*

105

SPRING-FLOWERING CROCUS
*Crocus versicolor*

DWARF JAPANESE CEDAR
*Cryptomeria japonica* 'Globosa Nana'

Golden Bunch produces clusters of up to 20 small, brilliant yellow or orange flowers. The 3-inch flowers and gray-green foliage of the chrysanthus hybrids appear together. The name means golden flower but these hybrids come in a variety of colors: Blue Beauty is a soft blue; E. A. Bowles is an hourglass-shaped clear yellow touched with bronze at the base of the petals; Goldilocks is a vivid yellow that is frequently double petaled. Moonlight has light-yellow petals that fade to ivory at their tips and are streaked with brown and purple; Princess Beatrix is blue flushed with violet at its petal tips and fading to white at its throat; and Zwanenburg Bronze has a brownish-maroon exterior along with a bright yellow interior.

The early crocus bears 1½-inch lilac or white blossoms that are streaked with purple. The Sieber crocus is available in many varieties including Firefly, a delicate lilac-to-pink crocus with bright orange stamens, and Hubert Edelsten, with rose-colored flowers. *C. laevigatus* has fragrant violet flowers. *C. versicolor,* the parent of many varieties, bears large 4- to 5-inch flowers with yellow-to-white petals that are delicately veined with purple.

HOW TO GROW. Crocuses grow in any well-drained soil in full sun or partial shade; those planted in full sun in locations protected from winter wind bloom earliest. Plant the bulblike corms in early fall, spacing them 2 to 6 inches apart and 2 to 4 inches deep. A light dusting of bone meal or 5-10-5 fertilizer after planting and each fall will nourish the corms for the following season of bloom. Allow leaves to ripen and wither before removing or mowing them; otherwise corm vigor is greatly reduced. Clumps may be dug and divided in early summer every three or four years for propagation, or they may be left undisturbed to spread naturally. Crocuses seed themselves but it takes three or four years before the corms develop to flowering size.

CROSS-LEAVED HEATH See *Erica*

CRYPTOMERIA
*C. japonica* and varieties (Japanese cedar, cryptomeria)

Stately evergreens with a formal, conical shape, Japanese cedars have fine-textured, bright green needles that turn to bronze, purple or blue during winter in colder areas. The branches of older trees, studded with round 1-inch cones, part to expose the shaggy red-brown bark on the trunks. These elegant trees grow as tall as 60 feet in Zones 5-9 but they need some protection from winter sun and drying winds in the northern part of their range. Although there is only one species, its varieties offer a wide choice of needle colors, sizes and forms.

The tips of the branches of the crested Japanese cedar, *C. japonica* Cristata, have thick fans of young growth that resemble bright green cockscombs. It grows slowly up to 12 feet high with a 4-foot spread and the trunks of older shrubs become deeply grooved.

*C. japonica* Globosa Nana, the dwarf round Japanese cedar, hardy in Zones 8-10 and the warm coastal areas of Zone 7, is conical when young but develops into a globe of foliage as it reaches its mature height of 3 to 6 feet. The rounded shape is enhanced by a slight droop of the branchlets. They are lined with needles that are yellow-green to deep green in summer and blue in winter.

HOW TO GROW. Japanese cedars grow in full sun or partial shade in moist but well-drained, slightly acid soil. They thrive in high humidity and do not do well where the air is polluted or hot and dry. Set out young plants in spring, choosing sites protected from winds. Keep the roots moist by watering weekly until they are well established. Maintain a 3- to 4-inch layer of organic mulch such as shredded bark or pine needles, and feed in the spring with cottonseed meal or a standard 5-10-5 garden fertilizer. Prune in the early spring only to maintain a central leader in trees; unnecessary pruning destroys the naturally informal appearance of the dwarf round Japanese cedar.

**CURLY HAZEL** See *Corylus*

## CYCLAMEN
*C. coum,* also called *C. atkinsii; C. orbiculatum* (Coum cyclamen)

A small-flowered cousin of the florist's showy potted plant, the Coum cyclamens provide winter delight for those willing to care for them and to stoop to enjoy them. Hardy in Zones 5-9, the 4- to 5-inch-tall plants carry tiny crimson buds from late fall into winter and bloom at various times depending on the climate. Starting in midwinter in the southern part of the plant's range and moving progressively north, the ¾-inch purple-spotted red, pink or white blooms appear like miniature butterflies among 3-inch kidney-shaped leaves. The leaves, sometimes marbled with silver or white, remain on the plants the year round except for a brief period in midsummer. These cyclamens grow from tubers, which increase in size each year, producing greater quantities of flower stems as they do so.

HOW TO GROW. Coum cyclamens grow best in a lightly shaded location protected from drying winter winds and hot summer sun. Plant the 1½-inch tubers in midsummer in well-drained soil enriched with humus; space them 6 to 10 inches apart and 1 to 2 inches deep. Be careful not to plant the tubers upside down — remnants of the old roots will mark the bottom. After the blooms fade, mulch Coum cyclamens with an inch of compost to nourish the tubers and to protect them from cycles of freezing and thawing in the following winter. Cyclamens are grown from seed; the tubers require 18 months to reach flowering size.

## CYTISUS
*C. praecox* (Warminster broom); *C. scoparius* (Scotch broom, common broom)

The brooms, with tall whisks of slender green branches, add both color and texture to a winter-garden scene. Although these shrubs are deciduous, their brightly colored stems make them seem evergreen; inconspicuous leaves only ⅓ to ½ inch long drop early in autumn. Brooms are particularly suited to coastal areas from Zone 5 southward. The vigorous young shoots of Warminster broom grow erect, then softly arch as they reach 5 to 6 feet in height. The slender green stalks are among the first of the brooms to burst forth with pale yellow blossoms in the spring. The dense Scotch broom grows upright to a height of 4 to 8 feet and spreads rapidly. Its flowers are larger and a brighter yellow color than those of the Warminster broom.

HOW TO GROW. Brooms thrive in full sun and in dry, sandy, acid soils, which they enrich with nitrogen that is produced by nodules on their roots. Good drainage is essential. Brooms flower on the stems from the previous season, and stems more than a year old cannot be rejuvenated with pruning. Their sparse roots make brooms difficult to transplant. Purchase small container-grown plants rather than shrubs with soil balls, and plant in the early spring.

COUM CYCLAMEN
*Cyclamen coum*

SCOTCH BROOM
*Cytisus scoparius*

**D**

**DAGGER PLANT** See *Yucca*

*For climate zones and frost dates, see maps, pages 148-149.*

WINTER DAPHNE
*Daphne odora*

COMMON PERSIMMON
*Diospyros virginiana*

## DAPHNE

*D. mezereum* (February daphne); *D. odora* (winter daphne)

On cold, crisp mornings in mid- to late winter, the sweet, rosy fragrance of the waxy blossoms of daphnes perfumes the winter garden. They should be planted near walkways, front doors or other spots where their fragrance can be readily enjoyed. A deciduous shrub growing 18 to 36 inches tall, the February daphne has ¼-inch rosy-purple flowers growing in small clusters along the upper sides of its branches. The flowers, which last up to three weeks, appear before the 2- to 3-inch wedge-shaped, gray-green leaves. In milder parts of its range in Zones 4-9, this shrub blooms in midwinter but buds open later in colder areas. Like those of all daphnes, its bark, leaves and small, bright red berries, which ripen in late spring, are all poisonous.

Winter daphne, considered the most fragrant of all the daphnes, is an evergreen shrub with glossy, narrow leaves 3 inches long. Hardy in Zones 7-9, it grows from 3 to 6 feet tall and has an equal spread. The clusters of ½-inch pink-to-red flowers bloom at the tips of the branches. The variety Marginata, with its leaves edged in yellow, is particularly hardy and adds an additional color note to the winter garden.

HOW TO GROW. Daphnes grow well in partial shade in a well-drained, acid soil with a pH of 5.0 to 5.5. Mulch the shrubs with a 2- to 3-inch layer of wood chips, peat moss or shredded bark to keep their roots cool in summer and to prevent frost heaving in winter. Plant balled-and-burlaped shrubs with strong root systems. Once established, daphnes require little pruning or other special care. These shrubs are subject to a collar rot virus, which can be prevented by making sure that the soil has good drainage and by allowing the ground to dry thoroughly between summer waterings.

## DARLEY HEATH See *Erica*
## DAVID MAPLE See *Acer*

## DIOSPYROS

*D. virginiana* (common persimmon)

A deciduous tree well suited to city environments by virtue of its medium size and tolerance of pollution, the common persimmon has a rounded crown that gains grace with age as its crooked branches become slightly pendulous. Its attractive winter silhouette is enhanced by the rugged mosaic pattern of its bark. Almost black, the bark is checkered by deep fissures; the spaces between the small rectangular blocks on young trees are sometimes orange.

Native to the eastern and southeastern United States, the common persimmon is hardy in Zones 5-10, where it grows 35 to 60 feet tall with a spread about half as wide. Female trees bear brightly colored, edible fruits that may cling to the branches until early winter. Yellow to red-orange, the round, 1- to 2-inch fruits are very astringent until the first hard frost; then they ripen into the soft and sweet "food of the gods," the translation of its Latin name. Persimmons bear male and female flowers on separate trees, so both are necessary for fruit production. The narrow, oval foliage is coppery when young and matures into glossy green, leathery leaves. In fall, the leaves turn yellow. Varieties recommended for fruit include Garrettson, Early Golden and Killen.

HOW TO GROW. The common persimmon grows best in full sun in moist, well-drained soil, with a neutral to slightly alkaline pH of 6.5 to 7.5. Because of their long taproots, persimmons are difficult to transplant. Set out small balled-and-burlaped trees in the spring, in a ratio of 1 male tree for every 20 females in order to ensure good fruit production. Feed young trees each spring with a balanced garden fertilizer such as 10-10-10. Persimmons are notably pest-free. Pruning is seldom required except to remove dead or crossing branches.

DOGWOOD See *Cornus*
DOUGLAS FIR See *Pseudotsuga*

# E

EASTERN RED CEDAR See *Juniperus*
EBONY SPLEENWORT See *Asplenium*

## ELAEAGNUS

*E. pungens* (thorny elaeagnus); *E. umbellata* (autumn elaeagnus)

The evergreen thorny elaeagnus and the deciduous autumn elaeagnus are large shrubs tough enough for use as windbreaks or seaside plantings. Each offers different landscaping traits to the winter gardener.

The attractive leaves of the thorny elaeagnus are broad, glossy, olive-green ovals with wavy margins. The undersides of the 1½- to 4-inch leaves are covered with tiny silver and brown scales. Maculata is a variety with yellow leaves edged in green, while Variegata has green leaves with edges that are streaked yellow and white. The leaves line spiny twigs that are also dotted with brown scales. Drooping clusters of gardenia-scented, silver-to-white flowers perfume the garden in fall and develop into ¾-inch brown fruits that turn red in spring. Hardy in Zones 7-10, thorny elaeagnus grows in sprawling mounds 8 to 12 feet tall with a similar width. All thorny elaeagnus are fast-growing and adaptable to difficult growing conditions, although the two variegated types are more subject to damage from winter winds or extreme cold. Thorny elaeagnus is often sheared into hedges.

When the autumn elaeagnus drops its leaves, its yellow-to-brown twigs, occasionally spiny, add both color and texture to the winter landscape. Tiny brown berries that follow cream-colored spring flowers ripen to scarlet in the fall and will hang on the shrub through the winter unless eaten by birds. Hardy in Zones 3-8, the autumn elaeagnus grows 12 to 18 feet tall and as wide. In summer, its branches are covered with wavy-edged leaves 1 to 4 inches long that are silver when young, and later become pale or dark green above while remaining silver underneath.

HOW TO GROW. Both the thorny elaeagnus and the autumn elaeagnus grow best in full sun although either will tolerate partial shade. They survive in a wide range of soils under moist or dry conditions, but growth is fastest in a sandy, well-drained soil. Plant young shrubs in the fall or spring. Regular fertilizing is unnecessary in average soils; in poor soils, feed with a balanced fertilizer such as 10-10-10 once a year in the spring. Prune to shape or maintain size in the spring. Propagate from cuttings or seeds.

ELM, CHINESE See *Ulmus*
ELM, WINGED See *Ulmus*
ENGLISH BOX See *Buxus*
ENGLISH IVY See *Hedera*
ENGLISH OAK See *Quercus*

## ERANTHIS

*E. hyemalis* (winter aconite); *E. tubergeniana* (Tubergen winter aconite)

Winter aconites, relatives of buttercups, carpet flower beds with a cheery midwinter blanket of yellow, honey-scented flowers. Hardy in Zones 4-9, their twiggy tubers send up 2- to 4-inch stems topped by tight yellow balls that open into

VARIEGATED THORNY ELAEAGNUS
*Elaeagnus pungens* 'Variegata'

WINTER ACONITE
*Eranthis hyemalis*

*For climate zones and frost dates, see maps, pages 148-149.*

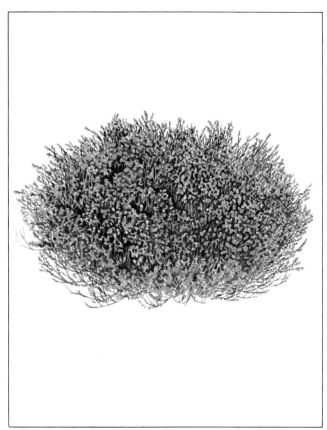

**KING GEORGE SPRING HEATH**
*Erica carnea* 'King George'

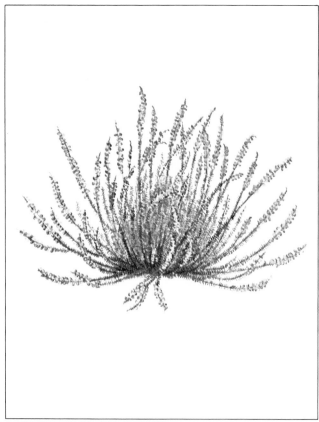

**SPRINGWOOD WHITE SPRING HEATH**
*Erica carnea* 'Springwood White'

shiny yellow cups surrounded by leafy ruffs. In a short time the carpet disappears until the following winter. The Tubergen winter aconite is a robust hybrid with slightly larger flowers and bronze-tinted leaves and stems. Although they are too small to be of note singly, winter aconites are stunning massed in rock gardens or under trees.

HOW TO GROW. Winter aconites thrive in moist but well-drained soil enriched with leaf mold in partially shaded sites sheltered from strong winds. Plant the tubers in fall 3 to 4 inches apart and 1 inch deep in clumps. Soak dry tubers in water overnight before planting. Propagate winter aconites at any season by digging up tubers with their soil, dividing them and replanting immediately so the roots do not dry. Undisturbed clumps spread into large mats with seedlings; new plants can be grown from seed to bloom in three years.

## ERICA
*E. carnea* and varieties (spring heath); *E. darleyensis* (Darley heath); *E. tetralix* (cross-leaved heath)

The dense, needle-like evergreen foliage of the heaths, persisting despite cold and snow, delights winter gardeners. In the milder parts of their ranges, spring heath and Darley heath begin blooming in early winter, bearing clusters of ¼-inch bell-shaped flowers among tiny leaves. In colder zones, colorful flower buds decorate the branches until they open in mid- to late winter or early spring.

Hardy from Zones 5-7, spring heath has red, purple or white flowers amid ¼-inch-long medium-green leaves. A slow-growing shrub, it seldom becomes more than a foot tall with a spread of twice its height. Spring heath can be used as accent plants in flower borders, grouped in rock gardens or massed as a ground cover. Choice varieties for winter gardens include King George, about 1 foot tall with crimsom flowers; Springwood Pink, 8 inches tall with deep pink flowers; Springwood White, 8 inches tall with white flowers; and Vivellii, 8 inches tall with blood-red flowers. Vivellii's foliage turns bronze in winter.

The Darley heath, which grows from Zone 6 southward, has pale purplish-pink blossoms. Though its flowers are less striking than those of the spring heath, it grows more rapidly, eventually reaching 2 feet in height. The fuzzy, gray-green leaves of the cross-leaved heath survive severe winter conditions from Zones 3-7. It forms low mounds 6 to 12 inches high that are as much as 24 inches across. Unlike spring heath and Darley heath, cross-leaved heath is not a winter bloomer but is covered with dense clusters of tiny red flowers from early summer to midautumn.

HOW TO GROW. Heaths grow best in full sun in Zones 3-7, but will also tolerate partial shade. Heaths thrive in a well-drained mixture of 1 part peat moss, 1 part coarse sand and 1 part garden soil; spring and cross-leaved heaths require an acid soil with a pH between 4.5 and 5.5, while Darley heath tolerates alkaline conditions. Avoid cultivating around the shallow root system, but to suppress weeds and protect the roots from extremes in temperature, maintain an inch-thick mulch of wood chips, pine needles or shredded bark. Darley heath should not be pruned; clip off dead flowers only. After spring heath and cross-leaved heath bloom, shear them to one half or one third of their original height just as new growth begins to encourage bushiness. Plant heaths in early spring, spacing them 2 to 3 feet apart and watering them well until their root systems are established. Propagate by dividing shrubs with a spade in spring, by rooting cuttings taken in summer, or by ground-layering branches.

**EULALIA See *Miscanthus***

## EUONYMUS

*E. alata* (winged euonymus); *E. fortunei* and varieties (winter creeper); *E. japonica* and varieties (evergreen euonymus)

Euonymuses include a wide variety of landscaping materials for winter interest ranging from creeping evergreen vines to deciduous shrubs with distinctively shaped branches.

From Zone 3 southward, the winged euonymus offers a unique visual texture to winter gardeners. When its scarlet leaves drop in autumn, the angular, corky flanges, or wings, that line this shrub's branches and twigs become clearly visible. The structure is particularly striking in colder northern regions when snow is trapped along the flanges and the shrub presents an interwoven pattern of brown and white. Winged euonymus grows into a vase-shaped shrub 8 to 9 feet tall. Its oval, 1- to 3-inch leaves turn a fiery scarlet in autumn, just as its bright red, pink or white fruits ripen and burst to reveal their orange seeds.

The evergreen common winter creeper is a rambling vine that trails across the ground or over banks and walls, rooting as it goes. Hardy in Zones 5-10, it has shiny, dark green oval leaves ½ to 1½ inches long. It can be trained to grow up a wall or house. As a ground cover, common winter creeper grows about a foot high, up to 20 feet in length and 6 feet in width. The oval, 1- to 2-inch leaves of the variety Coloratus turn a deep reddish-purple in winter. Minima has dainty leaves that are less than ½ inch long, making it a fine-textured ground cover. The prominent white edging on the leaves of Silver Queen make it a conspicuous winter plant. A form of *E. fortunei vegeta,* Emerald 'n Gold, grows up to 4 feet tall and has leaves edged with yellow.

Evergreen euonymus, a dense, rounded shrub up to 15 feet tall, is grown from Zone 7 southward for its splendid, lustrous foliage. Varieties distinctive for winter color include *E. japonica* Aureo-variegatus, with yellow leaves edged in green, and *E. japonica* Albo-marginatus, with green leaves edged in white. Evergreen euonymus is tolerant of salt air.

HOW TO GROW. Euonymuses grow in full sun or partial shade in any well-drained soil. Plant in early spring. Mulch with wood chips or shredded bark to keep soil moist and to protect roots from temperature extremes. While euonymuses rarely need pruning, they can be shaped at any time in mild climates or in spring in colder regions by cutting branches back and thinning older growth. Euonymuses are subject to attacks by scale insects. In spring before new leaf buds open, prune infested branches and spray with a dormant oil, adding an insecticide such as malathion to increase the effectiveness of the treatment.

## EUROPEAN BEECH See *Fagus*
## EUROPEAN BIRCH See *Betula*
## EUROPEAN HORNBEAM See *Carpinus*
## EUROPEAN WILD GINGER See *Asarum*

# F

## FAGUS

*F. grandifolia* (American beech); *F. sylvatica* and varieties (European beech)

A mature, silver-barked beech, with its massive trunk, low branches, spreading crown and gnarled surface roots, presents a noble picture in a winter landscape. The glossy oval and sometimes serrated summer leaves turn a handsome bronze in the fall and often cling to the tree into winter. Inconspicuous flowers ripen in fall into small nuts encased in prickly husks. Beeches grow slowly, reaching 15 or 20 feet in 10 years and mature heights of 50 to 100 feet only after 50 years or more. The American beech grows in Zones 3-9 and

PURPLE WINTER CREEPER
*Euonymus fortunei 'Coloratus'*

EMERALD 'N GOLD WINTER CREEPER
*Euonymus fortunei vegeta* 'Emerald 'n Gold'

*For climate zones and frost dates, see maps, pages 148-149.*

COPPER BEECH
*Fagus sylvatica* 'Atropunicea'

BLUE FESCUE
*Festuca ovina glauca*

develops a crown taller than it is wide. The European beech grows from Zone 5 southward with a spreading form as wide as it is high. The European beech variety Pendula, a weeping form, has branches that droop to the ground; the variety Fastigiata, also called Dawckii, has a columnar shape; the variety Atropunicea, called copper or purple beech, has purple or copper-red leaves and unusual whorled bark.

HOW TO GROW. Beeches grow best in full sun or light shade in well-drained, acid soils or soils enriched with peat moss or leaf mold; avoid wet sites and clay soil. Train young trees to a single trunk or leader and remove the lower branches if a high crown is desired. Remove suckers that grow from the roots of the American beech. Mature beeches need only maintenance pruning to remove brittle or damaged wood or to thin crowded branches; prune in summer because beeches bleed if cut any other time. Beeches are hard to transplant.

FALSE CYPRESS, HINOKI See *Chamaecyparis*
FALSE CYPRESS, LAWSON'S See *Chamaecyparis*
FALSE CYPRESS, SAWARA See *Chamaecyparis*
FEATHER REED GRASS See *Calamagrostis*
FERN, CHRISTMAS See *Polystichum*
FERN, LEATHER See *Polystichum*
FERN, SOFT SHIELD See *Polystichum*
FESCUE, BLUE See *Festuca*

FESTUCA
*F. ovina glauca* (blue fescue)

Whether standing alone as accents or lining the border of a garden bed, wiry clumps of blue fescue are uniquely ornamental in the winter garden. Retaining their silvery-blue color year round, this 4- to 10-inch-tall perennial grass forms rounded tufts of thin, fine blades. Thin stems up to 1 foot tall carry blue-purple summer flower spikes that ripen into flat fans of seeds but do not remain standing through the winter. Grown from Zones 3-9, blue fescue does not spread into carpets but remains in neat clumps or tufts. Tolerant of wind and salt spray, it is useful in seashore gardens.

HOW TO GROW. Blue fescue grows well in full sun or partial shade in any soil, but its color is most distinct and its growth most lush in full sun and in poor, fairly dry soils. Plant blue fescue in spring or fall, setting the plants 6 to 12 inches apart depending on the pattern desired. Since the tufts will not spread to fill in the spaces between them, use a light mulch around the plants to help deter weeds. Propagate blue fescue from seed or by dividing the tufts in spring or fall.

FILBERT, AMERICAN See *Corylus*
FIR See *Abies*
FIR, DOUGLAS See *Pseudotsuga*
FRAGRANT HONEYSUCKLE See *Lonicera*

# G

GALANTHUS
*G. elwesii* (giant snowdrop); *G. nivalis* (common snowdrop); *G. plicatus*

Snowdrops are undaunted by snow, pushing up through it to forecast the coming end of winter and reviving even when buried by a late storm. Local climate, warm periods and the amount of exposure to wind and sun affect the blooming time of these woodland bulbs across their wide range from Zones 3-9. The translucent flower bells, made up of three short greenish inner petals and three longer, pointed outer white petals, dangle from slender stalks rising above gray-green leaves that wither in late spring. The giant snowdrop grows 10 to 18 inches tall, bearing 1¼-inch flowers marked with green at their base; its leaves resemble wide green straps. The common snowdrop, 7 to 12 inches high, bears white, faintly green-tipped, inch-long flowers above grassy foliage. *G. plicatus* is similar to the common snowdrop but has deeper green markings on its inner petals. The bulbs multiply rapidly and the different species are effective when intermixed in rough grass or under deciduous trees.

HOW TO GROW. Plant snowdrops from late summer to early fall in moist but well-drained soil where they will be partially shaded. Space the bulbs 2 to 4 inches apart and 2 to 3 inches deep. Allow the foliage to wither naturally after the flowers fade, to provide nourishment for the bulbs. Left undisturbed, snowdrops develop long-lived colonies. They can be propagated by digging the bulbs as the foliage yellows, removing the tiny offsets that grow beside older bulbs and replanting immediately. New plants can also be grown from seed to bloom in four years.

## GAULTHERIA
*G. procumbens* (wintergreen, checkerberry, teaberry); *G. shallon* (salal, shallon)

Winter gardeners enjoy both the handsome evergreen foliage and the waxy berries of wintergreen and salal. Grown from Zones 4-8, wintergreen is an excellent ground cover, spreading to form dense mats 3 to 6 inches tall. The 2-inch, oval leathery green leaves that tip the end of each stem become shaded with bronze in fall and remain so throughout the winter. White bell-shaped flowers bloom in late spring and are followed in fall by round, scarlet berries that last all winter. These edible berries have a flavor that has given wintergreen the common name of teaberry. Its leaves, when crushed, have a spicy aroma.

Salal, a shrub native to the Pacific Coast, grows 2 to 6 feet tall depending upon the soil and the exposure to the sun. It is hardy in Zones 8 and 9. The oval dark green leaves, up to 4 inches long, hide the edible purple-to-black fruits that follow clusters of small white or pink spring flowers. Salal's handsome, leathery foliage is used decoratively and sold by florists as "lemon leaves."

HOW TO GROW. Both wintergreen and salal do best in partial shade in a moist but well-drained acid soil. When grown in poor soils or full sun, salal does not reach its full height. Look for moss to determine the best location for planting wintergreen, since both thrive under similar conditions. Neither of the plants requires pruning. Set nursery-grown plants out in spring or autumn, spacing them 1 to 2 feet apart. Propagate additional plants from seed or from cuttings taken in the summer. Wintergreen can also be divided and transplanted.

GIANT SNOWDROP See *Galanthus*
GINGER, EUROPEAN WILD See *Asarum*
GINGER, MOTTLED WILD See *Asarum*
GLORY-OF-THE-SNOW See *Chionodoxa*
GOLDEN-RAIN TREE See *Koelreutaria*
GRAY BIRCH See *Betula*
GREEK ANEMONE See *Anemone*
GUM, BLACK See *Nyssa*
GUM, SOUR See *Nyssa*
GUM, SWEET See *Liquidambar*

# H

## HAMAMELIS
*H. intermedia; H. mollis* (Chinese witch hazel); *H. vernalis* (vernal witch hazel)

Gardeners in Zones 4-6 can depend on the deciduous

*For climate zones and frost dates, see maps, pages 148-149.*

COMMON SNOWDROP
*Galanthus nivalis*

WINTERGREEN
*Gaultheria procumbens*

**CHINESE WITCH HAZEL**
*Hamamelis mollis*

**ENGLISH IVY**
*Hedera helix*

witch hazels for fragrant winter flowers, delicate in appearance but able to resist icy winter blasts. Clusters of spidery flowers with curled, ribbon-like petals crowd the branches of these shrubs from early to late winter, depending on the zone and the severity of the season. The serrated leaves that follow the flowers turn yellow, orange or red in fall.

*H. intermedia* is a vigorous hybrid that grows as a shrub or a tree up to 30 feet tall. Its 1-inch yellow petals are tinged with copper and foliage turns yellow in fall. The variety Arnold Promise produces 1½-inch golden flowers and has leaves that turn rich red and yellow in fall. The variety Jelena produces large blossoms flushed with copper and has orange, bronze or red fall foliage. Ruby Glow is an unusual red-flowered witch hazel.

Chinese witch hazel grows slowly into a rounded, compact shrub with fuzzy twigs laden with 1- to 1¼-inch yellow flowers touched with red at their base. Among the most showy of the witch hazels, the Chinese witch hazel is also the least hardy; Zone 5 marks its northern limit. The variety Brevipetala is grown for its dense clusters of small ocher-colored flowers, while Primavera bears especially profuse pale-yellow fragrant flowers.

Vernal witch hazel is often the first shrub to bloom in the winter and continues to flower for as long as two months; its orange flowers are smaller but more fragrant than those of other witch hazels.

HOW TO GROW. Witch hazels grow in full sun or partial shade with moist but well-drained soil enriched with peat moss, leaf mold or dried manure. Prune after the flowers have faded, cutting back leggy branches and thinning crowded stems; overgrown shrubs can be rejuvenated by cutting them back severely. Witch hazel can be trained as a tree with a single or multiple trunks by staking its central stem or stems and removing competing branches for several years. Prune any suckers that sprout from the roots of grafted plants. Plant witch hazels in fall.

HARDY ORANGE See *Poncirus*
HARRY LAUDER'S WALKING STICK See *Corylus*
HAZEL, AMERICAN See *Corylus*
HAZEL, CHINESE See *Corylus*
HAZEL, CORKSCREW See *Corylus*
HAZEL, CURLY See *Corylus*
HAZEL, TURKISH See *Corylus*
HEATH, CROSS-LEAVED See *Erica*
HEATH, DARLEY See *Erica*
HEATH, SPRING See *Erica*
HEATHER, SCOTCH See *Calluna*
HEAVENLY BAMBOO See *Nandina*

### HEDERA
*H. helix* (English ivy)

English ivy is a handsome evergreen vine that will roam over rocks, cling to tree trunks, climb walls or provide a dense green carpet in the winter garden. Easily cultivated from Zone 5 southward, English ivy is one of the most popular garden vines. A single plant can grow 50 to 90 feet long, clinging to tree trunks or walls by means of tiny rootlets on the stems. Used as a ground cover, the lobed, triangular leaves, 2 to 4 inches across, grow into a lustrous mat 6 to 8 inches high. Of the numerous varieties of English ivy, three are considered especially attractive in winter gardens: Glacier, with small green leaves that are spotted with silver gray and edged with white; Gold Heart, with tapering dark green leaves and golden-yellow centers; and Baltic ivy, a small-leaved variety that is particularly tolerant of both direct sun and the severe cold weather that causes the leaves of other English ivies to turn brown.

HOW TO GROW. English ivy grows well in either full sun or partial shade, but direct winter sun combined with drying winds may burn its foliage. The vine thrives in a moist well-drained soil enriched with organic matter. Plant English ivy in the spring in soil mixed with leaf mold or peat moss to a depth of 6 to 8 inches. Set the plants 12 inches apart and mulch to discourage weeds until the ivy becomes dense enough to cover the area. Ivy is such a vigorous plant that it can be sheared at any time of the year; however, shearing in fall or winter may leave unsightly bare spots that will not fill in until new growth begins in the spring. Thin climbing vines regularly to lighten their weight; old heavy vines can pull down fences and gutters.

HELLEBORE, CORSICAN See *Helleborus*

## HELLEBORUS
*H. foetidus* (setterwort); *H. lividus corsicus* (Corsican hellebore); *H. niger* (Christmas rose); *H. orientalis* (Lenten rose)

Perennial evergreen hellebores brighten gardens with 2- to 5-inch flowers from late fall to early spring, depending on the species and climate. Plants bloom as soon as the ground thaws, so the warmer the climate and the more protected their position, the earlier they bloom. Growing 12 to 18 inches tall, hellebores have glossy, dark green leaves arranged in clusters like fingers on a hand. They are ideal in sites close to the house where they can be easily seen during the winter and are protected from harsh winter winds.

The setterwort grows 1½ to 2 feet tall and blooms from midwinter to late spring in Zones 5-8. Each flower stem is crowded with clusters of drooping flower bells ½ to 1¼ inches across in shades of green, purple or yellow-green marked with purple. The leathery, dark green leaves are handsome all year.

The Corsican hellebore bears clusters of pale green, bowl-shaped flowers 2½ inches across in late winter in Zones 7-9. The flowers, dangling above sharply toothed, leathery leaves, are sometimes tinged with purple.

Hardy in Zones 3-8, the Christmas rose bears a yellow-centered, white flower sometimes tinged with pink on each of its red-spotted stalks. The 2- to 4-inch flowers bloom from late fall to early spring, even poking up through snow, and last up to a month. Its serrated leaves are divided into seven or nine segments. The variety Altifolius has flowers up to 5 inches across.

When the Lenten rose blooms from late winter to mid-spring, each flower stalk bears two to six creamy green flowers 2 to 3 inches wide that fade to brown. The flowers of the variety Atrorubens are brown-to-purple outside and green-to-purple inside. Isolde has pale rose flowers; Larissa has deep rose blooms; Snowdrift offers white flowers; the Millet hybrid group has flowers with speckles and stripes. The medium green leaves have seven to nine toothed segments. Although this species is hardy in Zones 3-9, its foliage is more sensitive to cold than the other hellebores.

HOW TO GROW. Grow hellebores in partial shade in the summer; some winter sun encourages blooming. The soil should be moist but well drained, neutral to slightly alkaline, and enriched with leaf mold or compost. Fertilize in the spring and again in the fall with a complete, balanced fertilizer and sprinkle ground limestone around the plants every three to four years. A 2-inch organic winter mulch will not only encourage earliest bloom but will also keep soil from splashing on the flowers. In the summer, maintain a 1-inch

CORSICAN HELLEBORE
*Helleborus lividus corsicus*

CHRISTMAS ROSE
*Helleborus niger*

*For climate zones and frost dates, see maps, pages 148-149.*

CLIMBING HYDRANGEA
*Hydrangea anomala petiolaris*

EVERGREEN CANDYTUFT
*Iberis sempervirens*

thick layer of compost or leaf mold around the plants to conserve moisture and provide nutrients. Remove old, unattractive foliage in the spring.

Plant hellebores in early spring, setting them 12 to 18 inches apart. Dig a hole deep enough so their roots can hang straight down rather than be spread out. Place the crown — where the stem and roots meet — 1 inch below the soil surface. Plants take two to three years to become established and mature to flowering size; do not divide the clumps unless the plants are very crowded after six or seven years. Then dig them up in late summer or fall and keep four to five growth buds to each division. Hellebores will sometimes sow themselves but seedlings take three to four years to flower. Take care in handling hellebores since all parts of the plants, especially their roots, are poisonous.

HEMLOCK, CANADA See *Tsuga*
HEMLOCK, CAROLINA See *Tsuga*
HICKORY, SHAGBARK See *Carya*
HOLLY See *Ilex*
HOLLY GRAPE, LEATHER-LEAVED See *Mahonia*
HOLLY GRAPE, OREGON See *Mahonia*
HONEYSUCKLE, FRAGRANT See *Lonicera*
HONEYSUCKLE, WINTER See *Lonicera*
HORNBEAM See *Carpinus*
HORNBEAM, AMERICAN See *Carpinus*

## HYDRANGEA

*H. anomala petiolaris,* also called *H. petiolaris* (climbing hydrangea); *H. quercifolia* (oak-leaved hydrangea)

Long after their splendid white flowers have faded and died, their shredding red-brown bark gives these hydrangeas winter interest in gardens in Zones 5-9. Climbing hydrangea is a vine that may reach 75 feet in height with lateral branches 3 to 4 feet long. It clings to trees, walls or other structures by means of rootlets, which can cause damage to wooden surfaces. This vine is also frequently used as a tall ground cover to hide old walls, tree stumps or rock piles. Oak-leaved hydrangea grows to a height of 6 feet with lobed, 4- to 8-inch dark green leaves that are silvery underneath and turn a rich red or purple before falling in the autumn. Oak-leaved hydrangea grows in spreading clumps. The shaggy bark on older stems shows to best advantage when the shrub is used as a specimen planting.

HOW TO GROW. Climbing hydrangea and oak-leaved hydrangea grow in either full sun or partial shade in moist but well-drained soil mixed with compost, peat moss or leaf mold. Prune climbing hydrangea in winter or early spring before new growth starts in order to keep it at the desired size and shape. Prune oak-leaved hydrangea only to control its height, clipping it just after the flowers fade since new flower buds form on the previous season's growth. Plant hydrangeas in spring or fall; newly planted climbing hydrangeas require one or two seasons before they begin major growth. Both hydrangeas can be propagated from cuttings taken in late spring or early summer or by digging and transplanting rooted suckers from the base of older plants.

# I

## IBERIS

*I. sempervirens* (evergreen candytuft)

The lustrous-leaved mats of evergreen candytuft hug the ground, drift gracefully across rocks, or take a firm hold in crevices among paving stones or along walks. Although its woody stems may bend and take root whenever they touch moist soil, this perennial does not spread enough to be useful as a ground cover unless the plants are closely spaced — a single plant may become up to 2 feet across and from 9 to 12 inches high. Grown from Zone 4 southward, evergreen candytuft has narrow, 1½-inch leaves that are evergreen in milder areas and usually last through most of the winter in the colder zones before turning brown. The plants are virtually covered with 1½- to 2-inch flat clusters of tiny white flowers in the early summer. There are several varieties, including Little Gem, under 6 inches tall; Snowflake, with thick stems and leaves; and Christmas Snow, which bears a second crop of flat flower clusters in the fall.

HOW TO GROW. Evergreen candytuft grows best in full sun in rich, well-drained sandy soil with a pH of 6.0 to 7.5. Set the plants 6 to 18 inches apart in early spring. To encourage thick foliage, shear the plants lightly after they flower. For best bloom and the fastest growth, work equal parts of leaf mold or peat moss, fresh soil and sand into the topsoil around the plants each spring. Established mats of candytuft do not transplant well. Start new plants by rooting summer cuttings in moist vermiculite or by sowing seeds in the beds where the plants are desired in spring. After the seeds germinate, thin the seedlings to stand 6 to 9 inches apart.

## IDESIA
*I. polycarpa* (iigiri tree)

Undamaged by frost, a profusion of brilliant red-orange berries hanging in grapelike clusters along tiered spreading branches bedeck the iigiri tree into the winter months. Hardy as a shade or specimen tree from Zone 6 southward, this deciduous tree grows into a pyramidal shape 45 to 50 feet tall. The broad, toothed leaves about 6 inches long somewhat resemble those of the catalpa, and turn yellow before dropping in fall. Only female trees produce berries, but the sexes cannot be differentiated until the trees mature and begin to flower, about 15 years after they are planted.

HOW TO GROW. The iigiri tree grows in any well-drained soil in full sun. Train young trees to a single trunk by choosing a top leader and removing competing branches. An iigiri can be transplanted with little difficulty.

## INTERMEDIATE YEW See *Taxus*

## ILEX
*I. aquifolium* (English holly); *I. cornuta* (Chinese holly, horned holly); *I. crenata* (Japanese holly); *I. decidua* (possum haw); *I. glabra* (inkberry); *I. opaca* (American holly); *I. serrata* (finetooth holly, Japanese winterberry); *I. verticillata* (winterberry, black alder)

The red, yellow or black berries that decorate gray-barked branches through the cold season have made hollies and their relatives winter-garden favorites. The evergreen species offer another premium — glossy green or variegated winter leaves that are often spiny and scalloped. The species listed here are neatly shaped shrubs or trees that bear inconspicuous but fragrant clusters of tiny white, sometimes green-tinged flowers in spring or early summer. While a few species are self-pollinating, only the females of most species produce berries and there must be at least one nonfruiting male within 100 feet of the females in order to ensure good pollination.

The English holly is the Christmas classic whose brilliant red berries and deep green leaves have become a holiday symbol. From Zone 7 southward, this slow-growing evergreen may take 10 years to grow from seed into a 6-foot shrub but it is long-lived and ultimately becomes a handsome, pyramidal tree 30 to 50 feet tall. The parent species

IIGIRI TREE
*Idesia polycarpa*

BURFORD HOLLY
*Ilex cornuta* 'Burfordii'

*For climate zones and frost dates, see maps, pages 148-149.*

**JAPANESE HOLLY**
*Ilex crenata*

**WINTERBERRY**
*Ilex verticillata*

has red berries and glossy green, 1- to 3-inch spiny-edged leaves that are wavy when young. There are numerous varieties that have other characteristics. Argentea-marginata has oval leaves edged with silver, for example, while Fructo-luteo bears bright yellow fruits.

Chinese holly produces large red berries ⅜ inch across in full, long-lasting clusters. The shiny green leaves, 1½ to 5 inches long, are a distinctive rectangular shape and have such long, strong spines that this evergreen is sometimes known as the horned holly. From Zone 7 southward the Chinese holly is a broad, dense shrub 5 to 9 feet high at maturity. The variety Burford has drooping branches and darker green, rounded leaves with fewer spines.

Finely toothed, 1-inch oval leaves give the evergreen Japanese holly a resemblance to boxwood. A densely twiggy, spreading, easy-to-grow shrub 20 feet tall at maturity, it tolerates shearing and is often used as a hedge plant in Zones 7-9. The tiny ¼-inch berries are black.

The self-pollinating possum haw is a 5- to 10-foot-tall deciduous shrub or a small tree up to 30 feet tall in Zones 5-8. When in fruit, it suggests a cherry tree and the bright scarlet berries cling to silvery branches long after the 1- to 2½-inch pointed oval leaves have fallen in autumn.

The female inkberry has erect, angular stems lined in fall with small black berries. Males are evergreen but the leaves of females may turn maroon or purplish in winter. The oval, glossy leaves, 1 to 2 inches long, are slightly toothed at their tips. Quick to reach their 9-foot height, inkberries can be cut to the ground for rejuvenation if they become too large for the garden. They grow in Zones 3-9.

The 1½- to 3½-inch spiny-edged leaves of the American holly have glossy green tops with dull, yellow-tinged undersides. Hardy in Zones 6-9, they spread into bushy or conical trees 40 to 50 feet tall. Small bright red berries ornament the dense foliage long into winter. Among the hundreds of named varieties are Goldie, with yellow fruits, and Miss Helen and Old Heavyberry, both bearing unusually abundant crops of large scarlet berries.

In Zones 5-9, the deciduous fine-tooth holly bears a profusion of tiny red berries only ⅙ to ⅛ inch across. It grows up to 15 feet tall with finely serrated 1- to 3-inch leaves. With similar leaves, the winterberry also bears clusters of ¼-inch red berries in great quantities. A deciduous shrub, winterberry grows 5 to 10 feet tall and 15 feet wide in Zones 3-9.

HOW TO GROW. Hollies grow best in moist, acid soils supplemented with peat moss or leaf mold; inkberry and winterberry will tolerate wet soils. Most hollies grown in full sun produce the best berries and have the most pronounced leaf color but the American holly grows best in partial shade and winterberry will produce its berries in shade as well as sun. All hollies should be watered well in fall, then mulched with oak leaves, wood chips, pine needles or compost before the ground freezes. Choose sites protected from winter winds. Hollies need little pruning except to remove dead or damaged branches; often cutting a few Christmas decorations is sufficient. Plant in spring or fall in a ratio of 1 male plant to every 10 females. Buy plants from nurseries that grow the sexes separately, since males and females are indistinguishable except when in flower. Hollies are frequently grown as hedges; set 18-inch plants at 3-foot intervals and clip branch tips during the second spring to encourage bushiness.

## IRIS

*I. bakerana* (Baker iris); *I. danfordiae* (Danford iris); *I. histrioides major* (Harput iris); *I. reticulata* (netted iris) (all called reticulata iris, bulbous iris)

Miniature reticulata irises bloom with the early squills, snowdrops, crocuses and winter aconites to signal that frost has left the ground. Each bulb produces a single 1- to 3-inch flower with three erect and three hanging petals above immature swordlike or grassy leaves that later grow 12 to 18 inches long before withering in early summer. Hardy from Zone 5 southward, reticulata irises are effective grouped in rock gardens or as accents along paths.

The 4-inch Baker iris has a fragrant flower with erect deep violet petals and purple-spotted hanging petals. Only 2 to 4 inches tall, the Danford iris has bright yellow flowers while the Harput iris, 4 inches tall, has brilliant blue ones; both bloom as their leaves break through the soil. Blooming slightly later than other reticulata species, the 6-inch netted iris has fragrant, deep violet flowers with yellow blotches on its drooping petals. The netted iris has many hardy varieties in colors from light blue to deep purple.

HOW TO GROW. Reticulata irises grow best in full sun although they will grow in partially shaded areas in the southern part of their range. Dry soil and excellent drainage are needed; otherwise, the bulbs must be dug up after the foliage dies and stored until fall. Plant the bulbs in early fall, spacing them 4 inches apart and 3 inches deep. Dust the bed with bonemeal or 5-10-10 fertilizer when the plants emerge in the spring. Allow the clumps to increase for about five years or until flowering slackens, then dig up the bulbs and set them farther apart. Propagate additional plants by removing the small bulblets or offsets that develop at the base of the old bulbs.

IRONWOOD See *Carpinus*
IVY, ENGLISH See *Hedera*

# J

JAPANESE ANDROMEDA See *Pieris*
JAPANESE BARBERRY See *Berberis*
JAPANESE CEDAR See *Cryptomeria*
JAPANESE MAPLE See *Acer*
JAPANESE RED PINE See *Pinus*
JAPANESE ROSE See *Kerria*
JAPANESE YEW See *Taxus*
JASMINE, PRIMROSE See *Jasminum*
JASMINE, WINTER See *Jasminum*

## JASMINUM
*J. mesnyi*, also called *J. primulinum* (primrose jasmine); *J. nudiflorum* (winter jasmine)

These two jasmines, one evergreen, the other deciduous, are rambling shrubs equally desirable in winter gardens for their winter bloom. Primrose jasmine, hardy in Zones 8-10, produces fragrant 2-inch yellow flowers, frequently double-petaled, among glossy, 3-inch evergreen leaves. The whip-like stems of winter jasmine, 3 to 8 feet high, bear 1-inch star-shaped yellow flowers from midwinter to early spring, depending on the variety and the severity of the winter. The winter jasmine grows in Zones 6-9 and, if given a protected spot, in Zone 5 as well. Though deciduous, this shrub has young stems that remain green throughout the winter, providing a color foil for the flowers. Both jasmines can be grown as informal shrubs or can be trained to trellises. They are also effective when allowed to trail from the tops of walls or banks.

HOW TO GROW. Jasmines grow best in full sun and in a well-drained, even slightly dry soil. In northern areas, give plants a sheltered position against a south or southwest wall to shield them from the chilly winter and early-spring winds,

DANFORD IRIS
*Iris danfordiae*

HARPUT IRIS
*Iris histrioides major*

*For climate zones and frost dates, see maps, pages 148-149.*

**WINTER JASMINE**
*Jasminum nudiflorum*

**HEDGEHOG JUNIPER**
*Juniperus chinensis* 'Echiniformis'

which otherwise may ruin the flowers. Mulch the shrubs in northern areas with 2 inches of organic matter such as wood chips or shredded bark to protect the roots from extreme temperature changes.

Plant primrose jasmine in spring, winter jasmine in autumn or early spring. Jasmines flower on the previous season's growth. Prune the canes immediately after they flower or cut the branches in midwinter and bring them indoors to force the flowers into bloom; cut away the dead canes and any excessively twiggy growth.

### JUNIPER See *Juniperus*

### JUNIPERUS

*J. chinensis* and varieties (Chinese juniper); *J. horizontalis* and varieties (creeping juniper); *J. scopulorum* and varieties (Rocky Mountain juniper); *J. virginiana* and varieties (eastern red cedar)

Tough evergreen junipers and red cedars tolerate wind, drought, pollution, seashore conditions and poor soil to remain attractive year round. There are varieties suitable for all climate zones in North America, with sizes and shapes ranging from ground covers to large trees. The foliage may be shades of green, blue or yellow in summer, sometimes changing to another shade in winter. The female plants carry attractive blue-gray berries through the winter. On young plants, the tiny needles are spiky and stand away from the twigs; on mature plants, they are pressed closely against the twigs like overlapping shingles. Sometimes both adult and juvenile foliage are found on the same plant. The red-brown bark is thin and peels off in shreds; with age it becomes deeply grooved. Generally slow growing, junipers can be used in the landscape as background plants, windbreaks, ground covers, hedges or specimens.

The Chinese juniper is a large cone-shaped tree growing up to 60 feet tall with dense dark green foliage. Male plants are narrower than the females, which bear purple-brown berries ⅓ to ⅜ inch across. Hardy in Zones 4-9, this species has attractive varieties. Among them is Echiniformis, the hedgehog juniper, a rounded dwarf variety that becomes 1 to 2 feet high and slightly wider. It is hardy in Zones 4-10. Torulosa, the Hollywood juniper, grows in Zones 5-10 and has dark green, scalelike leaves clustered along twisted, irregular branchlets that give the plant a tufted appearance. Forming a narrow cone shape, it grows to about 6 feet in height as a multistemmed shrub or as tall as 15 to 25 feet as a tree with a central leader. Variegata, the variegated Chinese juniper, has blue-gray branchlets that are tipped with cream or white. Hardy in Zones 5-9, it has almost vertical branches that form an egg-shaped shrub 9 to 20 feet tall; with pruning it can be kept 6 to 8 feet tall.

Creeping juniper's trailing branches form mats 5 to 10 feet wide. The main branches lie flat against the ground and sometimes take root, but the 12- to 18-inch branchlets grow straight up. Hardy in Zones 2-9, it makes a good, dense ground cover of blue-green foliage that is not damaged by direct sun in either the summer or winter. It has tiny blue-black berries. There are many varieties, some with unusual winter coloration. The variety Douglasii, known as the Waukegan juniper, has steel-blue foliage that becomes purple in the winter; it grows 6 to 9 inches tall and spreads 10 to 12 feet. Plumosa, the Andorra juniper, forms an open-centered shrub 2 feet tall and 6 feet wide; its branchlets are feathery with erect needles that turn gray-green in summer, bronze in the fall, and a bright rose-to-violet in the winter. The Bar Harbor juniper, in contrast, has its needles pressed closely against thin V-shaped branchlets that are gray-green in summer, mauve in winter.

The Rocky Mountain juniper is a narrow, conical tree up to 35 feet tall with blue-green leaves that become gray, purple or silver blue in the winter. It can be pruned into a hedge or it can be kept small by removing branches at the trunk. Tolleson's weeping juniper has branches that droop. Blue Heaven is a dense tree that grows 20 feet tall in as many years with silver-blue to dark blue-green foliage and berries. Gray Gleam forms a narrow column of silver-green foliage 15 to 20 feet tall whose color intensifies in the winter; this juniper is used for both formal and informal hedges. Rocky Mountain junipers grow best in Zones 4-9 in the western parts of the United States.

The eastern red cedar is a reliable species in Zones 4-9 in the eastern portions of the country. It is a slender, pyramidal tree that grows 75 to 90 feet tall, broadening and losing its lower branches with age. With shearing, it can be kept compact and used for hedges and background plantings. Its dark green leaves turn bronze or brown in the winter. The variety Burkii, the Burk red cedar, grows 30 feet tall and half as wide with gray-blue foliage that turns purple or becomes a more intense blue in the winter. This dense, conical red cedar is hardy in Zones 5-9. The 20- to 30-foot Canaert red cedar has bunches of cordlike foliage that emerge yellow green, then turn dark green. Hardy in Zones 4-9, it forms an informal, spreading tree when left unpruned. Skyrocket, an aptly named variety, is perhaps the slimmest of any columnar juniper. It grows about 25 feet tall but is only 2 feet wide. The foliage has a silvery or blue-gray cast.

HOW TO GROW. Although partial shade is tolerated, junipers and red cedars grow best and develop their best color in full sun. They grow in a wide range of soils but do best in sandy, dry, well-drained locations with slightly alkaline soil. They will naturally grow in symmetrical shapes but respond well to pruning or shearing. Shape trees by removing competing leaders, cutting errant branches back to a fork, or removing upper branches at the trunk to let more light and air reach lower limbs. Prune shrubs or ground covers in summer or fall if they require it for shaping or for controlling their spread. Plant junipers and red cedars in the spring, setting out both male and female plants if berries are desired, and maintain a 2- to 4-inch layer of organic mulch such as wood chips or shredded bark.

# K

## KERRIA

*K. japonica* (Japanese rose)

The Japanese rose is a rounded deciduous shrub with slim, arching stems that are 3 to 5 feet tall and remain a bright green through the winter. The stems of the variety Aureovittata are green- and yellow-striped. In the spring, golden roselike flowers 1 to 2 inches across bloom at the tips of the previous year's growth. Pleniflora is a taller variety than its parent and bears double-petaled blooms over a longer period of time. It is more cold tolerant. These three kinds of Japanese rose have coarsely toothed, wedge-shaped leaves, 1½ to 4 inches long, that turn from bright green to yellow in fall. Japanese roses are used as foundation plantings, specimen shrubs or in a shrub border. Although they are hardy in Zones 5-9, the branch tips are sometimes damaged by severe cold in Zones 5 and 6.

HOW TO GROW. Japanese roses flower best in partial shade but they will grow in deep shade or sun. Although they adapt to a wide range of soils, growth is fastest in a moist but well-drained soil enriched with peat moss or leaf mold. Plant

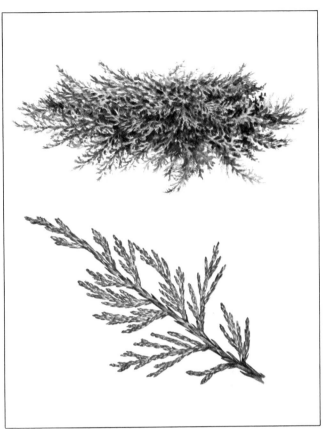

**BAR HARBOR JUNIPER**
*Juniperus horizontalis* 'Bar Harbor'

**JAPANESE ROSE**
*Kerria japonica*

*For climate zones and frost dates, see maps, pages 148-149.*

GOLDEN-RAIN TREE
*Koelreuteria paniculata*

CRAPE MYRTLE
*Lagerstroemia indica*

Japanese roses in spring in positions protected from strong winter winds. Yearly pruning is important to encourage the growth of new, more brightly colored stems and to ensure the greatest number of flowers. Clip off winter-killed branch tips in early spring before flowers appear. When the flowers fade, remove the stems that have flowered at ground level. Propagate Japanese roses from cuttings of new growth taken in late spring or early summer, by ground layering or by dividing the clumps of stems in spring or fall.

**KINNIKINICK** See *Arctostaphylos*

## KOELREUTERIA
*K. paniculata* (golden-rain tree)

Papery seed pods hanging like tiny lanterns from the uppermost branches of its asymmetrical crown make the golden-rain tree a picturesque accent in a winter garden. Despite their delicate appearance, the 2-inch-long three-sided pods last through winter. Mature trees have rough bark that stands out handsomely when the trees drop their leaves in fall. The golden-rain tree, hardy in Zones 5-10, grows rather fast—an 8- to 10-foot tree grows to 20 feet in five or six years. At maturity a golden-rain tree is seldom more than 30 feet tall, with a spread nearly equaling its height. Each of its 8- to 15-inch leaves is composed of 1- to 3-inch paired leaflets that unfold red in spring, turn green in summer and sometimes become yellow in autumn. Masses of yellow flowers in summer are followed by seed pods that at first are pale green, then turn pinkish and finally become rusty brown. This small- to medium-sized tree makes an effective accent outside a window, near a terrace or in another spot where its asymmetrical form is the center of interest.

HOW TO GROW. The golden-rain tree grows in full sun in any well-drained soil. Trees taller than 12 feet should be planted balled and burlaped with the soil around the roots intact; smaller saplings can be planted bare-rooted. Or start trees from seed. Prune young trees in winter to develop strong scaffold branches; older trees rarely need pruning.

# L

**LACE-BARK PINE** See *Pinus*

## LAGERSTROEMIA
*L. indica* (crape myrtle)

Erect clumps of thick stems with angular branches and twigs that form an irregularly rounded crown up to 20 feet high characterize deciduous crape myrtles in the winter landscape. The smooth tan bark on the trunk and older branches flakes to reveal paler bark beneath. Gardeners from Zone 7 southward prize the late summer 6- to 12-inch clusters of crinkled flowers in hues from white to pink, red or lavender that are borne profusely until autumn. The oval 1- to 2-inch privet-like leaves unfurl with a bronze tint, become green, then turn red, orange and yellow in fall.

HOW TO GROW. Crape myrtles grow in any moist but well-drained soil supplemented with leaf mold or peat moss; they require full sun. Mulch the soil under the shrubs with 2 inches of organic material such as wood chips, shredded bark or pine needles to protect the roots from frost and to maintain cool and moist soil during the growing season. In early spring, prune winter-damaged branches and thin out several of the new stems that grow from the base of the shrub; each fifth year, thin out several older stems. Oversized or winter-killed shrubs may be cut to the ground for rejuvenation. To develop an ornamental-tree form of crape myrtle, train a young plant to a single trunk until it reaches about 6 feet and pinch back top growth during the growing season to develop a round, bushy head. Plant container-grown plants in spring.

**LAVENDER COTTON** See *Santolina*
**LEATHER FERN** See *Polystichum*
**LEATHER-LEAVED HOLLY GRAPE** See *Mahonia*
**LENTEN ROSE** See *Helleborus*

## LEUCOTHOË

*L. fontanesiana,* also called *L. catesbaei* (drooping leucothoë)

With deep bronze-maroon leaves on gracefully arching branches, drooping leucothoë contributes both color and form to a winter garden. Cultivated in Zones 4-9, this broad-leaved evergreen shrub grows 6 feet tall but is most attractive when it is pruned to a more compact 3-foot height. The glossy, 7-inch-long leaves are popular in flower arrangements. In late spring leucothoë bears 2- to 3-inch clusters of small, bell-shaped flowers resembling lily of the valley. The flowers hang from the undersides of the branches, giving the shrub its common name.

Nana is a dwarf variety that grows only 18 inches tall and spreads 6 feet wide. It has deep green leaves 2 to 3 inches long that also turn bronze-maroon in fall and winter. Nana is often planted where the taller species would become ungainly unless pruned. Girard's Rainbow is a multicolored variety with new, bright red shoots that change to pink, then become green, yellow or copper in fall and winter. Drooping leucothoë can be used in front of larger trees or shrubs to camouflage trunks or stems that have become unsightly, or as a ground cover on shady banks. It is at its best in a woodland setting, but will tolerate city conditions and can be used as a border plant around terraces.

HOW TO GROW. Drooping leucothoë grows best in partial shade in a moist, acid soil mixed with peat moss. It grows in full sun, but without some protection from strong winter sun, its leaves may burn. In severe winters, the shrub sometimes loses some of its upper leaves. Plant drooping leucothoë in early spring in Zones 4 or 5, in either spring or fall in Zones 6-9. Set the plants 4 feet apart and mulch them with leaves or wood chips. Fertilize young shrubs annually in spring with cottonseed meal or fertilizer recommended for acid-loving plants such as holly or rhododendrons. Prune established shrubs in spring by removing a few of the older canes at ground level to keep the plants growing vigorously and at the proper height. If drooping leucothoë becomes overgrown and straggly, cut the stems off at ground level. To start new plants, divide a plant with a spade in early spring. Drooping leucothoë can also be propagated by rooting cuttings taken in spring in moist sand or vermiculite.

**LILY-OF-THE-VALLEY BUSH** See *Pieris*
**LILY-TURF, CREEPING** See *Liriope*

## LIQUIDAMBAR

*L. styraciflua* (sweet gum)

From a tapering trunk, the sweet gum tree branches symmetrically to form a dense pyramidal shape about two thirds as wide as its 60- to 80-foot height. Fragrant, amber-colored resin seeps through deep fissures in the gray bark of the trunk; mature branches have a rough, warty surface and older twigs develop distinctive corky flanges. In winter, this handsome skeleton is decked with prickly brown seed balls, 1½ inches across, that are often used indoors as Christmas decorations. These seed clusters follow inconspicuous, petal-less green flowers that appear among the star-shaped 4- to 7-inch leaves in spring. A glossy, dark green through the sum-

*For climate zones and frost dates, see maps, pages 148-149.*

DROOPING LEUCOTHOË
*Leucothoë fontanesiana*

SWEET GUM
*Liquidambar styraciflua*

**CREEPING LILY-TURF**
*Liriope spicata*

**FRAGRANT HONEYSUCKLE**
*Lonicera fragrantissima*

mer, this foliage turns splendid shades of orange, scarlet and bronze in fall, with all three colors sometimes on the same tree. The sweet gum grows from Zone 5 southward; in Zones 9 and 10 the bright leaves cling into winter. Its rate of growth depends on soil moisture; trees along riverbanks or in bottomlands may grow 30 feet tall in six to eight years, while this same growth takes 10 to 15 years in drier areas.

HOW TO GROW. Sweet gums thrive in full sun in moist but not wet soil enriched with peat moss or leaf mold. The soil must be deep to accommodate the long, fleshy roots. Prune sweet gum trees during the winter to avoid bleeding. In pruning a young tree, remove branches that compete with the main trunk; as the tree grows, thin out branches that are spaced too closely. Sweet gums that are dug with a large soil ball are easy to transplant in spring.

## LIRIOPE
*L. muscari* (big blue lily-turf), *L. spicata* (creeping lily-turf)

Lily-turfs form dense clumps of grasslike leaves that stand throughout the winter. Big blue lily-turf is a rather coarse-leaved plant hardy from Zone 6 southward. The arching leaves, ¾ inch wide and 18 inches long, keep their dark green color in winter. The variety *L. muscari* Variegata has yellow-striped foliage. Spikes of lilac flowers blossom in the center of each clump in early autumn, followed by small black fruits. Creeping lily-turf, with deep green leaves ¼ inch wide and 6 to 12 inches long, is a more finely textured plant that spreads by means of creeping underground stems. The leaves turn pale yellow-green in very cold weather in Zones 4-7; in the milder climates of Zones 8-10 their color does not change. In summer, creeping lily-turf bears tiny white or lilac flower spikes above the leaves. Lily-turfs are often used as ground covers in shady areas or to edge flower beds and walkways. Though they look like grasses, they cannot be walked on because they would be damaged.

HOW TO GROW. Both lily-turfs grow best in partial shade, but they can be grown in deep shade and will tolerate full sun if the soil is moist enough. These species also thrive in dry sites and tolerate salty seaside locations. Plant lily-turfs in any good garden soil in spring or fall, spacing clumps about 12 inches apart. As new leaves of big blue lily-turf appear in spring, clip old foliage to maintain an attractive appearance. Creeping lily-turf can be mowed once a year in spring. To start new plants, divide the clumps in spring, summer or fall.

## LITTLELEAF BOX See *Buxus*

## LONICERA
*L. fragrantissima* (fragrant honeysuckle, winter honeysuckle); *L. standishii* (Standish honeysuckle)

Extraordinarily sweet-smelling flowers and stiff leathery leaves make fragrant honeysuckle and Standish honeysuckle good winter-garden shrubs. In Zones 5 and 6, their leaves usually cling until midwinter, though in some years the foliage remains throughout the season, and the flowers bloom in late February to very early spring. In Zones 7-9 these honeysuckles bloom as early as January and the leaves are fully evergreen. Fragrant honeysuckle becomes 6 to 8 feet in height and breadth and has oval, dull green leaves 1 to 3 inches long. The ¾-inch-long, creamy white flowers appear on stems that grew the previous year. A rounded shrub growing 4 or 5 feet tall, the Standish honeysuckle has spiny hairs on its young branches and peeling bark on its older ones. The oval leaves, 3 to 4 inches long, are also hairy and its flowers are similar to those of the fragrant honeysuckle, though somewhat smaller. The ¼-inch red fruits that ripen in the summer on both species are quickly eaten by birds.

Whether used in shrub borders, as hedges or as specimens, these honeysuckles should be planted near a walkway or house where the flowers can be easily enjoyed. These two species require little maintenance, tolerate city conditions and are relatively pest-free. Their branches are often cut and forced into bloom indoors.

HOW TO GROW. Vigorous honeysuckles thrive in full sun; they will also grow in partial shade though they will have fewer flowers. They grow best in a well-drained soil enriched with organic matter such as peat moss or leaf mold. Plant the shrubs in fall and mulch them with a 2- to 4-inch layer of wood chips or bark mulch. Prune honeysuckles immediately after flowering to develop an open fountain shape, to thin out old stems and to remove suckers. Propagate from cuttings or by ground-layering.

# M

## MAGNOLIA

*M. grandiflora* (Southern magnolia, bull bay); *M. macrophylla* (bigleaf magnolia, large-leaved cucumber tree); *M. virginiana,* also called *M. glauca* (sweet bay)

Renowned for the sweetly fragrant flowers that sometimes bloom year round in mild climates, deciduous and evergreen magnolias make splendid winter attractions.

The southern magnolia, found in Zone 7 southward, is a massive evergreen tree that grows more than 90 feet tall and spreads half as wide in a striking, pyramidal form. The thick, polished, 8-inch leaves have downy, rust-colored undersides in striking contrast to the creamy white flowers up to 10 inches across that bloom in spring and summer. Where night temperatures do not fall below about 40°, occasional blooms appear in fall and winter. Erect, cone-shaped seed pods covered with velvety down and filled with flat red seeds follow the flowers. Both the pods and the leaves are popular indoor winter decorations. It can take 15 years for ordinary seedlings of the species to blossom, but grafted varieties such as Majestic Beauty, Russet, St. Mary and Samuel Sommer produce flowers in two to three years. In the northern limits of its range, wet snow clinging to the broad leaves can weigh down and damage smaller branches.

Known for its huge, 1- to 3-foot-long leaves — the largest of any North American tree — the bigleaf magnolia is prized in winter, without its foliage, for its distinctive vase shape and its smooth yellowish bark, peeling to reveal silvery gray patches. Growing up to 50 feet in Zones 6-10, this magnolia also boasts the biggest flowers of any magnolia. The 10- to 12-inch-wide cream-colored flowers appear from midsummer to early fall and are followed by cucumber-shaped seed pods filled with red seeds. Because strong winds can tatter its leaves and make the tree unsightly, the bigleaf magnolia requires a sheltered position in the garden.

The sweet bay is a handsome tree for winter gardens in Zones 8-10, where it keeps its glossy, 3- to 5-inch-long leaves year round. It grows rapidly to a height of 40 to 60 feet in the southern parts of its range. In Zones 5-7, sweet bay is deciduous and matures at a height of 25 feet. The fragrant 3-inch flowers that appear in early summer are followed by 2-inch red seed pods.

HOW TO GROW. Magnolias grow best in full sun in a moist, rich soil supplemented with peat moss or decaying leaves. Plant container-grown trees at any time; move balled-and-burlaped ones into the garden in early spring. Set the plants in the ground at exactly the same level they were growing in the nursery and water thoroughly after planting. To encour-

LARGE-LEAVED CUCUMBER TREE
*Magnolia macrophylla*

*For climate zones and frost dates, see maps, pages 148-149.*

OREGON HOLLY GRAPE
*Mahonia aquifolium*

SARGENT CRAB APPLE
*Malus sargentii*

age good growth, fertilize magnolias each spring with cotton-seed meal or a fertilizer recommended for acid-loving plants such as rhododendrons or camellias. Magnolias rarely need pruning; if trees need shaping, prune after flowering.

### MAHONIA
*M. aquifolium* (Oregon holly grape); *M. bealei* (leather-leaved holly grape, leather-leaf mahonia)

Shapely silhouettes, attractive evergreen foliage, tolerance of cold, and clusters of flower buds make holly grapes outstanding broad-leaved evergreen shrubs for winter gardens.

The glossy, spiny leaflets of the Oregon holly grape could be mistaken for the foliage of a true holly, although the plants are not related. Five to nine of these spiny leaflets make up each of the long leaves growing along its spreading stems. As the weather gets colder, the deep green foliage turns purple or bronze, an attractive foil for the light-green buds that cling to the plant throughout the winter and open into sweetly scented yellow flowers in early spring. The flowers develop into edible blue-to-black fruits that can be used to make a tangy jelly. Hardy in Zones 5-9, this shrub grows 2 to 3 feet tall in three or four years. The shrub ultimately reaches 6 feet but most gardeners keep it pruned to half that height to avoid tall, bare stems.

In Zones 6-9, the leather-leaved holly grape grows into a stately shrub 8 to 10 feet tall. Its erect stems are lined with long, stiff horizontal leaves composed of four to seven pairs of thick prickly leaflets. This species is green year round but, unlike the Oregon holly grape, has more showy spikes of flower buds in winter. Leather-leaved holly grape is particularly effective when grown against a wall or fence to display its angular form. In February and March extraordinarily fragrant lemon-yellow flowers fill the garden with their scent. The blue fruits ripen in late spring or early summer.

HOW TO GROW. Oregon holly grape and leather-leaved holly grape grow best in partial shade in a moist, but well-drained soil. They do well under trees where many other shrubs will not thrive. In the northern parts of their range, these shrubs must be sheltered from the strong winter sun, which can burn their leaves, and from dehydrating winter winds. Plant balled-and-burlaped shrubs in early spring. To encourage growth, fertilize in early spring with cottonseed meal or any other fertilizer formula recommended for acid-loving plants such as camellias or rhododendrons. If necessary, prune holly grapes in early spring before active leaf growth begins again. Cut young shrubs back to encourage bushy growth. Remove a few older canes from large shrubs and remove suckers to keep plants within bounds.

### MAIDENHAIR SPLEENWORT See *Asplenium*

### MALUS
*M. 'Bob White'* (Bob White crab apple); *M. 'Red Jade'* (Red Jade crab apple); *M. sargentii* (Sargent crab apple); *M. zumi calocarpa* (Zumi crab apple)

To attract birds to a winter garden, plant the crab apple. The ornamental red or yellow fruit of this small tree often lasts through most of the winter, providing a dependable food source; its dense thicket of intertwining branches offers welcome shelter. Crab apples are easy to grow and are among the most cold-resistant of flowering trees. Except for the Zumi crab apple, which is hardy only from Zone 5 southward, those recommended for winter settings grow in Zones 4-8. Most species grow from 15 to 25 feet tall, spreading just as wide when mature. A 6- to 8-foot tree usually is 15 to 20 feet high in about five or six years. The fruit, which varies in size and color according to species, can be used for jellies or left on the trees for birds or winter color.

Bob White crab apple is a round, intricately branched tree that grows 15 to 20 feet tall. In winter, a multitude of ⅝-inch-wide yellow fruits clings to its branches, and in summer, it is covered with masses of 1-inch white blossoms. Red Jade crab apple has a weeping form that is especially attractive in the winter landscape. It grows 15 to 20 feet tall and in autumn bears ½-inch bright red fruit that remains on the tree's drooping branches until early winter. The quantity of fruit tends to vary in two-year cycles, being abundant in one year and less so in alternate years. Red Jade's 1-inch-wide spring flowers are white.

Sargent's crab apple is a dwarf variety, growing only 6 to 8 feet tall. It has a curious, almost square form, its branches curving and spreading upward from a short, sometimes multiple trunk. In winter these branches intertwine in a picturesque zigzag pattern. The tree's ⅜-inch red fruit ripens in autumn and holds its color well into the winter. The spring blossoms are white, double-flowered and about ½ inch wide. The Zumi crab apple grows 20 to 25 feet tall, and it too bears masses of small berry-like fruit, ½ inch wide, in alternate years. The fruit is dull red, ripens in autumn, and clings to the tree through most of the winter. Small white blossoms appear in spring.

HOW TO GROW. Crab apples grow best in a sunny location and a moist, well-drained acid soil, pH 5.0 to 6.5. Young trees may be pruned in winter or early spring to improve their shape. Old trees seldom need pruning other than the annual removal of suckers.

MANZANITA, STANFORD See *Arctostaphylos*
MAPLE See *Acer*
MAPLE, CORAL-BARK JAPANESE See *Acer*
MAPLE, DAVID See *Acer*
MAPLE, PAPERBARK See *Acer*
MAPLE, STRIPED See *Acer*
MAPLE, THREAD-LEAF JAPANESE See *Acer*

## MISCANTHUS
*M. sinensis* (eulalia)

In a winter garden, where the dominant note is often the angular forms of bare trees and shrubs, the gentle lines and straw color of eulalia grass effectively soften the seasonal landscape. The long, gracefully arching leaves and stems of this ornamental grass end in feathery, fanlike fronds, often a foot long. A perennial found in Zones 4-10, eulalia grass grows in clumps that increase in size, but slowly. A 20-year-old clump may be only 4 feet across, although it can sometimes grow to 10 or 12 feet.

The slender leaves of the plant are less than an inch wide, but frequently grow to 2 to 3 feet in length; during the summer they are boldly marked with a white or yellow stripe, but the stripe patterns differ with variety. Variegatus, striped eulalia grass, has white or yellow stripes along the center of each leaf blade; Zebrinus, zebra grass, has interrupted bands of green and yellow; Gracillimus, maiden hair, grows in smaller clumps with narrower leaves. In early autumn, eulalia bears creamy white flowers in feathery 2-inch spikes, followed by the seed plumes.

HOW TO GROW. Eulalia grass grows best in a dry, sunny location and tolerates poor soil conditions. It needs little care once established; however, old stalks should be cut back to ground level each spring in order to make room for new growth. Additional plants are easily started from seed or by dividing root clumps.

*For climate zones and frost dates, see maps, pages 148-149.*

**EULALIA**
*Miscanthus sinensis*

**WHITE MULBERRY**
*Morus alba*

**WAX MYRTLE**
*Myrica cerifera*

## MORUS
*M. alba* (white mulberry), *M. alba* 'Pendula' (weeping mulberry)

The white mulberry tree, whose summer leaves nourish the silkworm, survives winter temperatures in Zones 4-10, and flourishes in such difficult conditions as drought and sandy seaside soils. In its standard form it is a round-topped tree with spreading limbs, growing rapidly to 50 feet tall. But for winter interest the weeping variety, Pendula, a grafted form, is especially recommended. Its slender branches arch outward and downward like the ribs of a giant umbrella, with older branches that are gnarled and twisted, forming a tree 8 to 15 feet high. In summer the mulberries are notable for their bright green, glossy leaves that take varying shapes depending on whether they are single-, double- or triple-lobed. They also produce edible white, pink or purple fruits shaped like blackberries.

HOW TO GROW. Mulberries do best in a well-drained garden loam, but will grow in poor, dry soils provided young trees are watered for the first several seasons, until their long roots become established. Plant mulberries in spring, training standard forms to one or several trunks by trimming unwanted side branches. The weeping form comes already grafted to a single trunk. As the standard trees grow, prune in winter to remove lower branches for headroom and to thin out the dense crown to let light and air inside. This will show off its branching pattern to better advantage in summer.

MOTTLED WILD GINGER See *Asarum*
MOUNTAIN ANDROMEDA See *Pieris*
MULBERRY, WEEPING See *Morus*
MULBERRY, WHITE See *Morus*

## MYRICA
*M. cerifera* (wax myrtle); *M. pensylvanica* (bayberry)

Abundant clusters of waxy, aromatic gray-white berries trim the winter branches of the neat, compact bayberry and wax myrtle shrubs, providing cold weather food for more than 70 species of birds that favor them in their diets. The berries, collected and boiled, yield the scent from which bayberry candles are made, though it requires 1½ quarts of berries to produce the wax for a single 8-inch candle. Bayberry, which is hardy in Zones 4-8, grows up to 10 feet tall and, though it is deciduous, its dark green, 3- to 5-inch-long leaves often cling to the plant well into winter without changing color. Wax myrtle, hardy in Zones 7-9, grows 30 feet tall with 3-inch evergreen foliage. Both species can be trained into tree form or sheared as hedge plants.

HOW TO GROW. Bayberries and wax myrtles grow best in full sun in sandy, well-drained acid soils, pH 4.5 to 5.5. They are frequently found wild along the sea, and are ideal for coastal gardens. Plant them in the spring as container-grown plants; wild specimens are difficult to transplant. Only females produce berries, but male plants are needed for pollination, so be sure to plant both kinds, usually in the ratio of 1 male plant for every 6 to 10 females. Both bayberry and wax myrtle produce flowers and berries on the current season's growth, so they should be pruned in the winter or early spring before the new growth starts. Thin out older branches, which can be used for indoor decoration. To train newly planted bayberry or wax myrtle into a tree form, select one to four stems and cut back all of the other branches; be especially watchful for suckers.

MYRTLE, CRAPE See *Lagerstroemia*
MYRTLE, WAX See *Myrica*

# N

## NANDINA

*N. domestica* (nandina, heavenly bamboo)

Nandina's vivid display of scarlet berries and, in cooler areas, its handsome bright red foliage add winter color to garden borders, where it is often planted. Though called bamboo, and similarly graceful in form, it is actually a relative of the barberry. It does well and is a useful hedge plant; planting in close proximity encourages cross-pollination and increases winter fruit production.

Nandina grows in Zones 7-10; farther north, its top dies but the roots occasionally survive the winter if they are in a protected place and are well mulched. When mature, in three to six years, it is a 5- to 6-foot shrub with compound, frondlike leaves, 18 to 20 inches long, divided into 1- to 2-inch feathery leaflets. The new foliage in early spring is tinged with pink or bronze, turning dark green in summer and deep bronze-red in autumn or winter. Its ¼-inch berries are borne in large graceful clusters at the end of the branches; they ripen in the fall and last well into the winter. Although normally red, the variety Alba bears creamy white fruits, which are especially effective when planted among red-fruited varieties. Nandina's spring flowers are white and bloom in upright clusters 8 to 15 inches long.

HOW TO GROW. Nandina does well in either full sun or partial shade and thrives in any moist, well-drained soil enriched with peat moss. In early spring, prune out older stems to ground level to encourage new growth. Propagate nandina by dividing root clumps.

## NORWAY SPRUCE See *Picea*

## NYSSA

*N. sylvatica* (pepperidge, sour gum, black gum, black tupelo)

A mature pepperidge tree has an unmistakable winter silhouette — the horizontal limbs growing along a tall, straight central trunk are forked and divided into a stiff zigzag pattern of smaller branches and twigs. The whole tree forms a blunted pyramid up to 100 feet tall. The dark, reddish-brown bark is thick and deeply fissured. These trees are hardy in Zones 5-9 and are valued not only for their sculptural winter outlines but also for their extreme tolerance of swampy conditions and for their autumn foliage color. Even in the warmer parts of its range, the tree's leathery, pointed 5-inch leaves turn vivid orange and scarlet. In summer dense foliage hides dark blue berries on female trees from all eyes but those of the birds.

HOW TO GROW. Pepperidge trees grow best in full sun and in moist, slightly acid soil, pH 6.0 to 6.5. They have shallow root systems and should therefore be planted in locations sheltered from strong wind. Pepperidge trees are not easy to establish. Plant saplings in early spring and train them to a single trunk by cutting back all leaders except the central one to half their length. Trim out some of the twiggy growth in fall for the first few years to thicken the branches. Remove any suckers that sprout from the roots.

# O

OAK See *Quercus*
ORANGE, HARDY See *Poncirus*
ORANGE, TRIFOLIATE See *Poncirus*
OREGON HOLLY GRAPE See *Mahonia*

## OSMANTHUS

*O. fortunei* (Fortune's osmanthus); *O. heterophyllus*, also called *O. aquifolium*, *O. ilicifolius* (holly osmanthus)

*For climate zones and frost dates, see maps, pages 148-149.*

HEAVENLY BAMBOO
*Nandina domestica*

PEPPERIDGE
*Nyssa sylvatica*

**HOLLY OSMANTHUS**
*Osmanthus heterophyllus*

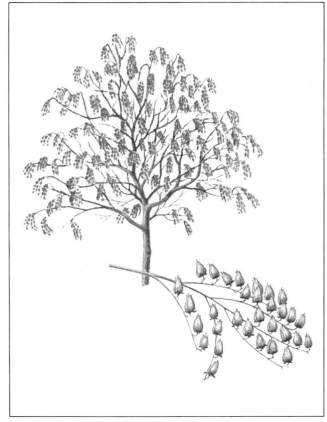

**SORREL TREE**
*Oxydendrum arboreum*

The dark, lustrous foliage of osmanthus, an evergreen shrub with prickly, holly-like leaves, is a winter-long addition to the garden, elegant as a clipped hedge or as single plants in a shrub border. Some gardeners even train osmanthus to grow flat against a wall as an espalier. Fragrant white flowers decorate the plants in spring or autumn, and are followed by small blue-black berries.

Fortune's osmanthus, a popular hybrid, grows in the mild climates of Zones 7-9. A vigorous plant, it can reach 12 feet in height if not clipped back, and is densely covered with 4-inch leaves. Holly osmanthus is slightly more cold-resistant, growing in Zones 6-10. It can become a 15-foot shrub in 10 years, but is often trimmed back to a more compact 5- or 6-foot height. Its 2½-inch dark green leaves closely resemble those of English holly, although one variety, Variegatus, has leaves edged with white.

HOW TO GROW. Osmanthus grows best in open, sunny locations in a moist, well-drained soil enriched with 1 part peat moss or leaf mold to 2 parts soil; in dry soils, the plants do better in partial shade. Prune at any time to maintain shape, cutting branches back to a side branch to avoid leaving unattractive stubs. Late-summer cuttings can be rooted to start new plants. Osmanthus can be damaged by severe or prolonged frosts in the zones where it is normally hardy.

### OXYDENDRUM

*O. arboreum* (sorrel tree, sourwood)

The sorrel tree's contributions to the winter landscape are many — an interesting shape and unusual bark and seed pods. Its upper branches form an irregular narrow crown spreading from the tree's often-multiple trunk. The bark is gray, flushed with red, and deeply furrowed when old. The pendulous clusters of seed pods are brownish-gray, sharply angled, and hang on the tree's bare branches in such profusion that they give the impression the tree is still in flower. Grown in Zones 5-8, the sorrel tree grows slowly and never becomes very tall. A 5- to 6-foot sapling usually takes 12 to 15 years to reach a height of 20 feet, and at maturity is 25 feet tall with a spread of 10 to 15 feet. In midsummer, tiny white bell-shaped flowers, resembling lilies of the valley, hang in 6- to 8-inch-long clusters at the end of the tree's branches. In fall, seed pods replace the flowers. The sorrel tree's 5- to 7-inch leaves are red when they open in spring, turning glossy green in summer and a richer red in the fall.

HOW TO GROW. The sorrel tree needs a sunny location to produce the most flowers and best fall colors, but it also tolerates partial shade. It grows well in a moist, well-drained acid soil, pH 5.8 to 6.5; the soil should be liberally mixed with peat moss or leaf mold. Pruning is seldom necessary.

# P

PAPERBARK MAPLE See *Acer*
PEPPERIDGE See *Nyssa*
PERIWINKLE See *Vinca*
PERSIMMON, COMMON See *Diospyros*

### PHELLODENDRON

*P. amurense* (Amur cork tree)

The handsome Amur cork tree, hardy in Zones 4-8, cantilevers its scaffold of huge branches far out over the garden; indeed, the open crown often has a spread wider than the tree's 30- to 50-foot height. Its bark, which is smooth when young, soon develops the deeply furrowed corklike texture that gives the tree its name. Silvery flower buds decorate the female Amur cork tree in winter and swell to produce inconspicuous clusters of yellow-to-green flowers in early summer, followed by small black berries. Though the berries attract birds, some gardeners consider the fruit messy and prefer the nonfruiting male tree. The 10- to 15-inch leaves are deeply divided into as many as 13 leaflets and cast lacy open shade under which grass will grow. Both the leaves — bright green in summer, yellow in autumn — and the berries have a scent reminiscent of turpentine.

HOW TO GROW. The Amur cork tree requires full sun in almost any deep fertile soil. Plant a sapling in spring, in a location protected from late spring frost. Provide a 2- to 3-inch mulch around the young tree, keeping the mulch about an inch from the trunk to forestall rot. Remove branches with narrow crotches as the young tree grows, to develop strong horizontal scaffold branches.

## PICEA
*P. abies* and varieties (Norway spruce); *P. glauca* and varieties (white spruce); *P. pungens* and varieties (Colorado spruce)

Growing with almost perfect symmetry, spruces are dense conical evergreens with stiff horizontal branches lined with attractive cones in winter. Well-suited to cold climates and able to withstand severe winds, they are one of the most commonly planted evergreen specimen trees. Crowded together, however, they lose their lower branches and their attractive silhouettes. Spruces are used as hedges, background plantings or as specimens; dwarf varieties are often planted in rock gardens. The dense appearance of spruces is due to sharply pointed square needles that radiate from all sides of the twigs and remain on the trees for many years. When the needles finally fall, their leaf bases remain to give the twigs a rough texture. Spruces have brown, pendulous cones 2 to 6 inches long that ripen in one season and drop to the ground. Their thin bark is scaly with vertical grooves.

Hardy in Zones 2-7, the Norway spruce withstands heat and drought better than other spruces. Growing quickly, it reaches 75 feet in 50 years and ultimately may become 150 feet tall. Drooping twigs clad with dark green needles give it a graceful appearance with age, and as the red-brown bark chips off the trunks of mature trees, dark gray-to-purple squares develop. Pendula, the weeping Norway spruce, has a drooping central stem and branches.

The white spruce is the species that is most widely used for windbreaks and open screens because it tolerates more crowding than other spruces. It grows 70 to 90 feet tall in Zones 2-8 and has ascending branches and drooping twigs lined with short, pale blue-green to light-green needles. The variety Conica, the dwarf Alberta spruce, is an excellent landscape ornamental that forms a very dense, compact pyramid 6 to 7 feet tall in 15 to 20 years. With time, it may grow 15 feet tall and 8 feet wide. Light-green needles only ½ inch long give this spruce a particularly fine-textured appearance. The dwarf Alberta spruce is sensitive to bright winter sun combined with strong winds.

Growing in Zones 2-8, the Colorado spruce has thick horizontal layers of branches that develop into a broad pyramid 50 or more feet tall in 35 to 50 years. The color of the inch-long needles ranges from dark green through blue to almost white in this tree's many varieties. The variety Argentea, called the Colorado silver spruce, has silver-white foliage and grows 6 feet tall and 3 feet wide in 10 years. Seedlings with blue foliage are usually sold as the variety Glauca or the Colorado blue spruce. Hoops blue spruce has silver-blue leaves, while the especially compact Moerheim blue spruce has intensely blue needles and is more resistant to pollution than other blue spruces.

*For climate zones and frost dates, see maps, pages 148-149.*

**AMUR CORK TREE**
*Phellodendron amurense*

**DWARF ALBERTA SPRUCE**
*Picea glauca* 'Conica'

MOERHEIM COLORADO SPRUCE
*Picea pungens* 'Moerheimii'

JAPANESE ANDROMEDA
*Pieris japonica* 'Dorothy Wyckoff'

HOW TO GROW. Spruces grow best in full sun; grown in shade, they may lose their lower branches. A moist but well-drained, deep acid soil is best; they survive in dry sandy soils if watered weekly for several years until their deep roots are well established. Plant spruces in the spring or fall and fertilize with cottonseed meal each spring thereafter. Pruning is seldom needed except to remove rival central leaders or an occasional branch that spoils the outline of the plant.

## PIERIS

*P. floribunda* (mountain andromeda); *P. japonica* (Japanese andromeda, lily-of-the-valley bush)

A snow-laden garden is the perfect backdrop for the andromedas' conspicuous clusters of white or rose flower buds and glossy evergreen foliage. Mountain andromeda, growing in Zones 4-7, has 2- to 4-inch oblong leaves; its creamy white buds cluster along upright flower stems at the end of its branches. In early spring, the buds open into nodding white flowers. When mature, mountain andromeda is 5 to 6 feet tall. The less hardy Japanese andromeda, found in Zones 6-8, grows 4 to 6 feet tall and has 3-inch, oval leaves. It comes in a number of varieties with differing winter colors. The foliage, buds and stems of Dorothy Wyckoff are tinged red all winter, for instance, while the seasonal appeal of Pink Bud is its appropriately colored pink buds. Japanese andromeda's foliage is bronze-green in spring, becoming true green in summer. Its bud clusters are pendulous rather than erect and open into white flowers resembling lilies of the valley.

HOW TO GROW. Andromedas grow in either shade or sun, but they produce more buds when planted in a partly sunny location. They should be protected from the wind. The shrubs grow best in a moist, acid soil, with a pH of 5.5 to 6.5, enriched with ample peat moss or leaf mold. Fertilizer is not usually necessary, but weak plants may be strengthened in the spring with a light application of cottonseed meal or with a fertilizer recommended for rhododendrons, azaleas and camellias. Andromeda roots also benefit from a permanent 3- to 4-inch mulch of wood chips, chunky peat moss, compost or ground bark. Prune the shrubs only to shape them and remove seed capsules immediately after the flowers bloom. Additional plants are easily propagated from stem cuttings of new or old wood.

PIN OAK See *Quercus*
PINE See *Pinus*

## PINUS

*P. bungeana* (lace-bark pine); *P. densiflora* and varieties (Japanese red pine)

Among the most widely grown evergreen conifers, pines are broad, conical trees when young; with age they become rounded or flat topped. There are also dwarf varieties. The thin needles, 1 to 12 inches long, grow in tufts or bundles of two, three or five. Their woody, often spiny cones take several years to ripen and cling to the branches for a few more years after opening. Pine bark may be gray or red-brown and is sometimes flaky or scaly. Pines are used as specimen plants, windbreaks and hedges; the small forms are used as foundation plantings or accent plants.

The lace-bark pine has unusual, patchy bark that falls off in irregularly shaped flakes to create a mottled pattern of gray, rust, white and green. A dense, flat- or round-topped tree that grows 30 to 50 feet, with upright branches, it frequently has multiple trunks. Although hardy in Zones 4-6, its long, slender branches are weak and sometimes break under heavy loads of snow and ice. The 2- to 4-inch needles in bundles of three are a glossy dark green and the oval 3-inch cones are tan.

Japanese red pine grows 100 feet tall or more. It is a flat-topped tree with contorted branches covered with scaly, red-orange bark. In its native Japan, it is frequently thinned heavily to reveal the shape of its branches. Hardy in Zone 5 southward, its paired 3- to 5-inch needles change color with the seasons: they are yellow or pale green in winter and light-gray to blue-green or bright green in summer. The 2-inch tan cones grow in clusters. The variety Oculus-draconis, the dragon's-eye pine, has needles banded with yellow; observed from its tip, a needle appears as concentric circles of yellow and green, hence the pine's name. Umbraculifera, the Tanyosho pine, grows in Zones 4-8 with a rounded head of branches that spread like the spokes of a windblown umbrella. As broad as it is tall, the Tanyosho pine becomes 10 to 15 feet tall but can be kept smaller with pruning. The 3- to 5-inch needles may be blue-green, gray-green or yellow-green, and its green-to-brown bark flakes off to expose yellow or orange layers underneath. Its dark brown cones are produced in great numbers even by young trees.

HOW TO GROW. Pines grow best in full sun and will survive in almost any soil, even poor dry ones, as long as they are well drained and acid. Sandy or gravelly soils with low fertility encourage slow, compact growth and dense foliage. Plant in spring or fall, mixing a small amount of peat moss into the planting hole. To control their shape and rate of growth, pinch off a portion of the central bud, or candle, of new growth in spring, beginning when the pine is one third the desired size. For more severe pruning, use hand clippers to remove branches at the point where side branches originate. Do not prune back beyond the point on the branches where needles grow because no new shoots will develop.

PLANE TREE, AMERICAN See *Platanus*

POLYSTICHUM

PLATANUS

*P. occidentalis* (American plane tree, sycamore, buttonwood, buttonball)

When plane trees drop their broad, hand-shaped leaves in fall, their mottled bark contributes texture and color to winter gardens. The thin brown outer bark flakes off to reveal dark green, yellow and white inner layers. Their irregularly shaped crowns of crooked branches are decked with prickly, inch-wide seed balls that dangle from slender stems throughout winter before dispersing hundreds of tiny, fluffy seeds. A long-lived, fast-growing tree hardy from Zone 4 southward, the plane tree develops a coarse, open silhouette with ascending young branches and horizontal older ones. It grows up to 100 feet tall and almost as wide. Often found growing along stream banks, the plane tree is also used for street plantings and as a shade tree in spacious gardens.

HOW TO GROW. The plane tree grows best in full sun in a moist but well-drained, deep, fertile soil. It will grow under dry conditions in almost any soil and in partial shade, but its growth will be slower. Plant plane trees in spring. Prune in winter to remove crowded or crossing branches or to maintain a central leader. Plane trees are susceptible to anthracnose and twig canker diseases. Prune affected twigs, rake up diseased leaves after they drop, and burn the debris. To increase resistance to disease, fertilize young trees in spring using a balanced fertilizer such as 10-10-10.

POLYSTICHUM

*P. acrostichoides* (Christmas fern); *P. adiantiforme*, also called *P. coriaceum*, *P. capense*, *Aspidium capense*, *Ru-*

TANYOSHO PINE
*Pinus densiflora* 'Umbraculifera'

AMERICAN PLANE TREE
*Platanus occidentalis*

*For climate zones and frost dates, see maps, pages 148-149.*

**CHRISTMAS FERN**
*Polystichum acrostichoides*

**HARDY ORANGE**
*Poncirus trifoliata*

*mohra adiantiformis* (leather fern); *P. munitum* (western sword fern); *P. setiferum,* also called *P. angulare* (soft shield fern)

Stiff and bushy, evergreen polystichums form symmetrical crowns of fronds along creeping stems called rhizomes that are covered with brown scales. Easy to grow in shady areas, these ferns are used to disguise foundations, in borders, under trees and in rock gardens. The foliage is attractive in winter floral arrangements and wreaths.

Growing 1 to 3 feet tall in crowns 2 or more feet wide, the fronds of the Christmas fern are light-green when young, dark green when mature. Tapering to a point, each 3- to 5-inch-wide frond is composed of paired leaflets with slightly serrated edges. There is a characteristic bump or ear on the topmost edge of each leaflet near the central stalk. The stalks are white when young and become brown with age. The Christmas fern is hardy in Zones 3-8.

The dark green leather fern has fronds 2½ to 3 feet tall and almost as wide that are composed of many coarsely toothed leaflets. With age, silver-white scales on the stems darken and the fronds become rough and stiff. The leather fern is hardy in Zones 8-10.

Similar to the Christmas fern, the western sword fern grows 2 to 4 feet tall with up to 100 fronds in a clump. Its long, narrow leaflets, which are up to 5 inches long, have spiny edges and a small bump on their upper edges. It is hardy in Zones 7-10.

The soft shield fern has a softer, finer texture than the other polystichums. Its arching 1- to 2½-foot fronds are composed of many finely cut, dark green leaflets and grow in clumps 3 to 5 feet wide. Hardy in Zones 8-10, it tolerates dry conditions better than the other polystichums.

HOW TO GROW. Polystichums grow best in partial shade, although the Christmas and the western sword ferns will tolerate deep shade. They prefer a cool, moist, well-drained soil, preferably rocky or sandy, with a pH of 5.5 to 6.6. Plant in spring, first preparing a bed composed of 2 parts leaf mold or peat moss, 1 part builder's sand and 1 part garden soil. Maintain an organic mulch of leaf mold or shredded bark. Cut off dead or damaged fronds at any time. Fertilize in spring and again in midsummer with a light dusting of bone meal or use fish emulsion at half strength. Propagate by dividing large clumps in early spring.

## PONCIRUS
*P. trifoliata* (hardy orange, trifoliate orange)

A complex pattern of smooth, dark green branches and thorns studded with yellow-orange fruits makes the hardy orange a striking and unusual deciduous tree for a winter garden. As its name suggests, the hardy orange is a close relative of the more tender citrus trees. It grows in Zones 7-10 and in the coastal areas of Zone 6. Seldom growing more than 20 feet tall, it has several main stems with thin, gray-brown bark that splits lengthwise to reveal narrow, wavy stripes of dark green bark. The formidable woody thorns, from ½ to 2½ inches in length, punctuate the flattened branches at frequent intervals. The 2-inch fruits, fuzzy and green before they ripen in fall, look like miniature oranges but are bitter, though very fragrant when cut open.

In Zones 9 and 10 the fruits remain on the tree for most of the winter; farther north, they may drop in early winter. In spring, before foliage appears, the tree produces fragrant 2-inch white flowers. In summer the hardy orange has dark green, leathery leaves composed of three oval or oblong leaflets 2 to 3 inches long. It is an excellent choice for barrier hedges because of its sharp thorns and dense growth.

HOW TO GROW. The hardy orange grows best in full sun but will tolerate partial shade. Plant in spring or early fall in a moist, well-drained acid soil. When setting out a hedge, allow about 3 feet between plants. Hardy oranges respond well to pruning and may be sheared into formal shapes. The new branches that appear after pruning are a brighter green than older ones. Propagate from seed or by rooting cuttings taken in summer in a mixture of sand and compost.

PRIMROSE JASMINE See *Jasminum*

## PRUNUS

*P. laurocerasus* (cherry laurel); *P. maackii* (Amur choke-cherry); *P. serrula* (paperbark or birchbark cherry); *P. subhirtella* 'Autumnalis' (autumn-flowering Higan cherry); *P. subhirtella* 'Pendula' (weeping Higan cherry)

In winter these cherry trees offer landscape effects as varied as evergreen foliage, colorful bark, weeping forms and even an occasional winter blossom. The four deciduous cherry trees listed here tend to grow fast; an 8-foot tree reaches 20 feet in six to eight years. The cherry laurel is an evergreen shrub or small tree that also grows quickly, becoming about 12 feet tall in five to six years; if unpruned it may reach 25 feet in height. The cherry laurel, hardy in Zones 7-10, has shiny, dark green leaves 4 to 6 inches long. Its dense foliage makes it an ideal plant for hedges or windbreaks. Besides the winter beauty of its foliage, the cherry laurel offers small white flower clusters in spring that are followed by purple fruits. The bark, leaves and fruit are poisonous if eaten. The Schipka cherry laurel is hardier than the species, surviving winters in Zones 5 and 6. It has smaller leaves than the cherry laurel and grows 8 feet tall.

The Amur chokecherry, among the most cold-resistant of deciduous cherries, grows in Zones 2-9 and may become 45 feet tall. Its glossy red-brown bark is particularly striking when the tree is bare. In spring the Amur chokecherry has 2- to 3-inch clusters of small white flowers followed by small purple-black fruit in summer.

The paperbark cherry grows in Zones 5-8 and becomes 30 feet tall, its branches spreading upward from multiple trunks. When its leaves fall in autumn, they expose the tree's brilliant shiny red bark, considered the most ornamental of cherry barks. Its white blossoms appear in late spring. The tree is hard to find in American nurseries. Higan cherries, both the autumn-flowering and the weeping varieties, grow in Zones 5-9, where they become 30 feet tall when mature. The autumn-flowering Higan cherry is a dense, rounded tree with drooping branches growing from a single trunk; snow laden, it is a delicate and attractive winter sight. As its name implies, this tree flowers in the fall as well as in early spring, bearing light-pink 1½-inch blossoms that may occasionally open in winter during warm spells. The graceful weeping Higan cherry has cascades of hanging branches, spreading in a parasol pattern from single or multiple trunks. Its 1½-inch pink flowers appear in early spring.

HOW TO GROW. All cherries grow well in full sun but the evergreen cherry laurels will also tolerate partial shade and salty seaside conditions as well. The deciduous cherry trees adapt to almost any well-drained garden soil; for the cherry laurels the soil should be enriched with peat moss or leaf mold. Cherry trees need little pruning, but when it is required, prune in spring after flowering, cutting back small branches to the main stem. Cherry laurels may be pruned into formal shapes; it is preferable to do this with hand clippers rather than with shears, to avoid cutting leaves and spoiling the natural line of the plant.

*For climate zones and frost dates, see maps, pages 148-149.*

**SCHIPKA CHERRY LAUREL**
*Prunus laurocerasus* 'Schipkaensis'

**HIGAN CHERRY**
*Prunus subhirtella*

**DWARF DOUGLAS FIR**
*Pseudotsuga menziesii* 'Densa'

**PIN OAK**
*Quercus palustris*

## PSEUDOTSUGA

***P. menziesii*** and varieties, also called ***P. douglasii, P. mucronata, P. taxifolia*** (Douglas fir, Douglas spruce red fir)

Conical evergreens familiar as Christmas trees, graceful Douglas firs have closely spaced, flat, aromatic dark green needles. Their branches curve gently upward when young, then droop slightly with age. Brown 4-inch cones hang from the upper branches of mature trees through the winter. Their red or dark brown bark becomes deeply ridged and corky as the tree ages.

The broad, cone-shaped Douglas fir becomes 40 to 100 feet tall in 50 years or more in Zones 5 and 6, growing 1 or 2 feet a year when young. The trees are useful as tall screens because they do not lose their lower branches. They can also be sheared into hedges. Glauca is a more cold-tolerant variety that originates high in the Rocky Mountains and is hardy in Zones 4-6. About 40 feet tall at maturity, it has blue-green needles, 2-inch brown cones, and dull gray bark that becomes black and deeply furrowed with age. Because of its shallow roots, it needs protection from strong winds.

Pendula, the weeping Douglas fir, is a variety that has drooping branches and is hardy in Zones 5 and 6. Densa is a dwarf Douglas fir that grows into a broad, flat-topped shrub 3½ feet tall. Thick with branches that are lined with blue-green needles, it is an excellent plant for rock gardens or low hedges in Zones 4-6. It is most attractive when allowed to grow naturally rather than being sheared.

HOW TO GROW. Douglas firs grow best in full sun in a moist but well-drained, slightly acid soil. Plant trees in spring and fertilize young plants each spring thereafter by sprinkling cottonseed meal or 5-10-5 fertilizer around the base of the tree. Prune Douglas fir hedges in early spring before new growth begins. Remove rival leaders from trees at any time. Propagate from seeds.

# Q

## QUERCUS

***Q. alba*** (white oak); ***Q. imbricaria*** (shingle oak); ***Q. palustris*** (pin oak); ***Q. robur*** (English oak)

The majestic oak trees, their massive trunks and branches sometimes centuries old, are magnificent in winter. When their leaves drop in autumn, they reveal handsome, often wide-spreading forms, which dominate the garden. The trees have sturdy branches that resist ice and wind damage, and rough bark that catches and holds snow. Leaves are deeply lobed and jagged in outline but vary in shape and size with the species. Also depending on species, they may turn yellow, red, purple or brown in the fall. All oaks bear acorns, which often take one or two years to mature before dropping.

The white oak, found in Zones 4-8, grows 50 to 80 feet tall, its huge limbs sweeping horizontally from the tree's short trunk. The tree's spread equals or surpasses its height. Growing slowly, an 8- to 10-foot white oak reaches 20 to 25 feet in 10 to 12 years. When placed some distance from a house, winter views of the entire tree are impressive, with its scaly, grayish-white bark and its widely separated branches tapering into smaller branches and twigs. The white oak's 3- to 5-inch leaves are purple tinged with red in autumn, and cling to the tree well into winter.

The shingle oak grows in Zones 5-9 where it becomes 50 to 60 feet tall when mature, spreading just as wide. It grows slowly, an 8- to 10-foot tree reaching 20 to 25 feet in 10 to 12 years. Its slender branches form a conical or pyramidal shape when young, but with age the tree becomes more rounded. It holds its low-growing branches beginning just above ground level and can therefore be sheared into a clipped hedge or tall windbreak. Its lustrous green leaves turn red-brown in autumn and remain on the tree through most of the winter.

The pin oak is one of the most symmetrical of oaks. Near the top of the tree, its many slender branches slant upward; midway down, they spread horizontally; along the lower trunk they droop, often touching the ground. Twigs on the branches are short and pinlike, giving the tree its common name, and are so dense and numerous that the pin oak, even when bare, will camouflage an unsightly view. Found in Zones 4-9, the pin oak grows rapidly, an 8- to 10-foot tree reaching 20 to 25 feet in five or six years; eventually it becomes 60 to 70 feet tall with a 25- to 40-foot spread. Its autumn foliage is dull red; the leaves sometimes cling to the branches through the winter.

The English oak, hardy in Zones 5-8, is normally an open, broad-headed tree with a short, thick trunk. It grows rapidly: an 8- to 10-foot tree reaches 20 feet in six to eight years and eventually becomes 60 to 80 feet tall. But it is more often used in the variety, *Q. robur fastigiata,* which has a slender, columnar shape and is only 50 to 60 feet tall when mature, with a 20-foot spread. In this form it is frequently chosen instead of the Lombardy poplar when a more permanent landscape accent is desired. None of the English oaks is notable for fall color.

HOW TO GROW. All oaks grow well in full sun and an average, somewhat acid soil, pH 5.5 to 6.5. Prune young trees in winter or early spring to establish their shapes. Old trees rarely need pruning except to remove dead branches or those that are so low that they interfere with the use of the ground underneath them.

# R

RED CEDAR, EASTERN See *Juniperus*
RED PINE, JAPANESE See *Pinus*
REED GRASS, FEATHER See *Calamagrostis*

## RHODODENDRON

*R. mucronulatum* (Korean rhododendron, Korean azalea); *R.* 'P.J.M.' (P.J.M. rhododendron)

Two especially cold-tolerant rhododendrons, the deciduous Korean rhododendron and the evergreen P.J.M. rhododendron, a hybrid, grow farther north than most other rhododendrons. Often the earliest blooming of the rhododendrons, the Korean rhododendron is a narrow, upright shrub 6 to 8 feet tall. It bears clusters of 1½-inch magenta flowers at the tip of each bare branch in midwinter in Zones 9 and 10 along the Pacific Coast; blooms occur later in Zones 5-8. The narrow, 1- to 3-inch leaves that unfold after the flowers fade turn yellow and crimson in the fall. Cornell Pink is a variety with clear pink flowers.

The P.J.M. rhododendron, hardy in Zones 4-10, is a billowy, rounded shrub that grows about 6 feet tall. Its rosettes of evergreen leaves 1½ to 2 inches long change from dark green to a deep mahogany or purplish-bronze in the cold weather. The P.J.M. rhododendron bears profuse clusters of lavender-pink flowers in early spring.

HOW TO GROW. Korean rhododendron grows best in partial shade; the P.J.M. rhododendron grows best with full sun in summer but requires some shade from strong winter sun to prevent its leaves from burning. To prevent flowers from being killed by a freeze, plant the Korean rhododendron in a shady location so that its buds will not open prematurely during a warm sunny spell. Both shrubs need a moist, well-drained humus-filled soil with a pH of 4.5 to 5.5 enriched with peat moss or leaf mold. To protect their shallow root

P. J. M. RHODODENDRON
*Rhododendron 'P.J.M.'*

*For climate zones and frost dates, see maps, pages 148-149.*

**JAPANESE ROSE**
*Rosa multiflora*

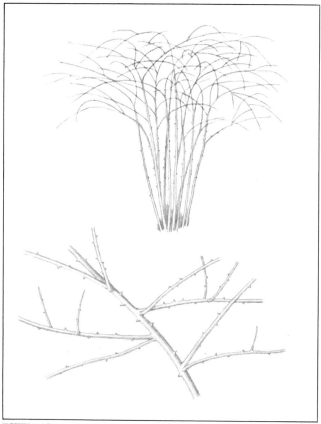

**WHITEWASHED BRAMBLE**
*Rubus cockburnianus*

systems, keep the soil around rhododendrons cool and moist with a 2- to 3-inch-thick mulch of wood chips, oak leaves or pine needles. Transplant in spring or fall, setting the shrubs in wide, shallow holes about an inch higher than they grew in the nursery. Rhododendrons seldom require pruning, but pinch off faded flowers for the greatest vigor. Evergreen rhododendrons can be propagated by rooting cuttings taken in early spring or summer. Deciduous rhododendrons are propagated by softwood cuttings taken in early spring or summer, or by seed.

**RIVER BIRCH** See *Betula*

### ROSA
*R. multiflora* (Japanese rose); *R. omeiensis* (Omei rose); *R. virginiana* (Virginia rose); *R. wichuraiana* (memorial rose)

The beauty of the four rose species recommended here does not end when their flowers fade in the spring and summer. Brightly colored fruits called hips, prickles and stems are among the winter attractions that are offered by these species.

The Japanese rose rambles across winter gardens and attracts birds with its masses of ¼-inch red hips that ripen after its 1-inch white, early summer blooms fade. A dense plant with arching stems up to 10 feet long, the Japanese rose is grown in Zones 5-9 in gardens that are large enough to accommodate its vigorous growth.

The Omei rose has prominent red prickles that stand out along its stems all winter long. The shrub grows up to 12 feet in Zones 6-9 and bears small 1-inch flowers in early summer followed in fall by unique pear-shaped red fruits on yellow stalks. The variety Pteracantha, with especially conspicuous red prickles, is known as the Wingthorn Omei rose.

The Virginia rose is attractive in all seasons. The 3- to 6-foot bright red stems and ½-inch red hips are handsome in winter settings in Zones 3-9. In spring, 2- to 3-inch magenta or pink flowers cover the shrub and in autumn, the glossy foliage turns scarlet and orange.

The memorial rose is a creeping shrub with semievergreen foliage, which trails across steep or rocky slopes in dense mats of shiny leaves seldom more than a foot tall. The foliage stays green all year long in Zones 8 and 9 but does not last throughout the winter in Zones 6 and 7, although the rose is hardy there. The shrub spreads rapidly, its stems growing several feet longer every year. The memorial rose is among the last of the roses to bloom. The 2-inch white flowers that appear in the late summer are followed by tiny red hips in the fall.

HOW TO GROW. Japanese, Omei and Virginia roses grow best in full sun; the memorial rose will grow in full sun or partial shade. All of these rose species need a well-drained soil supplemented with leaf mold, compost or peat moss. Plant them in the spring, setting the plants 5 to 8 feet apart. These vigorous plants have little need of fertilizer, but will benefit from an application of compost in spring. Cut the Virginia rose to the ground in early spring to maintain plants at a 3-foot height if desired. Prune the other species in early spring to remove dead canes and inward growing branches or to shorten overly tall stems. Additional plants can be started by removing rooted suckers with a spade in early spring or by rooting cuttings taken in late spring or early summer in moist sand or vermiculite.

ROSE See *Rosa*
ROSE, CHRISTMAS See *Helleborus*
ROSE, LENTEN See *Helleborus*

## RUBUS
*R. biflorus; R. cockburnianus* (both called whitewashed bramble)

Brambles are best known for the sweet summer and fall crops of berries that several species such as blackberries and raspberries have to offer. But ornamental species with waxy white stems and twigs are winter attractions as well, especially when they stand out against a backdrop of evergreens. Known as the whitewashed brambles, *R. biflorus* and *R. cockburnianus* are erect deciduous shrubs that grow in Zones 3-8 as fountains of spiny stems and twigs coated with a white, waxlike substance. *R. biflorus* grows 8 to 10 feet tall with 4- to 8-inch leaves that are dark green above, white beneath; its stems bear ¾-inch white midsummer blossoms and round yellow fruits when the plant is two years old. *R. cockburnianus* is an 8- to 10-foot shrub with an especially bushy top. When its 5- to 8-inch saw-toothed leaves drop, they reveal stems and twigs coated with a pure white wax, sometimes tinged with blue. Small, purple, star-shaped flowers appear in 4- to 5-inch clusters in summer on the 2-year-old stems and are followed by small black fruits.

HOW TO GROW. *R. biflorus* and *R. cockburnianus* grow in full sun in any good, loamy soil. Cut the stems back to the ground after their second year when they flower and fruit for new, more vigorous canes. New plants are easily started by dividing plants with a spade or by rooting cuttings taken in early spring.

# S

SAFFRON, SPRING-MEADOW See *Bulbocodium*
SALAL See *Gaultheria*

## SALIX
*S. alba* 'Chermesina' (redstem willow); *S. alba* 'Tristis' (golden weeping willow); *S. discolor* (pussy willow); *S. matsudana* 'Tortuosa' (corkscrew willow)

The contributions of willows to winter landscapes range from the colorful twigs and drooping forms of the redstem and golden weeping willows to the ornamental catkins of the pussy willow and the peculiarly twisted branches of the corkscrew willow. Willows are among the earliest trees to leaf out in spring and among the last to lose their foliage, which turns a soft yellow before falling in autumn.

Found in Zones 2-9, the redstem and golden weeping willows are fast-growing deciduous trees; a 9- to 10-foot sapling reaches 20 feet in 3 years and when mature is often 50 to 75 feet tall. The limbs branch from a massive, crooked trunk and taper to delicate, trailing twigs that are bright red in the redstem willow and yellow on the golden weeping willow. As the redstem willow's young branches mature, their red color fades, but the bark of the golden weeping willow remains yellow throughout the tree's life.

The pussy willow's furry, pearl-to-gray catkins, which are actually petalless flowers, appear in late winter on this 8- to 10-foot-tall deciduous shrub. The 1-inch-long catkins grow on separate male and female plants; male pussy willows bear more catkins than the females. Grown in Zones 2-9, the plant is frequently used as a specimen shrub or combined with other kinds of shrubs in a border. The branches can be cut in the winter and brought indoors, where the catkins are easily forced into bloom. The catkins are also attractive in dried-flower arrangements.

The corkscrew willow is a unique deciduous tree with olive-green, contorted branches twisting upward. In Zones 4-9, it grows into a 30-foot tree. Clothed in its narrow, twisted 3-inch leaves, the corkscrew willow has only ordinary orna-

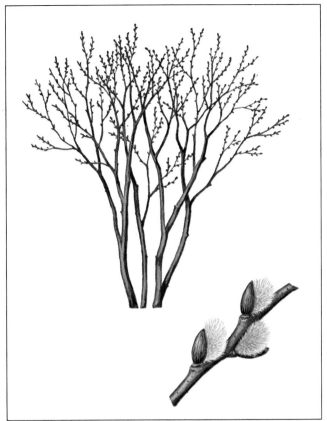

PUSSY WILLOW
*Salix discolor*

CORKSCREW WILLOW
*Salix matsudana* 'Tortuosa'

*For climate zones and frost dates, see maps, pages 148-149.*

mental value, but in winter, its asymmetrical branches stand out in distinctive patterns.

HOW TO GROW. All willows grow best in full sun in any good garden soil supplemented with peat moss, compost or leaf mold. Willow trees are especially well suited to wet soils, but they should not be planted closer than 50 feet to drain or sewer lines since their roots may quickly clog them. Trim the lower branches of young redstem and golden weeping willows to allow adequate headroom beneath the pendulous boughs. Pussy willows can be kept small by periodically cutting them back to within 4 to 6 inches from the ground after their flowers fade. The corkscrew willow needs little pruning except to remove broken branches. Start new willows by rooting cuttings taken in spring in moist sand.

## SANTOLINA

*S. chamaecyparissus* (lavender cotton); *S. virens* (green lavender cotton)

Among evergreen plants the aromatic, silver-gray foliage of lavender cotton is unique. Its pale color contrasts strikingly with the green shades of standard evergreens when they are planted together in borders or in rock gardens. A compact, shrubby perennial hardy from Zone 7 southward, lavender cotton has delicate leaves that are ⅛ inch wide and 1 to 1½ inches long. It will grow 2 feet tall and spread 3 feet wide but is usually sheared to half that size for a more formal shape and denser growth. Green lavender cotton is similar in size and shape to lavender cotton but has dark green leaves. In summer, both plants bear yellow, button-like flowers. The stems of these two species, said to repel moths, produce an oil used in perfume.

HOW TO GROW. Lavender cottons develop their color best when grown in full sun in any light, well-drained sandy soil where their roots remain relatively dry. Set out in spring, spacing plants 18 to 24 inches apart. If a formal shape is desired, cut the plants back to a height of 4 to 6 inches each spring. Lavender cottons can also be sheared in summer, though this will prevent flowering. Start new plants from stem cuttings taken in spring or fall.

## SARCOCOCCA

*S. hookeriana* 'Digyna' (Himalayan sarcococca); *S. hookeriana* 'Humilis' (dwarf Himalayan sarcococca); *S. ruscifolia* (sweet box)

In shaded evergreen shrub borders or as a ground cover, the leathery, lance-shaped foliage of the sarcococcas stands out handsomely in a winter garden. Fragrant white flowers blossom among the leaves on the lower branches from late winter to early spring. Small blue or black fruits follow the flowers. Himalayan and dwarf Himalayan sarcococcas grow in Zones 5-7; dwarf Himalayan sarcococca is slightly more cold resistant. A 6-foot-tall shrub when mature, Himalayan sarcococca bears white flowers with cream-colored stamens. Dwarf Himalayan sarcococca grows in billows of foliage 1 to 3 feet tall and is often used as a ground cover; its white flowers have prominent pink stamens. Sweet box, *S. ruscifolia,* grows 6 feet tall in Zones 8-10. The shrub's berries ripen in fall to a deep scarlet.

HOW TO GROW. Heavy snows in the northern limits of their range may damage the stems of sarcococcas; sweep the snow gently off plants. Sarcococcas grow best in partial-to-deep shade in a rich, well-drained soil. Plant sarcococcas intended as ground covers 9 to 12 inches apart in spring; plant border shrubs 2 to 3 feet apart. Mulch the ground around the plants with shredded bark or wood chips to keep the roots moist. Prune sarcococcas only to remove dead

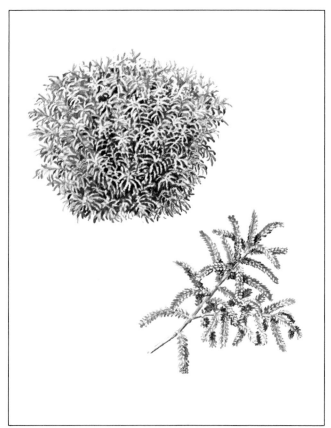

LAVENDER COTTON
*Santolina chamaecyparissus*

HIMALAYAN SARCOCOCCA
*Sarcococca hookeriana* 'Digyna'

branches. New plants are easily started from cuttings taken in early summer, or by dividing the spreading underground roots of established plants in spring or late summer.

SAWARA FALSE CYPRESS See *Chamaecyparis*

## SCILLA
*S. bifolia* (two-leaved squill, twinleaf squill); *S. siberica* (Siberian squill); *S. tubergeniana* (Tubergenian squill)

The two-leaved and Tubergenian squills, with the winter aconites, brighten the last gray days of winter. The Siberian squill follows in early spring, but it flowers over a longer period of time.

The 3- to 4-inch-tall two-leaved squill, hardy from Zone 4 southward, has clusters of star-shaped blue, pink or white flowers with back-curving petals. The Siberian squill, hardy in Zones 4-8, has brilliant blue flower bells that dangle from 3- to 4-inch stems. The Tubergenian squill, hardy in Zones 3-10, bears pale blue flower stars on 5-inch stalks. The foliage of all the squills is ribbon-like and dies in early summer. Squills are attractive carpeting rock gardens or the ground beneath deciduous shrubs and trees. Bulbs colonize rapidly under favorable growing conditions.

HOW TO GROW. Squills grow in any well-drained garden soil in full sun or shade. Plant the bulbs in the fall, spacing them 8 to 10 inches apart and three times their own depth. Spread a thin layer of compost or dried manure after the blooms fade, to nourish the bulbs. Squills can be left undisturbed or they can be propagated by digging them in early summer, removing the tiny offsets that grow beside older bulbs, and replanting.

SCOTCH BROOM See *Cytisus*
SCOTCH HEATHER See *Calluna*
SETTERWORT See *Helleborus*
SHAGBARK HICKORY See *Carya*
SHALLON See *Gaultheria*
SHINGLE OAK See *Quercus*
SIBERIAN SQUILL See *Scilla*
SIBERIAN TEA See *Bergenia*

## SKIMMIA
*S. japonica* (Japanese skimmia); *S. reevesiana* (Reeves skimmia)

The bright scarlet berries of Japanese and Reeves skimmia ripen in autumn; birds, preferring other fruits, leave the colorful harvests for much of the winter. These low-growing evergreen shrubs form dense, billowy mounds of shiny oval foliage, which make an attractive, rough-textured ground cover when planted in front of taller, more open shrubs such as laurels and rhododendrons. Popular in warm-climate gardens where winter temperatures stay above 0°, both shrubs grow in Zones 7-10, with Reeves skimmia a slightly more cold-resistant plant. Japanese skimmia grows 2 to 4 feet tall with glossy 3- to 4-inch leaves. Only the female plants produce the masses of small red fruits but the 2- to 3-inch clusters of tiny white flowers that bloom in spring are larger and more fragrant on the male plants. Reeves skimmia is a smaller shrub, growing 18 to 24 inches in height; the ½-inch berries that ripen among its 4-inch leaves are not as bright as those of the Japanese skimmia, but both the male and female plants produce fruit.

HOW TO GROW. Skimmias require partial shade; to protect them from the strong winter sun that can burn their leaves, plant them on the north side of taller evergreens or a wall, or beneath densely branched deciduous trees. They grow best

*For climate zones and frost dates, see maps, pages 148-149.*

SIBERIAN SQUILL
*Scilla siberica*

JAPANESE SKIMMIA
*Skimmia japonica*

**CHINESE STRANVAESIA**
*Stranvaesia davidiana*

**HICKS YEW**
*Taxus media hicksii*

in a moist, acid soil enriched with peat moss or leaf mold. Plant skimmias in early spring, setting them 1½ to 3 feet apart; female Japanese skimmias need a male plant within 100 feet if they are to produce their berries. A permanent mulch of shredded bark, oak leaves or pine needles keeps the root system of skimmias cool and moist. Cultivating around the plants with any tool may damage the shallow roots; pull weeds by hand. Skimmias rarely need pruning. Start new plants from cuttings taken in spring or summer and rooted in moist sand.

SNOWDROP, COMMON See *Galanthus*
SNOWDROP, GIANT See *Galanthus*
SOFT SHIELD FERN See *Polystichum*
SORREL TREE See *Oxydendrum*
SOUR GUM See *Nyssa*
SOURWOOD See *Oxydendrum*
SPANISH BAYONET See *Yucca*
SPLEENWORT, EBONY See *Asplenium*
SPLEENWORT, MAIDENHAIR See *Asplenium*
SPRING HEATH See *Erica*
SPRING-MEADOW SAFFRON See *Bulbocodium*
SPRUCE, COLORADO See *Picea*
SPRUCE, NORWAY See *Picea*
SPRUCE, WHITE See *Picea*
SQUILL See *Scilla*
STANFORD MANZANITA See *Arctostaphylos*

STRANVAESIA

*S. davidiana* (Chinese stranvaesia)

Chinese stranvaesia is at its best in winter, when it bears abundant clusters of brilliant red berries with red stems among leathery green and red leaves. An irregularly shaped broad-leaved evergreen shrub with a wide spread, Chinese stranvaesia grows 10 feet high or more in Zones 7-10. Young foliage is tinged with red, then develops into lustrous 2- to 4-inch pointed oval dark green leaves. The ruddy color returns to some leaves with the onset of cold weather. The masses of round, ⅓-inch scarlet fruits cling to the shrub all winter. In spring, small white flowers bloom in clusters 4 inches across. Chinese stranvaesia, which grows with several main stems, can be espaliered against a wall. *S. davidiana undulata* is a more open, spreading variety with more resistance to cold than the species. *S. davidiana* Flava has yellow berries.

HOW TO GROW. Chinese stranvaesia grows best in full sun in a moist soil rich in organic matter. Plant the shrubs in spring or fall, spacing them 8 to 10 feet apart to allow for their vigorous wide growth. Little pruning is required. Propagate from seed or from cuttings taken in summer.

SWEET BAY See *Magnolia*
SWEET BOX See *Sarcococca*
SWEET GUM See *Liquidambar*
SWORD FERN, WESTERN See *Polystichum*
SYCAMORE See *Platanus*

# T

TAXUS

*T. baccata* and varieties (English yew); *T. cuspidata* and varieties (Japanese yew); *T. media* and varieties (intermediate yew, Anglo-Japanese yew)

Easy to grow, yews decorate winter gardens with their soft, bright green needles and pulpy, scarlet berries. Remarkable for their slow reliable growth under almost any condition, yews are planted as specimen shrubs, in hedges or as backgrounds for flower borders. Because they tolerate heavy shearing, yews are often shaped into formal topiaries. The inch-long needles line the sides of each twig to form flat sprays. Both the foliage and the ½-inch berries are highly toxic. Yews grow very slowly during their first five years but, once established, last indefinitely with minimal care. Only females produce berries.

The English yew is hardy in Zones 7-9. Unpruned, it forms a broad, rounded tree 15 feet tall with spreading branches and a short, thick trunk that is covered with attractive flaking reddish bark. The variety Stricta, called the Irish yew, has vertical branches packed into a narrow column of foliage; it may require tying to prevent heavy snow from bending and breaking upright branches. Spreading English yew, Repandens, is a slow-growing, flat-topped shrub with drooping branch tips; it is used as a ground cover or allowed to cascade over walls. It will grow 1 to 5 feet tall and spread 3 to 12 feet wide. Its leaves are longer and narrower than those of the species and are blue-green. Both the Irish and spreading English yews are hardy in Zones 6-8; the latter is considered the hardiest variety of English yew.

Fast-growing Japanese yew reaches 20 feet in height in as many years in Zones 5-8. Unpruned, it becomes an upright tree but it can be pruned and sheared into a multiple-stemmed shrub. The dull green needles banded yellow on their undersides are usually shorter than the needles of the English yew. Capitata, the upright Japanese yew, is a broadly conical, fast-growing yew. Densa, the dense spreading Japanese yew, is a flat-topped variety growing 4 feet tall and 8 to 20 feet wide. Female plants produce large quantities of berries. Nana, the dwarf Japanese yew, grows into a rounded or conical shrub 10 to 15 feet tall and 20 feet wide.

The intermediate yew is a hybrid between the English and Japanese yews. It is hardy in Zones 5-8. There are many forms, but the most common one is a broad column or narrow pyramid 20 or more feet tall with a central leader. The Berryhill yew is a female clone that resembles the dwarf Japanese yew. Brown's yew is a male clone that produces no berries and develops into a flattened globe. It grows 9 feet tall and 12 feet wide in 20 years. The Hicks yew, a narrow columnar plant excellent for hedges and screens, grows 20 feet tall in 20 years. Ward's yew is a spreading, flat-topped shrub that grows 8 feet tall and 20 feet wide.

HOW TO GROW. Yews grow in full sun to deep shade. They do best in a moist but well-drained, slightly acid soil. Plant balled-and-burlaped plants in early spring and container-grown plants at any time in the growing season. Set hedge plants 1½ to 2 feet apart. When planting, mix 1 part peat moss, compost or leaf mold to 2 parts soil. Fertilize young yews annually in spring with cottonseed meal or 5-10-5 fertilizer. Prune young plants frequently during the growing season for a more compact shape. To maintain a neat appearance, thin out by clipping off branches from inside the plant so no stubs will show. Yews are propagated from seed or from cuttings of named varieties.

TEA, SIBERIAN See *Bergenia*
TEABERRY See *Gaultheria*

THUJA

*T. occidentalis* and varieties (American arborvitae, white cedar)

Old-fashioned evergreens with a long-standing reputation for reliability in cold climates, arborvitaes grow in a dizzying array of shapes — conical, oval or vase-shaped trees, narrow columns, round globes, and dwarf shrubs. Their tiny, tightly overlapping leaves are arranged in feathery fans of flat fo-

UPRIGHT JAPANESE YEW
*Taxus cuspidata* 'Capitata'

*For climate zones and frost dates, see maps, pages 148-149.*

DOUGLAS ARBORVITAE
*Thuja occidentalis douglasii pyramidalis*

CANADA HEMLOCK
*Tsuga canadensis*

liage that is highly aromatic. Light yellow-green to dark green, this soft foliage responds well to shearing in hedges or screens. Strong winds, heavy snow or ice can break the branches of plants with vertical growth, but the damage can be minimized by loosely encircling the shrubs with plastic-coated wire for support in winter.

The American arborvitae grows into a broad or columnar tree up to 60 feet tall with dull dark green leaves marked with yellow on their undersides and hanging in curled sprays from short, ascending branchlets. Extremely hardy, it grows in Zones 2-8, although the foliage may be bronze or even brown in the northern parts of its range in winter. While the species, which is native to the Eastern United States, is not often grown in gardens, it is the parent of numerous varieties that are widely planted. Douglasii Pyramidalis, the Douglas arborvitae, is a dense conical tree growing 18 to 20 feet tall that maintains the rich green color of its curled and twisted fernlike foliage throughout the winter. Globosa, the dwarf American arborvitae, is an almost perfectly round shrub that grows only 4 feet tall in 20 years; it has densely packed sprays of dull green leaves. Woodwardii, Woodward globe arborvitae, is a rounded plant when young. It spreads to 20 feet as it matures to a height of 8 or 10 feet; it holds its flat sprays of dark green leaves vertically rather than horizontally as the other arborvitaes do.

HOW TO GROW. Arborvitaes need a sheltered position in full sun; the plants become thin when they are grown in the shade. Choose sites that are sheltered from strong winds and have fertile, moist, but well-drained soil. All plants are sensitive to air pollution. Plant arborvitaes in the fall or spring, mulching them with a 4-inch layer of organic matter to keep soil cool and moist. Water plants weekly until their roots are well established. Feed annually in spring with a light dusting of 5-10-5 fertilizer around the base. Pruning is seldom necessary, but arborvitaes can be sheared in early spring before new growth begins to keep them small or shape them into hedges. Arborvitaes can be propagated from seeds and cuttings; they root very quickly in moist sand or vermiculite.

TRIFOLIATE ORANGE See *Poncirus*

TSUGA

*T. canadensis* and varieties (Canada hemlock); *T. caroliniana* (Carolina hemlock)

Fine-textured Canada and Carolina hemlocks and their varieties are effective in naturalized settings when they are used either in groups or combined with other native plants such as the flowering dogwood or paper birch. They can also be grown as specimen trees or shrubs or trained into hedges. They are hardy in Zones 4-8, but their delicate foliage can be damaged by severe winter winds, strong winter sun or air pollution; therefore, care must be taken in choosing sites for them. Their drooping branchlets bear soft, flat, sharply pointed tiny needles that are banded with white on their undersides. New growth is pale or yellow-green and turns dark green when it matures. Hemlocks grow into narrow, conical silhouettes with slim downswept branches that rise slightly at the tips. Small brown cones hang from the limbs of older trees, which have deeply furrowed, scaly red bark.

The Canada hemlock will grow 50 feet tall and 25 feet wide in 30 years. Its pointed cone shape becomes somewhat rounded with age. There are many attractive varieties of the Canada hemlock. A widely grown variety is Pendula, also known as Sargent's weeping hemlock. A dense mound of soft hanging branches, this weeping tree grows 15 or more feet tall and spreads 40 or more feet across. Frequently used as a specimen plant or beside woodland pools, it must be staked until it is about 3 feet tall before it is allowed to cascade naturally. Albospica, the variegated Canada hemlock, is a slow-growing pyramidal shrub with white or cream-colored new growth; the color varies with soil and climate conditions and is most effective in the spring. Cole's prostrate hemlock is a dwarf plant that will almost flow over and around the stones in a rock garden; growing only 6 inches tall, it spreads 3 or 4 feet.

The Carolina hemlock is a slender tree that can grow 15 feet tall in as many years. At maturity it is about 40 feet tall. The ¾-inch needles wind in spirals around red-brown twigs to give the tree an especially soft and dense look.

HOW TO GROW. Hemlocks grow in full sun to deep shade and are frequently planted on the north side of buildings where they receive protection from winter sun and wind. A cool, moist, acid soil is best. Plant in the spring or fall, spacing hedge plants 24 inches apart and watering them frequently until their roots are well established. Maintain a 4-inch mulch of organic matter such as wood chips or bark. If their foliage becomes sparse or pale, fertilize the plants with a dusting of cottonseed meal or any of the garden fertilizers that are recommended for acid-loving plants such as camellias or hollies. To keep hemlocks to a desired height, prune them in the spring or early summer by cutting off unwanted branches inside the plant, using hand clippers. Hedges can be sheared closely since new shoots sprout readily from branch stubs. Additional hemlocks may be propagated from seeds or from cuttings.

TUBERGEN WINTER ACONITE See *Eranthis*
TUBERGENIAN SQUILL See *Scilla*
TUPELO, BLACK See *Nyssa*
TURKISH HAZEL See *Corylus*
TWINLEAF SQUILL See *Scilla*
TWO-LEAVED SQUILL See *Scilla*

# U

## ULMUS

*U. alatus* (winged elm); *U. parvifolia* (Chinese elm)

The high, arching branches of the vase-shaped elms cast exquisite shadows on snow-covered landscapes, and these two species offer other winter attractions as well. Snow settling on the winged elm outlines the corky wings that extend out from many of its branches, and the Chinese elm has beautifully mottled bark. The winged elm, native to the American South, is hardy in Zones 7-10. It is deciduous, growing 40 to 50 feet tall with a round and open form. In autumn its 2-inch green leaves fall to reveal the handsome, ornamental wings.

The Chinese elm, hardy in Zones 4-10, grows 40 to 50 feet high and equally wide. When mature, the bark on its trunk and larger limbs peels back, exposing a striking pattern of patchy, lighter bark underneath. The Chinese elm's thick, 1- to 3-inch leaves are bright yellow in spring and turn red in the fall, although in warmer climates this tree may keep its leaves through the winter. Unlike other elms, this species flowers in autumn.

HOW TO GROW. Elms grow best in full sun and in any moist, well-drained soil that is deep enough to allow the tree's wide-spreading roots to expand laterally without invading nearby shrubs and trees. Pruning, which is seldom required, should be done in the fall.

# V

## VERNAL WITCH HAZEL See *Hamamelis*

*For climate zones and frost dates, see maps, pages 148-149.*

CHINESE ELM
*Ulmus parvifolia*

LEATHERLEAF VIBURNUM
*Viburnum rhytidophyllum*

PERIWINKLE
*Vinca minor* 'Aureo-variegata'

## VIBURNUM

*V. rhytidophyllum* (leatherleaf viburnum); *V. tinus* (Laurustinus viburnum); *V. trilobum* (American cranberry bush)

Viburnums display the same variety of flowers, fruits and foliage in winter settings that make them versatile garden shrubs in other seasons. Gardeners use them in hedges, in borders or as single shrubs where they can enjoy the winter flowers, berries or shiny evergreen foliage offered by different species.

The leatherleaf viburnum, grown in Zones 5-10, is a loose, round 9-foot-tall shrub. The plant's 3- to 7-inch crinkled evergreen leaves grow in whorls along its stems and give the shrub a shingled appearance year round. In spring, leatherleaf viburnum bears flat clusters of light-pink flowers, followed by attractive red or black berries in autumn. The evergreen Laurustinus viburnum grows 10 to 20 feet tall in Zones 7 and 8, where its 3-inch clusters of white blossoms, sometimes tinged with pink, open in early winter. Metallic blue berries follow in late summer, eventually turning black. Dark green, glossy leaves, 1½ to 4 inches long, decorate the shrub year round. Laurustinus viburnums form excellent hedges that retain their handsome shape for years and seldom need pruning. The deciduous American cranberry bush grows 12 feet tall in Zones 3-9. Its edible, cranberry-like fruits ripen in late summer and cling well into winter. Clusters of white flowers bloom in late spring.

HOW TO GROW. Viburnums grow best in full sun in any well-drained soil. Laurustinus viburnum may become unsightly in winter, or even die, if the soil has been too wet during the previous summer. Since wind damages the leatherleaf viburnum's foliage, it looks its best when planted in protected sites. Plant bare-rooted, balled-and-burlaped or container-grown viburnums in spring, summer or fall, spacing hedge plants 2½ to 4 feet apart. Prune lightly only to remove dead branches. New plants are started from cuttings taken in late spring.

## VINCA

*V. major* (greater periwinkle); *V. minor* (common periwinkle, creeping myrtle)

The periwinkles stay green all winter, although their shiny leaves darken somewhat in hue. These robust, trailing plants spread rapidly, rooting at many places along their stems, a characteristic that makes them excellent for controlling soil erosion. They are used in almost any shady location as ground covers under trees, as borders along paths or in separate plantings by themselves. *V. major,* the less hardy species, is grown in gardens in Zones 8-10. It is 6 inches tall and in its common form has dark, lustrous green leaves 2 inches long; but the species also includes two varieties with attractive, conspicuous foliage: *V. major* Variegata, which has cream-white mottled leaves; and *V. major* Elegantissima, with leaves splattered white. All three forms bear large, dark blue funnel-shaped flowers in spring.

*V. minor,* sometimes called common periwinkle, is hardy in Zones 4-10, and is one of the most often-used evergreen ground covers in Northern gardens. It grows about 6 inches high with ¾-inch to 1½-inch leaves that taper to a point at each end. Dark green in its standard form, it too has varieties with more conspicuous foliage. *V. minor* Argenteo-variegata has white-bordered leaves; *V. minor* Aureo-variegata has leaves bordered with rich yellow. All three forms bear lilac-blue 1-inch flowers in early spring.

HOW TO GROW. Periwinkles grow in either sun or shade, but in the colder climates of Zones 4-7 some shade is preferable; the combination of sun and freezing temperatures tends to burn their foliage. They tolerate almost any soil condition, but spread faster and grow into more attractive plants in a moist, deep soil enriched with peat moss or leaf mold to a depth of about 6 inches. Set out periwinkles in spring, spacing them 12 to 18 inches apart. Once established they need little care, but for bushier growth their tips may be nipped off occasionally. Additional plants are easy to start from the offshoots that take root wherever the stems of periwinkle touch the ground.

# W

WARMINSTER BROOM See *Cytisus*
WEEPING MULBERRY See *Morus*
WHITE OAK See *Quercus*
WHITE SPRUCE See *Picea*
WHITEWASHED BRAMBLE See *Rubus*
WILD GINGER See *Asarum*
WINDFLOWER, GRECIAN See *Anemone*
WINGED ELM See *Ulmus*
WINTER ACONITE See *Eranthis*
WINTER CREEPER See *Euonymus*
WINTER HONEYSUCKLE See *Lonicera*
WINTERGREEN See *Gaultheria*
WINTERGREEN BARBERRY See *Berberis*
WINTERSWEET See *Chimonanthus*
WITCH HAZEL See *Hamamelis*

# Y

YELLOWWOOD See *Cladrastis*
YEW See *Taxus*

## YUCCA
*Y. aloifolia* (Spanish-bayonet, dagger plant); *Y. filamentosa* (Adam's-needle yucca)

The yucca, which is indigenous to the desert regions of the Southwest, is a fascinating plant for winter gardens in other parts of the United States and Canada as well. The plant's stiff swordlike leaves, often 2½ feet long and only 2 inches wide, keep their color, a dusty gray-green, all winter long. Bending under the weight of snow, and even without it, their bold silhouettes are an important contribution to the winter landscape. The larger of these two species, the Spanish-bayonet, grows only in Zones 8-10, its trunk eventually reaching a height of 8 feet. Among its many varieties are *Y. aloifolia* Marginata, whose leaves are edged with yellow; *Y. aloifolia* Tricolor, which has white or yellow bands bisecting each leaf; and *Y. aloifolia* Variegata, with white-striped foliage.

The Adam's-needle yucca grows in Zones 4-10, making it the most popular yucca for winter gardens. Much smaller than the Spanish-bayonet, it is only 3 feet tall when mature. Almost stemless, it has arching leaves that are 2½ to 3 feet long and about 1 inch wide. Long, curling threads hang from the plant's rigid leaves, which may also vary from the standard gray-green. Among varieties especially recommended for their contribution to the winter garden are *Y. filamentosa* Bright Edge, with narrow yellow bands along the borders of its leaves; *Y. filamentosa* Concava, with flat, 2- to 3-inch-wide leaves; *Y. filamentosa* Variegata, with white-striped foliage. In mid- to late summer, yuccas bear waxy white flowers along spikes 6 to 8 feet tall.

HOW TO GROW. Yuccas require as much sun as possible and grow best in a well-drained sandy soil; moisture standing around their roots is especially harmful in winter. New plants are started by separating well-rooted offshoots from the base of the plants, and replanting them in a new location.

*For climate zones and frost dates, see maps, pages 148-149.*

BRIGHT EDGE YUCCA
*Yucca filamentosa* 'Bright Edge'

# Appendix

# Climate notes for winter gardens

The most important principle in designing a successful winter garden is to select plants that will survive the winter of your region and at the same time will remain attractive. But even varieties within a given species can differ in their ability to withstand freezing temperatures, drying winds and strong winter sun.

To help you choose trees, shrubs, perennials, grasses, ground covers and bulbs that will grow reliably in your winter garden, the preceding encyclopedia keys each plant to the zone map below. The map divides the United States and Canada into 10 climate zones based on the average low winter temperatures experienced in each zone. Plants grown at the extreme northern limit of their range may require sheltered positions or deeper mulches than normal to get them through especially severe winters; those grown at the extreme southern end of their range may need protective shade or more frequent watering in summer to prevent the stresses that reduce their chances of surviving the colder months.

Use the maps at the right to determine when winter will begin and end in your garden. The top map indicates the average date of the first killing fall frost, the signal to hardier plants to prepare for the coming cold. The lower map shows the average dates of the last spring frost. By that time the flowers of early-blooming plants will have passed and the milder weather will prompt the evergreens to resume their summer foliage colors and the deciduous plants to bud out.

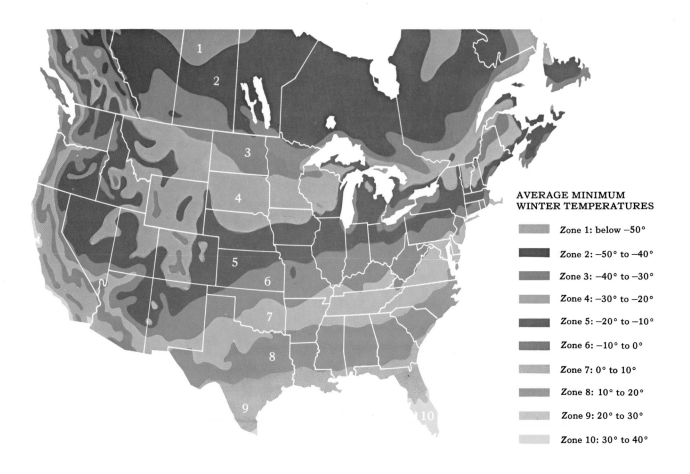

**AVERAGE MINIMUM WINTER TEMPERATURES**

Zone 1: below −50°

Zone 2: −50° to −40°

Zone 3: −40° to −30°

Zone 4: −30° to −20°

Zone 5: −20° to −10°

Zone 6: −10° to 0°

Zone 7: 0° to 10°

Zone 8: 10° to 20°

Zone 9: 20° to 30°

Zone 10: 30° to 40°

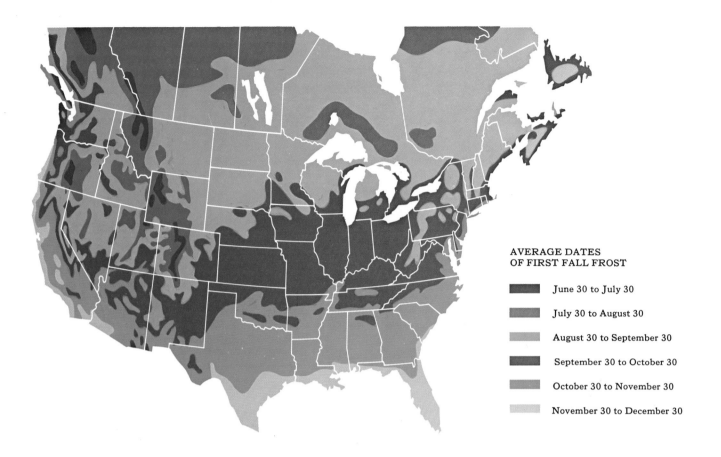

AVERAGE DATES
OF FIRST FALL FROST

- June 30 to July 30
- July 30 to August 30
- August 30 to September 30
- September 30 to October 30
- October 30 to November 30
- November 30 to December 30

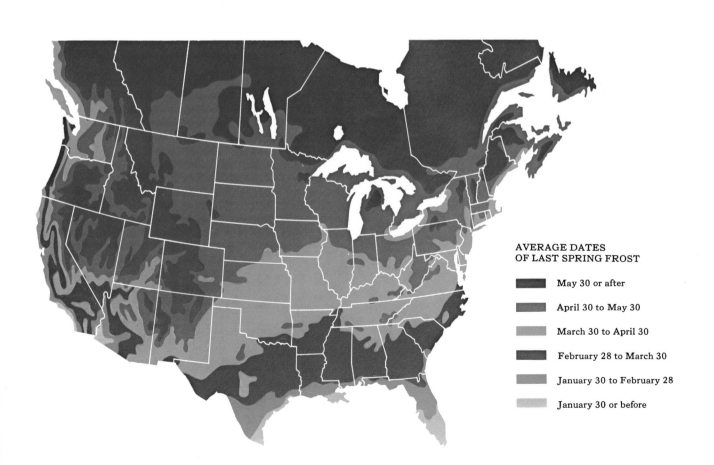

AVERAGE DATES
OF LAST SPRING FROST

- May 30 or after
- April 30 to May 30
- March 30 to April 30
- February 28 to March 30
- January 30 to February 28
- January 30 or before

# Characteristics of 239 winter-garden plants

| | PLANT HEIGHT | | | | WINTER TRAITS | | | | | | | | WINTER TOLERANCE | | | WINTER CARE | | | | SOIL NEEDS | | | | |
|---|---|---|---|---|---|---|---|---|---|---|---|---|---|---|---|---|---|---|---|---|---|---|---|---|
| | Under 1 foot | 1 to 3 feet | 3 to 6 feet | Over 6 feet | Distinctive foliage | Evergreen | Decorative fruit or pods | Distinctive branches or bark | Flowers | Fragrance | Pruning required | Heavy snow | Extreme cold | Winter sun | Wind | Mulching | Watering | Snow removal | Wind protection | Acid | Alkaline | Dry | Moist but well drained | Wet |
| ABIES CONCOLOR (white fir) | | | ● | ● | ● | ● | ● | ● | | ● | | | ● | | | | | | | ● | | | ● | |
| ABIES VEITCHII (Veitch fir) | | | ● | ● | ● | ● | ● | ● | | ● | | ● | ● | | | | | | | ● | | | ● | |
| ACER DAVIDII (David maple) | | | ● | ● | | | | ● | | | | | ● | | | | | | | ● | ● | | ● | |
| ACER GRISEUM (paperbark maple) | | | ● | ● | | | | ● | | | | | ● | | | | | | | ● | ● | | ● | |
| ACER PALMATUM 'DISSECTUM' (threadleaf Japanese maple) | | | ● | ● | | | | ● | | | | | ● | | | | | ● | ● | ● | | | ● | |
| ACER PALMATUM 'SANGOKAKU' (coral-bark Japanese maple) | | | ● | ● | | | | ● | | | | | ● | | | | | ● | ● | ● | ● | ● | ● | |
| ACER PENSYLVANICUM (striped maple) | | | ● | ● | | | | ● | | | | ● | ● | | | | | | | ● | ● | | ● | |
| ACER RUFINERVE | | | ● | ● | | | | ● | | | | | ● | | | | | | | ● | ● | | ● | |
| ANEMONE BLANDA (Greek anemone) | ● | | | ● | | | | ● | | | | | | ● | | | | | | ● | ● | | ● | |
| ANEMONE BLANDA 'RADAR' (Greek anemone) | ● | | | ● | | | | ● | | | | | | ● | | | | | | ● | ● | | ● | |
| ARCTOSTAPHYLOS STANFORDIANA (Stanford manzanita) | | | ● | ● | ● | | ● | | | | | ● | ● | | | | | | | ● | ● | ● | ● | |
| ARCTOSTAPHYLOS UVA-URSI (bearberry) | ● | | | ● | ● | ● | | | | | | ● | ● | | | | | | | ● | | | ● | |
| ARONIA ARBUTIFOLIA (red chokeberry) | | | ● | ● | | ● | | | | | | | ● | | ● | | | | | ● | ● | | ● | ● |
| ARONIA MELANOCARPA (black chokeberry) | | | ● | ● | | ● | | | | | | | ● | | | | | | | ● | ● | | ● | |
| ARONIA PRUNIFOLIA (purple chokeberry) | | | ● | ● | | ● | | | | | | | ● | | | | | | | ● | ● | | ● | |
| ASARUM EUROPAEUM (European wild ginger) | ● | | | ● | ● | | | | ● | | | | | | | | | | | ● | | | ● | |
| ASARUM SHUTTLEWORTHII (mottled wild ginger) | ● | | | ● | ● | | | | ● | | | | | | | | | | | ● | | | ● | |
| ASPLENIUM PLATYNEURON (ebony spleenwort) | | ● | | | ● | ● | | | | | | ● | | | ● | | | | | | | ● | ● | |
| ASPLENIUM TRICHOMANES (maidenhair spleenwort) | ● | | | ● | ● | | | | | | | ● | | | | | | | | | | ● | ● | |
| AUCUBA JAPONICA 'PICTURATA' (Japanese aucuba) | | | ● | ● | ● | ● | ● | | | | | | | | | | | | | ● | ● | | ● | |
| BERBERIS JULIANAE (wintergreen barberry) | | | ● | ● | ● | ● | | | ● | | | ● | ● | ● | ● | | | | | ● | ● | | ● | |
| BERBERIS THUNBERGII (Japanese barberry) | | | ● | | | ● | ● | | ● | | | ● | ● | ● | ● | | | | | ● | ● | | ● | |
| BERGENIA CORDIFOLIA (heartleaf bergenia) | ● | | | ● | ● | | | | | | | | | | | | | | | ● | ● | | ● | |
| BERGENIA CRASSIFOLIA (leather bergenia) | ● | | | ● | ● | | | | | | | | | | | | | | | ● | ● | | ● | |
| BETULA ALBO-SINENSIS (Chinese paper birch) | | | | ● | | | ● | | | | | | ● | | | | | | | ● | | | ● | |
| BETULA NIGRA (river birch) | | | | ● | | | ● | | | | | | ● | | | | | | | ● | | | ● | ● |
| BETULA PAPYRIFERA (canoe birch) | | | | ● | | ● | ● | | | | | | ● | ● | | | | | | ● | | | ● | |
| BETULA PENDULA (European white birch) | | | | ● | | | ● | | | | | | ● | ● | | | | | | ● | | ● | ● | |
| BETULA PENDULA 'YOUNGII' (Young's weeping birch) | | | | ● | | | ● | | | | | | ● | ● | | | | | | ● | | ● | ● | |
| BETULA PLATYPHYLLA | | | | ● | | | ● | | | | | | ● | | | | | | | ● | | ● | ● | |
| BETULA POPULIFOLIA (gray birch) | | | | ● | | | ● | | | ● | | | ● | ● | | | | | | ● | | ● | ● | |
| BULBOCODIUM VERNUM (spring-meadow saffron) | ● | | | | | | ● | | | | | | ● | ● | | | | | | ● | ● | | ● | |
| BUXUS MICROPHYLLA (littleleaf boxwood) | | ● | | ● | | ● | | | ● | | ● | | | | | ● | ● | ● | ● | ● | ● | | ● | |
| BUXUS SEMPERVIRENS (common box) | | | ● | | ● | | | | ● | ● | ● | | | | | ● | ● | ● | ● | ● | ● | | ● | |
| CALAMAGROSTIS EPIGEIOS HORTORUM (feather reed grass) | | ● | | ● | | | | | | | ● | | | ● | | | | | | | | ● | ● | |
| CALLUNA VULGARIS (Scotch heather) | | ● | | ● | ● | | | | ● | | | | | ● | | | | | | ● | | | ● | |
| CALLUNA VULGARIS 'BLAZE AWAY' (Blaze Away heather) | | ● | | ● | ● | | | | ● | | | | | ● | | | | | | ● | | | ● | |
| CALLUNA VULGARIS 'GOLDEN FEATHER' (Golden Feather heather) | | ● | | ● | ● | | | | ● | | | | | ● | | | | | | ● | | | ● | |
| CAMELLIA JAPONICA (common camellia) | | | ● | ● | ● | | | ● | | | | | | ● | | | | | | ● | | | ● | |
| CAMELLIA SASANQUA (sasanqua camellia) | | ● | | ● | ● | | | ● | | | | | | ● | | | | | | ● | | | ● | |
| CARPINUS BETULUS (European hornbeam) | | | ● | ● | | | ● | | | | | | ● | | | | | | | ● | ● | | ● | |
| CARPINUS CAROLINIANA (American hornbeam) | | | ● | ● | | | | | | | ● | | ● | | | | | | | ● | ● | | ● | |
| CARYA OVATA (shagbark hickory) | | | | ● | | | | ● | | | ● | | ● | | | | | | | ● | | | ● | |
| CEDRUS ATLANTICA (Atlas cedar) | | | ● | ● | ● | ● | | | ● | | | | ● | | | | | ● | | ● | ● | | ● | |
| CEDRUS ATLANTICA 'GLAUCA' (blue Atlas cedar) | | | ● | ● | ● | ● | | | ● | | | | ● | | | | | ● | | ● | ● | | ● | |
| CEDRUS DEODARA (deodar cedar) | | | ● | ● | ● | ● | | | ● | | | | ● | | | | | ● | | ● | ● | | ● | |
| CEDRUS LIBANI (cedar of Lebanon) | | | ● | ● | ● | ● | | | ● | | | | ● | | | | | ● | | ● | ● | | ● | |
| CHAMAECYPARIS LAWSONIANA (Lawson's false cypress) | | | ● | ● | ● | ● | | | | ● | | | | | ● | | | | | ● | | | ● | |
| CHAMAECYPARIS OBTUSA (hinoki false cypress) | | | ● | ● | ● | | | | | ● | | | | | ● | | | | | ● | | | ● | |
| CHAMAECYPARIS OBTUSA 'NANA GRACILIS' (dwarf false cypress) | | ● | | ● | ● | | | | | ● | | | | | ● | | | | | ● | | | ● | |

| Plant | Under 1 foot | 1 to 3 feet | 3 to 6 feet | Over 6 feet | Distinctive foliage | Evergreen | Decorative fruit or pods | Distinctive branches or bark | Flowers | Fragrance | Pruning required | Heavy snow | Extreme cold | Winter sun | Wind | Mulching | Watering | Snow removal | Wind protection | Acid | Alkaline | Dry | Moist but well drained | Wet |
|---|---|---|---|---|---|---|---|---|---|---|---|---|---|---|---|---|---|---|---|---|---|---|---|---|
| CHAMAECYPARIS PISIFERA 'FILIFERA' (thread sawara false cypress) | | | ● | | ● | ● | | | | | ● | | | ● | | ● | | | | ● | | | ● | |
| CHIMONANTHUS PRAECOX (wintersweet) | | | ● | | | | | | ● | ● | ● | | | ● | | ● | | | | ● | ● | | ● | |
| CHIONODOXA LUCILIAE (glory-of-the-snow) | ● | | | | | | | | ● | | | | ● | ● | | | | | | ● | ● | | ● | |
| CHIONODOXA SARDENSIS (glory-of-the-snow) | ● | | | | | | | | ● | | | | ● | ● | | | | | | ● | ● | | ● | |
| CLADRASTIS LUTEA (yellowwood) | | | ● | | | | ● | ● | | | | | | ● | | | | | | ● | ● | | ● | |
| CORNUS ALBA (Tatarian dogwood) | | | ● | | | | | ● | | | | | ● | ● | | | | | | ● | ● | | ● | |
| CORNUS ALBA 'SIBIRICA' (Siberian dogwood) | | | ● | | | | | ● | | | | | ● | ● | | | | | | ● | ● | | ● | |
| CORNUS FLORIDA (flowering dogwood) | | | ● | | | | | ● | | | | | | | | ● | | | | ● | | | ● | |
| CORNUS KOUSA (Kousa dogwood) | | | ● | | | | | ● | | | | | | | | ● | | | ● | ● | | | ● | |
| CORNUS SANGUINEA (blood-twig dogwood) | | | ● | | | | | ● | | | | | ● | | | | | | | ● | ● | | ● | |
| CORNUS SERICEA (red-osier dogwood) | | | ● | | | | | ● | | | | | ● | ● | | | | | | ● | ● | | | ● |
| CORYLUS AMERICANA (American hazel) | | | ● | | | | | ● | | | | | | | | ● | | | | ● | | | ● | |
| CORYLUS AVELLANA 'CONTORTA' (Harry Lauder's Walking Stick) | | | ● | | | | | ● | ● | | | | | ● | | ● | | | | ● | ● | | ● | |
| CORYLUS COLURNA (Turkish hazel) | | | ● | | | | | ● | ● | | | | | | | ● | | | | ● | ● | ● | ● | |
| COTONEASTER ADPRESSA (creeping cotoneaster) | | ● | | | | | ● | | | | | | ● | ● | | | | | | ● | ● | | ● | |
| COTONEASTER DAMMERI (bearberry cotoneaster) | | ● | | | | ● | ● | | | | | | | ● | | | | | | ● | | | ● | |
| COTONEASTER SALICIFOLIUS (willowleaf cotoneaster) | | | ● | | | ● | ● | | | | | | ● | ● | | | | | | ● | ● | ● | ● | |
| CRATAEGUS CRUS-GALLI (cockspur hawthorn) | | | ● | | | | ● | ● | | | ● | | ● | ● | | | | | | ● | ● | | ● | |
| CRATAEGUS PHAENOPYRUM (Washington hawthorn) | | | ● | | | | ● | ● | | | ● | | ● | ● | | | | | | ● | ● | | ● | |
| CRATAEGUS PHAENOPHYRUM 'FASTIGIATA' (Washington hawthorn) | | | ● | | | | ● | ● | | | ● | | ● | ● | | | | | | ● | ● | | ● | |
| CROCUS ANCYRENSIS (golden bunch crocus) | ● | | | | | | | | ● | | | | | | | | | ● | ● | ● | ● | | ● | |
| CROCUS CHRYSANTHUS | ● | | | | | | | | ● | | | | | | | | | ● | ● | ● | ● | | ● | |
| CROCUS IMPERATI (early crocus) | ● | | | | | | | | ● | | | | | | | | | ● | ● | ● | ● | | ● | |
| CROCUS LAEVIGATUS | ● | | | | | | | | ● | | | | | | | | | ● | ● | ● | ● | | ● | |
| CROCUS SIEBERI (Sieber crocus) | ● | | | | | | | | ● | | | | | | | | | ● | ● | ● | ● | | ● | |
| CROCUS VERSICOLOR (spring-flowering crocus) | ● | | | | | | | | ● | | | | | | | | | ● | ● | ● | ● | | ● | |
| CRYPTOMERIA JAPONICA (Japanese cedar) | | | ● | | ● | ● | ● | | ● | | | | | ● | | ● | | | | ● | | | ● | |
| CRYPTOMERIA JAPONICA 'GLOBOSA NANA' (dwarf Japanese cedar) | | ● | | | ● | ● | ● | | ● | | | | | ● | | ● | | | | ● | | | ● | |
| CYCLAMEN COUM (Coum cyclamen) | ● | | | | | ● | | | ● | | | | | | | ● | | ● | | | | | ● | |
| CYTISUS PRAECOX (Warminster broom) | | | ● | | | | | | ● | | | | | ● | | | | | | ● | | ● | | |
| CYTISUS SCOPARIUS (Scotch broom) | | ● | ● | | | | | | ● | | | | | ● | | | | | | ● | | ● | | |
| DAPHNE MEZEREUM (February daphne) | | ● | | | | | | | ● | ● | | | | ● | | | | | | ● | | | ● | |
| DAPHNE ODORA (winter daphne) | | ● | | | | ● | | | | ● | | | | ● | | | | | | ● | | | ● | |
| DIOSPYROS VIRGINIANA (common persimmon) | | | ● | | | | ● | ● | | | | | | ● | | | | | | | | ● | ● | |
| ELAEAGNUS PUNGENS 'VARIEGATA' (variegated thorny elaeagnus) | | | ● | ● | ● | | | | | | | | | | | | | ● | ● | ● | ● | ● | ● | |
| ELAEAGNUS UMBELLATA (autumn elaeagnus) | | | ● | | | | ● | ● | | ● | | | | ● | | | | ● | ● | ● | ● | ● | ● | |
| ERANTHIS HYEMALIS (winter aconite) | ● | | | | | ● | | | ● | | | | | | | | | ● | ● | ● | ● | | ● | |
| ERANTHIS TUBERGENIANA (Tubergen winter aconite) | ● | | | | | ● | | | ● | ● | | | | | | | | ● | ● | ● | ● | | ● | |
| ERICA CARNEA (spring heath) | ● | | | | ● | ● | | | ● | | | | | ● | | ● | | | | ● | | | ● | |
| ERICA CARNEA 'KING GEORGE' (King George spring heath) | | ● | | | ● | ● | | | ● | | | | | ● | | ● | | | | ● | | | ● | |
| ERICA CARNEA 'SPRINGWOOD WHITE' (Springwood White spring heath) | ● | | | | ● | ● | | | ● | | | | | ● | | ● | | | | ● | | | ● | |
| ERICA DARLEYENSIS (Darley heath) | | ● | | | ● | ● | | | ● | | | | | ● | | ● | | | | | | ● | ● | |
| ERICA TETRALIX (cross-leaved heath) | ● | | | | ● | ● | | | ● | | | | ● | ● | | | | | | ● | | | ● | |
| EUONYMUS ALATA (winged euonymus) | | | ● | | | | | ● | | | | | ● | ● | | | | | | ● | | | ● | |
| EUONYMUS FORTUNEI (winter creeper) | ● | | | | ● | ● | | | | | | | | ● | | ● | | | | ● | | | ● | |
| EUONYMUS FORTUNEI COLORATUS (purple winter creeper) | ● | | | | ● | ● | | | | | | | | ● | | ● | | | | ● | | | ● | |
| EUONYMUS FORTUNEI VEGETA 'EMERALD 'N GOLD' (Emerald 'n Gold winter creeper) | | ● | | | ● | ● | | | | | | | | ● | | ● | | | | ● | | | ● | |
| EUONYMUS JAPONICA (evergreen euonymus) | | | ● | | ● | ● | | | | | | | | ● | | ● | | | | ● | ● | | ● | |
| FAGUS GRANDIFOLIA (American beech) | | | ● | | ● | | | ● | | | | | | ● | | | | | | ● | | | ● | |
| FAGUS SYLVATICA (European beech) | | | ● | ● | ● | | | ● | | | | | | ● | | | | | | ● | | | ● | |

| | PLANT HEIGHT | | | | WINTER TRAITS | | | | | | | | WINTER TOLERANCE | | | WINTER CARE | | | | SOIL NEEDS | | | | |
|---|---|---|---|---|---|---|---|---|---|---|---|---|---|---|---|---|---|---|---|---|---|---|---|---|
| | Under 1 foot | 1 to 3 feet | 3 to 6 feet | Over 6 feet | Distinctive foliage | Evergreen | Decorative fruit or pods | Distinctive branches or bark | Flowers | Fragrance | Pruning required | Heavy snow | Extreme cold | Winter sun | Wind | Mulching | Watering | Snow removal | Wind protection | Acid | Alkaline | Dry | Moist but well drained | Wet |
| FAGUS SYLVATICA 'ATROPUNICEA' (copper beech) | | | ● | | ● | | ● | | | | | | | ● | | | | | | ● | | | ● | |
| FESTUCA OVINA GLAUCA (blue fescue) | ● | ● | | | ● | ● | | | | | | ● | ● | ● | | | | | | ● | ● | ● | | |
| GALANTHUS ELWESII (giant snowdrop) | | ● | | | | | | | ● | | | ● | ● | | | | | | | ● | ● | | ● | |
| GALANTHUS NIVALIS (common snowdrop) | ● | | | | | | | | ● | | | ● | ● | | | | | | | ● | ● | | ● | |
| GALANTHUS PLICATUS | ● | | | | | | | | ● | | | ● | ● | | | | | | | ● | ● | | ● | |
| GAULTHERIA PROCUMBENS (wintergreen) | ● | | | | ● | ● | ● | | | ● | | | | | | | | | | ● | | | ● | |
| GAULTHERIA SHALLON (salal) | | ● | ● | ● | ● | ● | ● | ● | | | | | | | | | | | | ● | | | ● | |
| HAMAMELIS INTERMEDIA | | | ● | | | | | ● | ● | ● | ● | | | | | | | | | ● | ● | | ● | |
| HAMAMELIS MOLLIS (Chinese witch hazel) | | | ● | | | | | ● | ● | ● | ● | | | | | | | | | ● | ● | | ● | |
| HAMAMELIS VERNALIS (vernal witch hazel) | | | ● | | | | | ● | ● | ● | ● | | | | | | | | | ● | ● | | ● | |
| HEDERA HELIX (English ivy) | ● | | | | ● | ● | | | | | | | | | | | | | | ● | ● | | ● | |
| HELLEBORUS FOETIDUS (setterwort) | | ● | | | ● | ● | | | ● | | | | | ● | | | | | ● | | ● | | ● | |
| HELLEBORUS LIVIDUS CORSICUS (Corsican hellebore) | | ● | | | ● | ● | | | ● | | | | | ● | | | | | ● | ● | ● | | ● | |
| HELLEBORUS NIGER (Christmas rose) | | ● | | | | ● | | | ● | | | | | ● | | | | | ● | ● | ● | | ● | |
| HELLEBORUS ORIENTALIS (Lenten rose) | | ● | | | | ● | | | ● | | | | | ● | | | | | ● | ● | ● | | ● | |
| HYDRANGEA ANOMALA PETIOLARIS (climbing hydrangea) | | | ● | | | | ● | ● | | | | | | | | | | | | ● | | | ● | |
| HYDRANGEA QUERCIFOLIA (oak-leaved hydrangea) | | ● | | | | | ● | ● | | | | | | | | | | | | ● | | | ● | |
| IBERIS SEMPERVIRENS (evergreen candytuft) | ● | | | | | ● | | | | | | | ● | | | | | | | ● | ● | | ● | |
| IDESIA POLYCARPA (iigiri tree) | | | ● | | | | ● | ● | | | | | ● | | | | | | | ● | ● | ● | ● | |
| ILEX AQUIFOLIUM (English holly) | | ● | ● | ● | | ● | ● | | | | | | ● | ● | ● | | | ● | ● | ● | | | ● | |
| ILEX CORNUTA (Chinese holly) | | ● | ● | ● | | ● | ● | | | | | | ● | ● | ● | | | ● | ● | ● | | | ● | |
| ILEX CORNUTA 'BURFORDII' (Burford holly) | | ● | ● | ● | | ● | ● | | | | | | ● | ● | ● | | | ● | ● | ● | | | ● | |
| ILEX CRENATA (Japanese holly) | | ● | ● | ● | | ● | ● | | | | | | ● | ● | ● | | | ● | ● | ● | | | ● | |
| ILEX DECIDUA (possum haw) | | | ● | ● | | | ● | | | | | | ● | ● | ● | | | ● | ● | ● | | | ● | |
| ILEX GLABRA (inkberry) | | | ● | ● | | ● | ● | | | | | | ● | ● | ● | | | ● | ● | ● | | | ● | ● |
| ILEX OPACA (American holly) | | | ● | ● | | ● | ● | | | | | | ● | ● | ● | | | ● | ● | ● | | | ● | |
| ILEX SERRATA (finetooth holly) | | | ● | ● | | | ● | | | | | | ● | ● | ● | | | ● | ● | ● | | | ● | |
| ILEX VERTICILLATA (winterberry) | | | ● | ● | | | ● | | | | | | ● | ● | ● | | | ● | ● | ● | | | ● | ● |
| IRIS BAKERANA (Baker iris) | ● | | | | | | | | ● | ● | | | ● | | | | | ● | | | | ● | | |
| IRIS DANFORDIAE (Danford iris) | ● | | | | | | | | ● | | | | ● | | | | | ● | | | | ● | | |
| IRIS HISTRIOIDES MAJOR (Harput iris) | ● | | | | | | | | ● | | | | ● | | | | | ● | | | | ● | | |
| IRIS RETICULATA (netted iris) | ● | | | | | | | | ● | ● | | | ● | | | | | | | | | ● | | |
| JASMINUM MESNYI (primrose jasmine) | | ● | | | | | | ● | ● | ● | | | ● | ● | | | | ● | | ● | ● | | ● | |
| JASMINUM NUDIFLORUM (winter jasmine) | | ● | ● | | | | | ● | ● | | | | ● | ● | | | | ● | | | ● | ● | ● | |
| JUNIPERUS CHINENSIS (Chinese juniper) | | | ● | ● | ● | ● | | | | | | | ● | | | | | | | | ● | ● | ● | |
| JUNIPERUS CHINENSIS 'ECHINIFORMIS' (hedgehog juniper) | | ● | | | ● | ● | ● | | | | | | ● | | | | | | | | ● | ● | ● | |
| JUNIPERUS HORIZONTALIS (creeping juniper) | | ● | | | ● | ● | ● | | | | | | ● | ● | | ● | | | | | ● | ● | ● | |
| JUNIPERUS HORIZONTALIS 'BAR HARBOR' (Bar Harbor juniper) | | ● | | | ● | ● | ● | | | | | | ● | | | | | | | | ● | ● | ● | |
| JUNIPERUS SCOPULORUM (Rocky Mountain juniper) | | | ● | ● | ● | ● | | | | | | | ● | | | | | | | | ● | ● | ● | |
| JUNIPERUS VIRGINIANA (eastern red cedar) | | | ● | ● | ● | ● | | | | | | | ● | | | | | | | | ● | ● | ● | |
| KERRIA JAPONICA (Japanese rose) | | ● | | | | | | ● | | | | | | | | | | ● | ● | ● | ● | | ● | |
| KOELREUTERIA PANICULATA (golden-rain tree) | | | ● | | | | ● | ● | | | | | | | | | | | | ● | ● | ● | ● | |
| LAGERSTROEMIA INDICA (crape myrtle) | | | ● | | | | | ● | | | | | | ● | | ● | | | | ● | ● | | ● | |
| LEUCOTHOË FONTANESIANA (drooping leucothoë) | | ● | | | ● | ● | | | | | | | | | | | | | ● | ● | | | ● | |
| LIQUIDAMBAR STYRACIFLUA (sweet gum) | | | ● | | | | ● | ● | | | | | | | | | | | | ● | | | ● | |
| LIRIOPE MUSCARI (big blue lily-turf) | | ● | | | ● | ● | | | | | | | ● | | | | | | | ● | ● | ● | ● | |
| LIRIOPE SPICATA (creeping lily-turf) | ● | | | | ● | ● | | | | | | | ● | | | | | | | ● | ● | ● | ● | |
| LONICERA FRAGRANTISSIMA (fragrant honeysuckle) | | | ● | | | | | | ● | ● | ● | | ● | | | | ● | | | ● | ● | | ● | |
| LONICERA STANDISHII (Standish honeysuckle) | | ● | | | | | ● | | ● | ● | ● | | ● | | | | ● | | | ● | ● | | ● | |
| MAGNOLIA GRANDIFLORA (southern magnolia) | | | ● | ● | ● | ● | | | ● | | | | ● | | | ● | ● | | ● | ● | | | ● | |

| Plant | Under 1 foot | 1 to 3 feet | 3 to 6 feet | Over 6 feet | Distinctive foliage | Evergreen | Decorative fruit or pods | Distinctive branches or bark | Flowers | Fragrance | Pruning required | Heavy snow | Extreme cold | Winter sun | Wind | Mulching | Watering | Snow removal | Wind protection | Acid | Alkaline | Dry | Moist but well drained | Wet |
|---|---|---|---|---|---|---|---|---|---|---|---|---|---|---|---|---|---|---|---|---|---|---|---|---|
| **MAGNOLIA MACROPHYLLA** (large-leaved cucumber tree) | | | ● | | | | ● | | | | | | | ● | | | | ● | ● | | | | ● | |
| **MAGNOLIA VIRGINIANA** (sweet bay) | | | ● | ● | | | | | | | | | | ● | | | | ● | ● | | | | ● | |
| **MAHONIA AQUIFOLIUM** (Oregon holly grape) | ● | ● | | ● | | ● | ● | | | ● | | | | ● | | | | ● | ● | ● | | | ● | |
| **MAHONIA BEALEI** (leather-leaved holly grape) | | | ● | ● | | ● | ● | ● | ● | ● | | | | ● | | | | ● | ● | ● | | | ● | |
| **MALUS 'BOB WHITE'** (Bob White crab apple) | | | | ● | | | ● | | | ● | | | | ● | | | | | ● | | | | ● | |
| **MALUS 'RED JADE'** (Red Jade crab apple) | | | | ● | | | ● | ● | | ● | | | | ● | | | | | ● | | | | ● | |
| **MALUS SARGENTII** (Sargent crab apple) | | | | ● | | | ● | ● | | ● | | | | ● | | | | | ● | | | | ● | |
| **MALUS ZUMI CALOCARPA** (Zumi crab apple) | | | | ● | | | ● | ● | | ● | | | | ● | | | | | ● | | | | ● | |
| **MISCANTHUS SINENSIS** (eulalia) | | | | ● | | | ● | | | ● | | | | ● | | | | | | | | ● | | |
| **MORUS ALBA** (white mulberry) | | | | ● | | | ● | | | | | | | | | | | | | | ● | ● | ● | |
| **MORUS ALBA 'PENDULA'** (weeping mulberry) | | | | ● | | | ● | | | ● | | | | | | | | | | | ● | ● | ● | |
| **MYRICA CERIFERA** (wax myrtle) | | | | ● | | ● | | | | ● | | | | ● | | | | | ● | | | | ● | |
| **MYRICA PENSYLVANICA** (bayberry) | | | | ● | | | ● | | ● | ● | | | | ● | | | | | ● | | | | ● | |
| **NANDINA DOMESTICA** (nandina) | | ● | | | ● | | ● | ● | | | | | | ● | | | | | ● | | | | ● | |
| **NYSSA SYLVATICA** (pepperidge) | | | | ● | | | ● | | | ● | | | | ● | | | | | ● | | | | ● | ● |
| **OSMANTHUS FORTUNEI** (Fortune's osmanthus) | | | | ● | ● | ● | | | | | | | | ● | | | | ● | ● | ● | | | ● | |
| **OSMANTHUS HETEROPHYLLUS** (holly osmanthus) | | | | ● | ● | ● | | | | | | | | ● | | | | ● | ● | ● | | ● | ● | |
| **OXYDENDRUM ARBOREUM** (sorrel tree) | | | | ● | | | | | ● | ● | | | | ● | | | | | ● | | | | ● | |
| **PHELLODENDRON AMURENSE** (Amur cork tree) | | | | ● | | | | ● | | ● | | | | ● | | ● | | | ● | | | | ● | |
| **PICEA ABIES** (Norway spruce) | | ● | ● | ● | ● | | | | | | | | ● | ● | | | | | ● | | | | ● | |
| **PICEA GLAUCA** (white spruce) | | ● | ● | ● | ● | | | | | | | | ● | | | | | ● | ● | | | | ● | |
| **PICEA GLAUCA 'CONICA'** (dwarf Alberta spruce) | | ● | ● | ● | ● | ● | | | | | | | | ● | | | | ● | ● | | | | ● | |
| **PICEA PUNGENS** (Colorado spruce) | | ● | ● | ● | ● | | | | | | | | ● | ● | | | | | ● | | | | ● | |
| **PICEA PUNGENS 'MOERHEIMII'** (Moerheim Colorado spruce) | | ● | ● | ● | ● | | | | | | | | ● | ● | | | | | ● | | | | ● | |
| **PIERIS FLORIBUNDA** (mountain andromeda) | | ● | | | ● | ● | | | | | | | | | | | | ● | ● | | | | ● | |
| **PIERIS JAPONICA 'DOROTHY WYCKOFF'** (Japanese andromeda) | | ● | | | ● | ● | | | | | | | | | | | | ● | ● | | | | ● | |
| **PINUS BUNGEANA** (lace-bark pine) | | | ● | ● | ● | ● | ● | | | ● | | | | ● | ● | | ● | | ● | | | ● | ● | |
| **PINUS DENSIFLORA** (Japanese red pine) | | | ● | ● | ● | ● | | | | ● | | | | ● | ● | | | | ● | | | | ● | |
| **PINUS DENSIFLORA 'UMBRACULIFERA'** (Tanyosho pine) | | | ● | ● | ● | ● | | | | ● | | | | ● | ● | | | | ● | | | | ● | |
| **PLATANUS OCCIDENTALIS** (American plane tree) | | | | ● | | | ● | ● | | | | | | ● | | | | ● | ● | ● | | | ● | |
| **POLYSTICHUM ACROSTICHOIDES** (Christmas fern) | ● | | | | ● | ● | | | | | | | ● | | | | | ● | ● | | | | ● | |
| **POLYSTICHUM ADIANTIFORME** (leather fern) | ● | | | | ● | ● | | | | | | | | | | | | | ● | | | | ● | |
| **POLYSTICHUM MUNITUM** (western sword fern) | ● | ● | | | ● | ● | | | | | | | | | | | | | ● | | | | ● | |
| **POLYSTICHUM SETIFERUM** (soft shield fern) | ● | | | | ● | ● | | | | | | | | | | | | | ● | | | ● | ● | |
| **PONCIRUS TRIFOLIATA** (hardy orange) | | | ● | | | | ● | ● | | ● | | | | ● | | | | | ● | | | | ● | |
| **PRUNUS LAUROCERASUS** (cherry laurel) | | | ● | | ● | ● | | | | | | | | ● | | | | | ● | ● | | ● | ● | |
| **PRUNUS LAUROCERASUS 'SCHIPKAENSIS'** (Schipka cherry laurel) | | | ● | ● | ● | ● | | | | | | | | ● | | | | | ● | ● | | ● | ● | |
| **PRUNUS MAACKII** (Amur chokecherry) | | | | ● | | | | ● | | | | | ● | ● | | | | | ● | ● | | | ● | |
| **PRUNUS SERRULA** (paperbark cherry) | | | | ● | | | | ● | | | | | | ● | | | | | ● | ● | | | ● | |
| **PRUNUS SUBHIRTELLA** (Higan cherry) | | | | ● | | | | ● | | | | | | ● | | | | | ● | ● | | ● | ● | |
| **PSEUDOTSUGA MENZIESII** (Douglas fir) | | | ● | ● | ● | | | | | ● | | | | ● | | | | | ● | | | | ● | |
| **PSEUDOTSUGA MENZIESII 'DENSA'** (dwarf Douglas fir) | | ● | | | ● | ● | | | | | | | | ● | | | | | ● | | | | ● | |
| **QUERCUS ALBA** (white oak) | | | ● | ● | ● | | ● | | | | | | ● | ● | ● | | | | ● | | | ● | ● | |
| **QUERCUS IMBRICARIA** (shingle oak) | | | ● | ● | ● | | ● | | | | | | ● | ● | ● | | | | ● | | | ● | ● | |
| **QUERCUS PALUSTRIS** (pin oak) | | | ● | ● | ● | | ● | | | | | | ● | ● | ● | | | | ● | ● | | | ● | |
| **QUERCUS ROBUR** (English oak) | | | | ● | | | ● | ● | | | ● | | | ● | ● | | | | ● | | | ● | ● | |
| **RHODODENDRON MUCRONULATUM** (Korean rhododendron) | | | ● | | | | | | ● | | | | | | | ● | | | ● | | | | ● | |
| **RHODODENDRON 'P.J.M.'** (P.J.M. rhododendron) | | ● | | ● | ● | ● | | | | | | | | | | ● | | ● | ● | | | | ● | |
| **ROSA MULTIFLORA** (Japanese rose) | | | ● | | | | ● | | | ● | | | | ● | | | | | ● | ● | | | ● | |
| **ROSA OMEIENSIS** (Omei rose) | | | | ● | | | ● | | | ● | | | | ● | | | | | ● | ● | | | ● | |

| | PLANT HEIGHT | | | | Distinctive foliage | Evergreen | WINTER TRAITS | | | | | WINTER TOLERANCE | | | | WINTER CARE | | | | SOIL NEEDS | | | | |
|---|---|---|---|---|---|---|---|---|---|---|---|---|---|---|---|---|---|---|---|---|---|---|---|---|
| | Under 1 foot | 1 to 3 feet | 3 to 6 feet | Over 6 feet | Distinctive foliage | Evergreen | Decorative fruit or pods | Distinctive branches or bark | Flowers | Fragrance | Pruning required | Heavy snow | Extreme cold | Winter sun | Wind | Mulching | Watering | Snow removal | Wind protection | Acid | Alkaline | Dry | Moist but well drained | Wet |
| ROSA VIRGINIANA (Virginia rose) | | ● | | | ● | ● | | | | | ● | | ● | ● | | | | | | ● | ● | | ● | |
| ROSA WICHURAIANA (memorial rose) | ● | | | | | | ● | ● | | | ● | | ● | | | | | | | ● | ● | | ● | |
| RUBUS BIFLORUS (whitewashed bramble) | | | ● | | | | | ● | | | ● | | ● | | | | | | | ● | ● | ● | ● | |
| RUBUS COCKBURNIANUS (whitewashed bramble) | | | ● | | | | | ● | | | ● | | ● | | | | | | | ● | ● | ● | ● | |
| SALIX ALBA 'CHERMESINA' (redstem willow) | | | ● | | | | | ● | | | ● | | ● | ● | | | | | | ● | ● | ● | ● | ● |
| SALIX ALBA 'TRISTIS' (golden weeping willow) | | | ● | | | | | ● | | | ● | ● | ● | ● | | | | | | ● | ● | ● | ● | ● |
| SALIX DISCOLOR (pussy willow) | | | ● | | | | | ● | | | ● | | ● | ● | | | | | | ● | ● | ● | ● | ● |
| SALIX MATSUDANA 'TORTUOSA' (corkscrew willow) | | | ● | | | | | ● | | | | | ● | | | | | | | ● | ● | ● | ● | ● |
| SANTOLINA CHAMAECYPARISSUS (lavender cotton) | | ● | | | ● | ● | | | | ● | ● | | ● | | | | | | | ● | ● | ● | | |
| SANTOLINA VIRENS (green lavender cotton) | | ● | | | ● | ● | | | | ● | ● | | ● | | | | | | | ● | ● | ● | | |
| SARCOCOCCA HOOKERIANA 'DIGYNA' (Himalayan sarcococca) | | | ● | | ● | ● | | | ● | ● | | | ● | | | | ● | | ● | ● | ● | | ● | |
| SARCOCOCCA HOOKERIANA 'HUMILIS' (dwarf Himalayan sarcococca) | | ● | | | ● | ● | | | ● | ● | | | | | | | ● | | ● | ● | ● | | ● | |
| SARCOCOCCA RUSCIFOLIA (sweet box) | | ● | | | ● | ● | | | ● | ● | | | | | | | ● | | ● | ● | ● | | ● | |
| SCILLA BIFOLIA (two-leaved squill) | ● | | | | | | | | ● | | | | ● | | | | | | | ● | ● | | ● | |
| SCILLA SIBERICA (Siberian squill) | ● | | | | | | | | ● | | | | ● | | | | | | | ● | ● | | ● | |
| SCILLA TUBERGENIANA (Tubergenian squill) | ● | | | | | | | | ● | | | | ● | ● | | | | | | ● | ● | | ● | |
| SKIMMIA JAPONICA (Japanese skimmia) | | ● | ● | | ● | ● | ● | | | | | | | | | | ● | ● | ● | ● | | | ● | |
| SKIMMIA REEVESIANA (Reeves skimmia) | | ● | | | ● | ● | ● | | | | | | | | | | ● | ● | ● | ● | | | ● | |
| STRANVAESIA DAVIDIANA (Chinese stranvaesia) | | | | ● | ● | ● | ● | | | | | | ● | | | | | | ● | ● | ● | | ● | |
| TAXUS BACCATA (English yew) | | | | ● | ● | ● | ● | | | | | | | | | | | ● | | ● | | | ● | |
| TAXUS CUSPIDATA (Japanese yew) | | | | ● | ● | ● | ● | | | | | | | | | | | | | ● | | | ● | |
| TAXUS CUSPIDATA 'CAPITATA' (upright Japanese yew) | | | | ● | ● | ● | ● | | | | | | | | | | | | | ● | | | ● | |
| TAXUS MEDIA (intermediate yew) | | | | | ● | ● | ● | | | | | | | | | | | | | ● | | | ● | |
| TAXUS MEDIA 'HICKSII' (Hicks yew) | | | | ● | ● | ● | ● | | | | | | | | | | | | | ● | | | ● | |
| THUJA OCCIDENTALIS (American arborvitae) | | | | ● | ● | ● | | | | | | ● | ● | | | ● | ● | ● | ● | ● | ● | | ● | |
| THUJA OCCIDENTALIS DOUGLASII PYRAMIDALIS (Douglas arborvitae) | | | | ● | ● | ● | | | | | | | ● | | | ● | ● | ● | ● | ● | ● | | ● | |
| TSUGA CANADENSIS (Canada hemlock) | | | | ● | ● | ● | | | | ● | | | ● | | | | | ● | ● | ● | | | ● | |
| TSUGA CAROLINIANA (Carolina hemlock) | | | | ● | ● | ● | | | | ● | | | ● | | | | | ● | ● | ● | | | ● | |
| ULMUS ALATUS (winged elm) | | | ● | | | | | ● | ● | | | | ● | | | | | | | ● | ● | | ● | |
| ULMUS PARVIFOLIA (Chinese elm) | | | ● | | | | | ● | ● | | | | ● | | | | | | | ● | ● | | ● | |
| VIBURNUM RHYTIDOPHYLLUM (leatherleaf viburnum) | | | ● | ● | ● | | | | | | | | ● | | | | | | ● | ● | ● | ● | ● | |
| VIBURNUM TINUS (Laurustinus viburnum) | | | ● | ● | ● | | | | ● | | | | ● | | | | | | | ● | ● | ● | ● | |
| VIRBURNUM TRILOBUM (American cranberry bush) | | | ● | | | | ● | | | | | ● | ● | | | | | | | ● | ● | ● | ● | |
| VINCA MAJOR (greater periwinkle) | ● | | | | ● | ● | | | | | | | | | | | | | | ● | ● | ● | ● | |
| VINCA MINOR (common periwinkle) | ● | | | | ● | ● | | | | | | | ● | | | | | | | ● | ● | | ● | |
| VINCA MINOR 'AUREO-VARIEGATA' (periwinkle) | ● | | | | ● | ● | | | | | | | | | | | | | | ● | ● | ● | ● | |
| YUCCA ALOIFOLIA (Spanish-bayonet) | | | ● | | ● | ● | | | | | | | ● | | | | | | | ● | ● | ● | | |
| YUCCA FILAMENTOSA (Adam's-needle yucca) | | ● | | | ● | ● | | | | | | | ● | | | | | | | ● | ● | ● | | |
| YUCCA FILAMENTOSA 'BRIGHT EDGE' (Bright Edge yucca) | | ● | | | ● | ● | | | | | | | ● | | | | | | | ● | ● | ● | | |

# Picture credits

The sources for the illustrations in this book are shown below. Credits from left to right are separated by semicolons, from top to bottom by dashes. Cover: Tom Tracy. 4: Frederick R. Allen. 6: John Neubauer, designed by Oehme, Van Sweden Associates. 8, 9: Linda Bartlett. 11-13: Henry Groskinsky. 14: Kim Steele. 16: Drawing by Kathy Rebeiz. 18: Map by John Drummond. 20: Foto Kiemer, Museum für Kunst und Gewerbe, Hamburg. 24-30: Drawings by Kathy Rebeiz. 33, 34: Linda Bartlett. 35: John Neubauer, designed by Oehme, Van Sweden Associates. 36-37: Linda Bartlett, designed by Frederick Peck. 38-39: Linda Bartlett. 40-41: John Neubauer, designed by Oehme, Van Sweden Associates. 42: John Neubauer. 43: Linda Bartlett. 44-46: Tom Tracy. 50-56: Drawings by Kathy Rebeiz. 59: Kim Steele. 60, 61: Horticultural Photography. 62, 63: John Zimmerman; John Neubauer. 64, 65: John Neubauer; Horticultural Photography. 66, 67: Horticultural Photography. 68, 69: John Neubauer. 70: Richard Jeffery. 72: Drawing by Joan S. McGurren. 75: Drawing by Kathy Rebeiz. 77-79: Malak, Ottawa. 80-83: Drawings by Kathy Rebeiz. 84: Tom Tracy. 86: Illustration by Eduardo Salgado. 88-147: Illustrations by artists listed in alphabetical order: Adolph E. Brotman, Richard Crist, Mary Kellner, Gwen Leighton, Rebecca Merrilees, Trudy Nicholson, Allianora Rosse, Eduardo Salgado, Ray Skibinski and Barbara Wolff. 148, 149: Maps by Adolph E. Brotman.

# Acknowledgments

The index for this book was prepared by Anita R. Beckerman. The editors also wish to thank: Mr. and Mrs. Frank H. Bailey, Charleston, S.C.; Woodbury Bartlett, South Hamilton, Mass.; Robert J. Black, Department of Ornamental Horticulture, University of Florida, Gainesville; Bill Brown, Coram, N.Y.; A. E. Bye, Old Greenwich, Conn.; Mr. and Mrs. T. E. Chase, Orting, Wash.; Mrs. Reuben Clark, Savannah, Ga.; James Cross, Environmentals, Cutchogue, N.Y.; Mr. and Mrs. Earl L. Dibble, Scarsdale, N.Y.; Fred Galle, Director of Horticulture, Calloway Gardens, Pine Mountain, Ga.; The Gambrill Family, Alexandria, Va.; Harold E. Greer, Greer Gardens, Eugene, Ore.; Pamela Harper, Seaford, Va.; Allen C. Haskell, New Bedford, Mass.; Dr. and Mrs. George C. Henny, Philadelphia, Pa.; Jerry Hill, Hill's Camellia Gardens, Arlington, Va.; Roland Jefferson, National Arboretum, Washington, D.C.; JoAnn Knapp, Locust Valley, N.Y.; Carlton Lees, New York Botanical Garden, The Bronx; Phyllis Luckritz, Alexandria, Va.; Sylvester G. March, National Arboretum, Washington, D.C.; Frederick McGourty, Jr., Brooklyn Botanic Garden, N.Y.; Dorothy Metheny, Seattle, Wash.; Everitt L. Miller, Director, Longwood Gardens, Kennett Square, Pa.; Mr. and Mrs. Ernest V. Montford, Savannah, Ga.; Oehme, Van Sweden Associates, Washington, D.C.; Frederick Peck, Chestnut Hill, Pa.; J. Liddon Pennock, Meadowbrook, Pa.; William Persen, Greenwich, Conn.; Lawrence J. Pierce, Seattle, Wash.; Suzanne Quinlan, Alexandria, Va.; Sally Reath, Devon, Pa.; Peter G. Rolland & Associates, Rye, N.Y.; Landon Scarlett, Longwood Gardens, Kennett Square, Pa.; Richard Simon, Bluemount Nurseries, Inc., Monkton, Md.; Marco Polo Stufano, The Bronx, N.Y.; Harry Swartz, Department of Horticulture, University of Maryland, College Park; Robert G. Titus, Planting Fields Arboretum, Oyster Bay, N.Y.; John van Bourgondien, Babylon, N.Y.; Mr. and Mrs. Lee Vollmer, Baltimore, Md.; Farol Hamer Wedel, Good Earth Nursery, Burke, Va.; Gerry Weinstein, New York, N.Y.

# Bibliography

Bailey, L. H., *Manual of Cultivated Plants*. Macmillian, 1940.

Bloom, Adrian, *Conifers for Your Garden*. Scribner's, 1972.

Bowles, E. A., *My Garden in Autumn and Winter*. London: David & Charles Reprints, 1973.

Chidamian, Claude, *Camellias for Everyone*. Doubleday, 1959.

Chittenden, Fred J., ed., *The Royal Horticultural Society Dictionary of Gardening*. 2nd Ed., Clarendon Press, 1974.

Everett, T. H., ed., *New Illustrated Encyclopedia of Gardening*. Greystone Press, 1967.

Formozov, A. N., *Snow Cover as an Integral Factor of the Environment and its Importance in the Ecology of Mammals and Birds*. Edmonton, Alberta: Boreal Institute (University of Alberta), 1969.

Graff, M. M., *Flowers in the Winter Garden*. Doubleday, 1966.

*Handbook on Bulbs*. Brooklyn Botanic Garden, 1966.

Lawrence, Elizabeth, *Gardens in Winter*. Harper Brothers, 1961.

Levitt, J., *Responses of Plants to Environmental Stresses*. Academic Press, 1972.

*Nursery Source Guide*. Brooklyn Botanic Garden, 1977.

Powell, Thomas and Betty, *The Avant Gardener*. Houghton Mifflin, 1975.

*Reader's Digest Encyclopaedia of Garden Plants and Flowers*. London: Reader's Digest Association, 1971.

Rosenberg, Norman J., *Microclimate: The Biological Environment*. Wiley, 1974.

Sakai, Li, *Plant Cold Hardiness and Freezing Stress*. Academic Press, 1978.

Schroeder, Marion, *The Green Thumb Directory*. Doubleday, 1977.

Schuler, Stanley, *The Winter Garden*. Macmillan, 1972.

Smith, Alice Upham, *Trees in a Winter Landscape*. Holt, Reinhart and Winston, 1969.

Staff of the L. H. Bailey Hortorium, Cornell University, *Hortus Third, A Concise Dictionary of Plants Cultivated in the United States and Canada*. Macmillan, 1976.

Steffek, Edwin F., *The Pruning Manual*. Little, Brown, 1969.

Taloumis, George, *Winterize Your Yard and Garden*. Lippincott, 1976.

Taylor, Kathryn S., and Edith W. Gregg, *Winter Flowers in Greenhouse and Sun-Heated Pit*. Scribner's, 1969.

Terres, John K., *Songbirds in Your Garden*. Thomas Y. Crowell, 1953.

Thomas, Graham Stuart, *Colour in the Winter Garden*. Charles T. Branford, 1957.

Underhill, Terry L., *Heaths and Heathers*. Newton Abbot, Great Britain: David & Charles, 1971.

Villiers, Trevor A., *Dormancy and the Survival of Plants*. London: Edward Arnold, 1975.

Welch, H. J., *Dwarf Conifers*. Faber and Faber, 1966.

Wilson, Helen Van Pelt, *Color for Your Winter Yard & Garden*. Scribner's, 1978.

Wyman, Donald, *Wyman's Gardening Encyclopedia*. Macmillan, 1977.

# Index